A Colorado River Reader

THE COLORADO RIVER

A Colorado River Reader

Edited by

Richard F. Fleck

The University of Utah Press

Salt Lake City

Printed on acid-free paper

Map of the Colorado River Basin by Lester Doré originally appeared in *High Country News.* Reprinted by permission of the artist.

Illustrations from *Canyons of the Colorado* by John Wesley Powell, 1895.

2000 01 02 03 04 05 06

5 4 3 2 1

LIBRARY OF CONGRESS CATALOGING-IN-PUBLICATION DATA

A Colorado River reader / [edited by] Richard F. Fleck.
p. cm.
Includes bibliographical references (p.).
ISBN 0-87480-647-X (paper : alk. paper)
1. Colorado River (Colo.-Mexico)—Description and travel—Anecdotes.
2. Natural history—Colorado River (Colo.-Mexico)—Anecdotes. 3. White-water canoeing—Colorado River (Colo.-Mexico)—Anecdotes. 4. Adventure and adventurers—Colorado River (Colo.-Mexico)—Anecdotes. 5. Colorado River (Colo.-Mexico)—History—Sources. I. Fleck, Richard F., 1937–

F788.C724 2000
917.91′3—dc21 00–021102

Contents

Richard F. Fleck

Preface

A sliver of moon clings to a wind-pocked sandstone cliff. A constant pulse of waves laps against the beach, teasing the scatters of driftwood there. Sparks from the campfire rise, dancing against a fixed field of shimmering stars. Reuben Ellis, Michael Mackey, river guide Melissa Scheel, and I lean toward the warmth of the fire, into a circle of light and warmth we've made on a small stretch of the upper Colorado. Only a day on the river, and already we can feel ourselves altering—our senses opening, our busy, troubled minds easing. Each of us relish a sense of our relative insignificance; we are mere specks on a segment of a mighty river, one that traverses high mountain valleys and desert playas over a course of 1,450 miles. Along the way, following the Green River from the Wind River Mountains of Wyoming and the old Grand River (now called Colorado) from the Never Summer Mountains of Colorado, the waters descend some 12,000 feet in elevation before reaching the Gulf of California. Here, along the stretch we've run today in southeastern Utah, the river is barely halfway to its destination.

A few hours earlier we had been tossing through white water rapids with Melissa at the oars, sluicing through gorges carved over thousands of millennia by the Colorado. Sudden breaks in the stone walls offered fleeting vistas of southeastern Utah's canyon country: distant red-rock buttes and mesas or the La Sal Mountains, their slopes laced with vertical snowfields. When the river calmed and slowed, our attention focused differently, on the nearer at hand: cliff swallows tending their mud-cone nests in the shoreline sandstone, a blue heron reviewing from a higher ledge our progress downstream.

Landfalls seem to shift our awareness yet again, inward, toward the places where nostalgia and metaphor reside. At one pull-out I recalled hiking with my son, Rich, atop Thunder Pass in the Never Summer Mountains and staring down at a twisting ribbon of snowmelt, birthplace of this canyon-making river. Our lunch stop today on a sandbar studded with Egyptian tamarisk in bloom had evoked in Reuben boyhood memories of growing up on an Imperial Valley ranch where rich green tamarisk honey had been his breakfast mainstay. This evening, having found this cottonwood-sheltered campsite for the night, we ambled beyond the shoreline into hills flaring orange in the setting sun. Melissa surprised us with some magic: She poured drops of water on a clump of cryptobiotic soil. Within seconds the soil flushed from drab gray to bright green, as though it possessed a kind of latent "green intelligence." I watched, imagining a cloudburst quenching these parched, gray hills, transforming them as a desert snake might be transformed into a bright plumed serpent.

Now, with stars glittering overhead, I crawl into my sleeping bag, and my mind drifts again to other hikes, one with my son down from the rim in Canyonlands National Park all the way to the snaking shoreline of the Green River, whose cool waters refreshed our tired and parched bodies; another as a tired and thirsty young man scrambling in desperation back up the Kaibab Trail after a long day's hike in the Grand Canyon. Hailstones pelting the ground provided me with much-needed water, saving my life, perhaps.

Tomorrow, I knew, we would face White's Rapids above Moab, Utah—-and not only rapids but suck holes dumping waves of icy water in our laps. But beyond the rapids would be flat stretches of river where our clothes would be dry and our skins would warm again, where we would find ourselves transfixed by nothing more than a turkey vulture, riding thermals above Moenkopi sandstone cliffs.

This night, in our sleeping bags around the fire, we had begun to appreciate the enduring value of river time in a modern age, and we knew we would feel the presence of the Colorado for months to come. Small wonder that such a river has generated, through storytellers and writers, a literary treasury.

This collection of writings about the Colorado River—arranged chronologically based on publication date*—is the first to encompass a span of time from Native American creation myth to contemporary nonfiction prose. The selections reflect a variety of approaches and voices: animistic mythology, narratives of exploration and conquest, and essays permeated by reverent wonder and the quest for harmony with the natural world now infusing the "New West." This volume also represents several distinctive sections of the river—from above the confluence of the lower Green (which Powell calls the upper continuation of the Colorado) and the upper Colorado (formerly the Grand) down to Cataract, Glen, Marble, and Grand Canyons and, finally, to the delta itself. The diverse writers represented here all have one important thing in common: an abiding respect for the Colorado River.

---

* With the exception of the pre-Columbian Paiute creation myth, Escalante's diary and R.B. Stanton's Down the Colorado, all selections are arranged by date of publication. The dates of publication for the pre-Columbian Paiute myth (1987), Escalante's diary of 1776 (published in English in 1976) and Stanton's 1880's notebook (1965) are much later than their composition dates that determined their placement in this anthology.

THE COLORADO RIVER BASIN

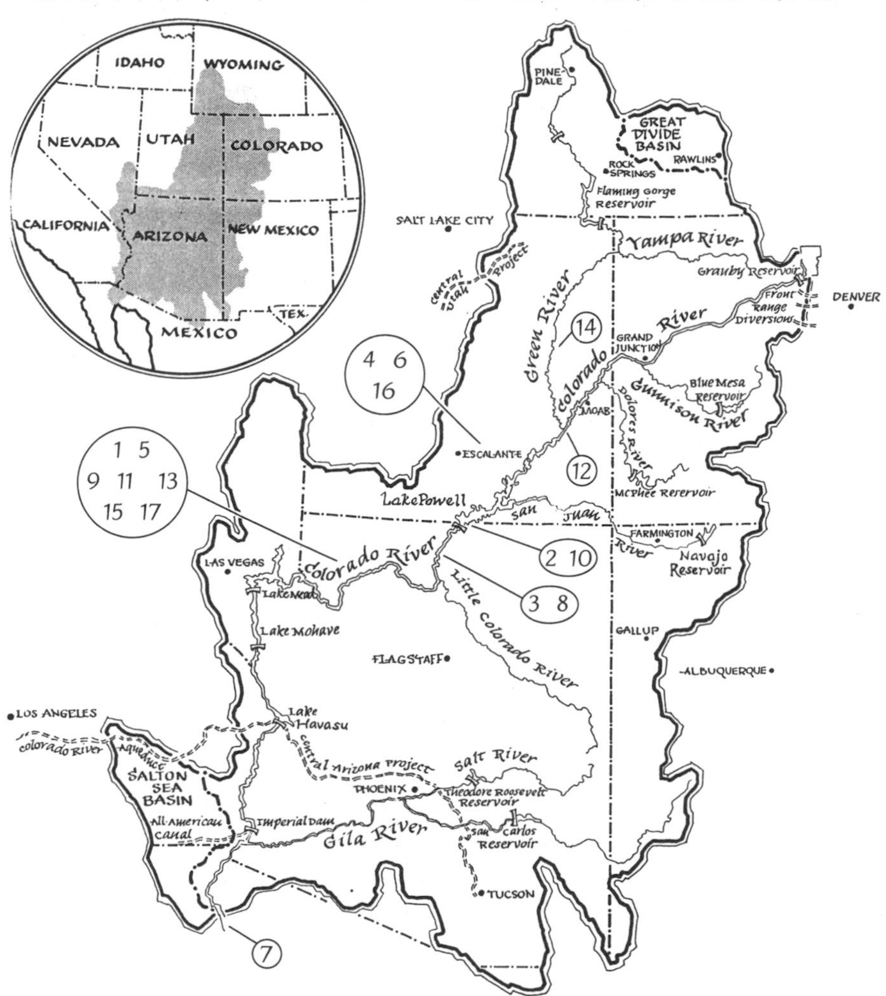

1 Paiute Indians
2 Silvestre Vélez de Escalante
3 John Wesley Powell
4 Robert Brewster Stanton
5 John C. Van Dyke
6 Frederick S. Dellenbaugh
7 Frank Waters
8 T. H. Watkins
9 John McPhee
10 Georgie White Clark
11 Philip L. Fradkin
12 Edward Abbey
13 Bill Beer
14 Ellen Meloy
15 Ann Zwinger
16 Colin Fletcher
17 Linda Hogan

The first selection, from Paiute tradition, provides us with an etiological tale couched in human terms that explains the origin of natural phenomena. In this story, lovers are separated by a chasm of anger and hatred. The rushing waters and vast canyon between Woman-Rock and Man-Rock (the tradition does not identify which particular stones the lovers signify) serve as a warning for couples who refuse reconciliation of their quarrels. William R. Palmer recorded the legend in eight-beat lines, suitable for drumbeat, from three Paiute tribal elders, who later scrutinized the text for accuracy. "Why the Grand Canyon Was Made" animates geological formations along the Colorado River with human spirit in memorable fashion.

Departing from this animistic view of the river and its canyons that seeks to explain the natural world in human terms, the text turns to a very different perspective, that of explorers whose intent was to describe and claim.

Fray Silvestre Vélez de Escalante, Fray Francisco Domínguez, and a crew of Hispanic and Indio laymen had been sent in 1776 by the Church in Mexico City to discover a direct route through the canyonland deserts from the missions at Santa Fe to those at Monterey on the California coast. While they were forced to return to Santa Fe after experiencing severe winter weather in the Grand Canyon region, they nonetheless made a memorable journey through the Colorado River canyon country, recorded in detail in Escalante's diary. The passage selected begins at Navajo Creek Canyon, a side canyon of Glen Canyon, with the expedition in search of a ford across the Colorado River. After enduring fearful lightning storms and blizzards that provoke fervent prayer from the party, the expedition finally succeeds in discovering a ford across a wide stretch of the Colorado River deep in Glen Canyon (now flooded by Lake Powell). Escalante's diary affords us a sense of the terror, reverent wonder, and awe for wild and unexplored terrain.

Major John Wesley Powell (1834–1902), a Civil War veteran and the first known explorer of substantial portions of the Colorado, departed with a company of nine men and wooden boats from Green River, Wyoming, in 1869. Powell followed the river's uncharted and uninterrupted course into the labyrinthine canyons of Utah and Arizona on two separate trips, which together constitute the narrative of *An Exploration of the Colorado River and Its Canyons* (1895). Powell's writing is an intriguing mixture of impassioned description and scientific exactitude. The selection from the chapter "From the Grand to the Little Colorado" focuses specifically on Marble Canyon below Glen Canyon. Dating from August 5 through August 12, 1869, the excerpt offers all of the attributes of Powell's writing style: his orderly Aristotelian description of varying textures of limestone and sandstone strata, and his decidedly aesthetic depiction of the "iridescent beauty" of shoreline marble pavement. Even though Powell's words succeed marvelously well in conveying a sense of place, he confesses his frustration over lacking the language capable of truly conveying the whole. In a later chapter, "Over the River," he writes: "The landscape is too vast, too complex, too grand for verbal description."

A narrative by Robert Brewster Stanton (1826–1918), "Cataract Canyon" taken from *Down the Colorado*, describes a later expedition, sponsored by Denver businessman Frank Brown in 1889 to Utah's canyonlands for the purpose of surveying a railway route along the shoreline of the Colorado. Since he had been a member of Powell's original government-sponsored exploring party in 1869, Stanton had great familiarity with the little-known terrain he describes. The Cataract Canyon portion of his book recounts the 304-foot descent compressed into a span of eighteen and a half miles of violent, roiling, tumbling water. Several mishaps are recounted, including Stanton's brush with death when his foot became wedged among rocks, trapping him in an isolated location. Stanton's narrative deftly captures the day-to-day struggle of an intrepid company of men in "frail boats" humbled by one of the most treacherous stretches of water on the Colorado. A second expedition, launched in December 1889 at Glen Canyon was also ill-fated. Only chief engineer Stanton and five of his men remained to reach the Gulf of California. While the survey was completed, no railway was ever built.

John C. Van Dyke's "Silent River," selected from *The Desert* (1901), frames the story of the Colorado as a dramatic set-piece with the river itself as the central protagonist, imbued with anthropomorphic and animistic qualities: the "silver laugh" of its source waters in alpine heights; its languid windings, like those of a "wounded snake," making its way through desert to the sea. Van Dyke (1856–1932), an art historian from Rutgers, applies words informed by the same sensibilities a painter uses choosing colors from his palette to evoke what he views as a living river. The moment of the Colorado's dissolution, when the blood-red waters are subsumed into the blue tide of the Gulf of Mexico (also known as the Sea of Cortez), is thus made vivid, even poignant. Yet his powers of observation are hardly limited to the visual. Van Dyke conveys the vastness that reduces the roaring Colorado to a silent stream:

> How deathly still everything seems! The water wears into soft banks, the banks keep sloughing into the stream, but again you hear no splashing. And the water is just as soundless. There is never a sunken rock to make a little gurgle. . . .

Frederick Dellenbaugh's (1853–1935) narrative "Wonderland of Crags" selected from *A Canyon Voyage* (1908) affords us a second perspective on

Major Powell's exploring expedition. His action-packed prose recounts the arduous two-week journey through Cataract Canyon, Utah, which included ascents with Powell and other members of the party to make topographic and photographic surveys of shoreline cliffs and the surrounding landscape. Powell's handicap—his right arm was lost in the Civil War—figures conspicuously in Dellenbaugh's account. On one excursion, Dellenbaugh lends his knee as a step, enabling Powell to negotiate a difficult descent on a narrow and perilous trail. Whether describing venomous scorpions seeking shade in caves, the taste of his coffee, or the brilliantly colored antediluvian formations of the desert, Dellenbaugh brings an engaging immediacy to his narrative.

Frank Waters (1902–1995), author of such widely acclaimed books as *The Man Who Killed the Deer* and *Book of the Hopi*, also wrote an American Rivers Series classic, *The Colorado* (1946), from which "Its Delta" has been selected. Waters believed that from the very landscapes of the American West emanate psychic energies that profoundly affect the human mind—a concept of the interrelationship of land and human spirit rare in its time, a reversal of Romantic projection. During the three days and four nights spent on a sweltering and overcrowded Mexican steamer, Waters directs his curiosity and his notable powers of observation to a wide-array of subjects: the idiosyncrasies and motley nature of the ship's crew and his fellow passengers; the landscapes through which the steamer passes—the dense vegetation and abundant bird life of the chaparral and the bleak, barren expanses of the delta itself; the disastrous effects of the tidal bore that races upstream from the sea for forty miles like a giant cobra rearing its head.

T.H. Watkins, conservationist and editor of the Wilderness Society's former journal *Wilderness*, provides us with a brief historic overview of recreational river running in the selection "River Runners" from *The Grand Colorado* (1969). Included are accounts about Julius Stone, first to run the river in 1909, as well as the pioneering Georgia White (aka Georgie Clark), whose reminiscences of commercial floating appear later in the anthology.

A float trip on the Colorado becomes the stage for a dramatic dialogue between two powerful archrivals, conservationist David Brower and Bureau of Land Reclamation Chief Floyd E. Dominy. "Encounters with an Archdruid," taken from John McPhee's book of the same name (1971), epitomizes, through Brower and Dominy, the environmental controversy spawned by the grand era of dam-building sixty years ago: Brower stresses the importance of a free flowing river, while Dominy emphasizes the need for clean hydro-electric power. One wants silt to cleanse the shorelines, and the other believes silt should be retained by a dam. While the conservationist sits on the edge of his seat with white knuckles as their raft bounds through rapids, the fed smokes a cigar and lets out cowboy whoops with every plunge.

McPhee serves as a keen literary witness to this encounter. His language comprises a unique blend of sardonic humor, geologic exactitude, and in-depth character analysis.

Georgie Clark's account of river running through Glen Canyon has been selected from *Georgie Clark: Thirty Years of River Running* (1977). Her career accomplishments are testaments to a life spent in intimate relationship with moving water: White was the first person to swim the rapids of the Grand Canyon in a life jacket and the first to run the white rapids consistently. She has run the rapids of the Grand Canyon more often than anyone else, and in 1955 she developed the oversized "G boat," becoming the first river runner to take large groups down the river. Her informal and chatty style portrays a strong sense of self-reliance and the spirit of conquest with which she met the challenges of the river and its canyons. While some of her activities might now seem anathema—such as widening "Moki" steps up Rainbow Bridge and encouraging tourists to "poke around" Anasazi sites, White's depiction of the unique essence of Glen Canyon reveals a deep respect for the land and its natural and human inhabitants. Because of her intense regard for this canyon, she condemns the construction of Glen Canyon Dam, lamenting that "The only reason they [dams] seem to exist is to keep the vast bureaucracy of the Bureau of Reclamation going and to provide a few outside jobs."

Philip Fradkin's "Canyon Country," taken from *A River No More* (1968), provides a contemporary view of the Colorado River following construction of the Glen Canyon Dam. In this section, Fradkin recalls a father-son adventure of eighteen days of blistering heat and chilly nights in the Grand Canyon. The trip prompts Fradkin to reflect on the stubborn and misguided efforts to subdue the river, which the government seems to view as "the ultimate ditch in the efficient transport of water." As Fradkin explains, among other effects, dams such as Glen Canyon profoundly alter and disrupt riparian ecology by holding back beach-building sediment and suppressing the flash floods necessary for the natural processes of plant and animal life in the "ephemeral zone."

The late Edward Abbey's account (from *Down the River*, 1982) of a November river trip the year Ronald Reagan was elected President epitomizes the essence of the canyonlands experience. The selection is also representative of Abbey's work—humorous, satirical, contemplative, and poetic, richly textured by carefully crafted scenes, the repartee of his companions, and, of course, Abbey's sardonic wit and intelligence. The piece constitutes an apotheosis of Henry David Thoreau, that "suburban coyote" and persona non grata who (like Abbey) took issue with the political, moral, and social conventions of his time. "Thoreau had many friends, we come to realize," Abbey writes, "if not one in his lifetime with whom he could truly, deeply share his life; it is we, his readers, over a century later, who must be and are his true companions."

"Rapids, Icewater and Fire," from *We Swam the Grand Canyon* (1988), renders the awesome force of the Colorado from an unprecedented and fascinating perspective. Bill Beer, along with his friend, Jim Dagget, floated 274 miles of the Colorado with nothing between them and the fifty-nine degree water but wet suits. In this selection the exhilaration of the adventure is obvious, but the perils and fears are palpable: the worries of the two men becoming separated from one another or their supplies in the churning river; the constant risk of frostbite and hypothermia; the immense power of rapids that toss and batter human bodies like so much flotsam. We, as much as they, find relief in their reaching night camp safely, where they share a meal wind-sprinkled with ashes and sand.

Ellen Meloy's "Gravity in a Fluid Medium," selected from *Raven's Exile* (1994), is a richly metaphoric depiction in autumn of the lower Green River's Desolation Canyon just north of the junction of the Green and Colorado Rivers. Desolation Canyon, with its plentiful array of bird life (but no ravens), is still a place of myth-making, despite the impact of dam-building and other human activities. Meloy and her ranger husband, Mark, spend an entire season in the canyon to determine just why that trickster raven exiles himself from this place where humans are present. Meloy's work is reminiscent of Edward Abbey's; both espouse the psychic necessity of the river experience, an experience central to so many other American authors including Henry Thoreau, Mark Twain, and Ernest Hemingway.

Ann Zwinger, one of our foremost literary naturalists, has authored such works as the award-winning *Run River, Run* (which follows the Green River from source to confluence), *Land Above the Trees*, *Wind in the Rock*, and *Beyond an Aspen Grove*. "Badger Creek and Running Rapids" is from *Down Canyon* (1995), perhaps the most meticulous and comprehensive book on the Colorado River in the Grand Canyon—an account of what is in and under the river as well as its surface features and shoreline. In this selection we are given exacting details of the features of rapids with downstream eddies and boils that force the river, and the rafter, momentarily to flow upstream. Why run the river at all? Zwinger explains,

> To someone who has not run a rapid before and questions the need to do so at all, the lure of this charging volume of water pouring toward your very own vulnerable, frangible body is difficult to explain . . . [it] give[s] an edge to living, a baptism that blesses with a reminder of mortality . . . once is enough for many, and forever not enough for some.

"Big Drop" by Colin Fletcher focuses on the more than twenty rapids of Cataract Canyon. Welsh-born Fletcher has become America's dean of desert authors with such literary landmarks to his name as *A Thousand Mile Summer* (a solo hike from Mexico to Oregon in eastern California), and *The Man Who Walked Through Time* (a solo hike, the first known, of the length of the Grand Canyon). In his latest book *River* (1997), Fletcher narrates the first-ever solo float trip from the source of the Colorado to the sea—no small accomplishment for a man in his late sixties suffering from recurrent bouts of the flu. Fletcher and his boat become the narrative "we" of his courageous journey, enlivened by the anxiety of each and every rapid of Cataract Canyon. Slower paced interludes, reminiscent of the changing complexion of the river itself, deftly incorporate stories of Fletcher's African farm life, his coming to America, and his treks in the California desert. The reader drifts with Fletcher and then is flung upon the white hell of foam until, coming at long last in the calm upper tongue of Lake Powell.

The last selection returns to a Native American perspective, this time from a contemporary writer. Linda Hogan, a poet and a member of the Choctaw tribe, is one of fifteen women writers who went down the river on separate trips between April and October 1997. Their thoughts form the fabric of *Writing Down the River: Into the Heart of the Grand Canyon* (1998). Hogan's "Plant Journey" is perhaps the most unusual piece of writing in the collection. Rather than focusing upon the adventure of white-water rapids gushing between vertical walls, she narrows her vision "to the small and nearly secret," acknowledging plants that have migrated into the canyon or have originated in the canyon. Of most interest to her is the very sacred datura plant, esteemed by tribal peoples for its ability to engender spiritual journeys to other realms, whose intimate beauty shines "with light and green intelligence." Despite the role datura plays in the ecosystem among canyon insect and bird pollinators, nontribal, commercial-minded settlers consider it a "noxious" weed. It is a short-sighted attitude stemming, perhaps, from the same utilitarian view of nature that turns rivers into hydroelectric generators. By Hogan's example, the long view may be, paradoxically, the view right under our own feet.

Whether you are aboard a raft, plunging through the river's tempestuous waters, or settled in an armchair a world away from them, this anthology will serve, it is my hope, to reinvigorate both mind and spirit. Taken as collective, these works stand as testaments that reflect our changing relationship with the natural world over time, testaments to the enduring and compelling power of the Colorado River upon the imagination.

Denver, Colorado
Spring 1999

Paiute Indian Legend

Why the Grand Canyon Was Made

"Why the Grand Canyon was Made" was recorded by William Rees Palmer from tribal elders. The second legend included in the original publication, "Three Days of Darkness," does not concern the Colorado River.

Ats-man-aka, ancient bow maker, sat near the brink of a mighty cliff and quietly plied his trade. To him his tribesmen came with offerings of skins and eagle feathers to exchange for the weapons his skill had learned to fashion. So long the old man had worked here that baskets of discarded flint had piled up about him. Today, as on days unnumbered before, Ats-man-aka sat and with pieces of broken flint patiently scraped and shaped the long rods of seasoned oak and cedar, then, as each was finished laid it carefully away. From time to time the bow maker fished out from the smoldering embers a hot rock, brushed the ashes off, and dropped it into a crude clay glue pot where steeped a batch of broken deer horns. Ats-man-aka was preparing to stretch and securely fasten to the backs of his bows the long strips of sinew that would give them the strength and snap of a steel spring.

Today, Ats-man-aka, the bow maker, was reflective. He looked silently over the ledge and down into the deep abyss. Slowly he raised his eyes to the distant wall across the canyon, then shook gently his old grey head and turned again to his task.

From *Two Pahute Indian Legends* by Dr. William Rees Palmer with research, supplementary information and editorial-commentary by Dr. Thomas Keith Midgley.

Before the wigwam hard by sat Mah-seep, the bow-man's daughter. Chu-ara, son of Ne-ab, sat there also. There had been hot words between them, but now they sat in silence. Mah-seep and Chu-ara had been sweethearts from childhood, but today jealousy had raised its ugly head and called forth tart words from the tongue of the angry maiden. The flare-up of his daughter's temper had occasioned the old man's reverie.

"My father is troubled," spoke the maiden.

"Why had he looked so long across the wide canyon?" asked Chu-ara.

Hearing them, the old man arose slowly to his feet, beckoned the speakers to follow, and led the way to a seat on a precarious rock that overhung the yawning canyon and exposed its awful vastness.

"Now," he said, "look into this cruel earth gash and let the hearts of my children listen to this legend of our fathers."

* * *

Before Tu-weap with life was gladdened
Tobats, god of all creation,
with Shinob, was holding council.
Tu-weap, the earth, had been created,
but nowhere were there any people.
There were trees and fruits and flowers,
but no animals to use them.
To-bats shaped the Indian Nung-wa,
out of earth and stone he made him,
God then skimmed from off the warm springs
vapor that like smoke, curled upward,
poured it in upon the man-form
'til the life within it quickened.
Then was man alive, but lonely,
restless and unsettled always.

Shinob, the second god in power,
held the wisdom and the magic
that could make all nature pleasant.
He it was that put the colors
in the flowers and the rainbow,
put the warmth into the sunshine,
and in the throats of birds their singing.

Shinob looked at lonely Nung-wa
then to Tobats paid a visit,

for he saw that Tobats' purpose
had been only half completed.
Tobats' man was never settled,
Ceaselessly he roamed the country
looking here and looking yonder,
never knowing what he sought for.

Tobats watching this was angered.
"What does the restless fellow want?
Tu-weap supplies his every need,
why can't the man be now content?"

"Contentment," said Shinob to Tobats,
"must have more than one to share it,
and a lonesome man is restless
seeking always for communion.
Give to Nung-wa a companion
who will balance all his frettings
and with sympathetic interest
enter into all his plannings."
Then for man they formed a maiden,
made her cheerful, made her sweet,
gave her laughter, love, and sunshine,
busy hands and willing feet.

Then one day the restless wanderer
found the woman God had made,
looked they wondering at each other,
but very shy and much afraid.
Another day Shinob came to them,
put her trembling hand in his,
told them they were for each other,
and must together live in peace.
Nung-wa built a wigwam for her
and children came to bless their home,
many tribes descended from them,
the man ceased aimlessly to roam.

* * *

The gods came once again to Tu-weap,
looked upon the tribes of men

saw them mingling like the beasts
promiscuously and without shame.
"Destroy them," shouted angry Tobats,
"for these are of the god-kind clan,
they disgrace our every purpose
we had when we created man."

"Do not destroy them," Shinob pleaded,
"man is the best thing we have made,
we must weld their hearts together
in communal love and pride.
With affection in their souls,
for matching soul-mates they will seek,
and finding them will cleave together
and all their evil ways forsake."

"Go, put love in their hearts," said Tobats,
"of two on whom to try your plan,
these to be the great example
of love at work in the heart of man."

* * *

Then among the youths and maidens
of the tribes in council, gathered
god Shinob, for observation,
passed unknown to make selection.
Found he two by nature suited
thus to live in ceaseless union.
Opening wide his bag of magic,
filled with softest ash of feathers,
poured he out upon these children,
all his medicine of love-mist,
filled Yan-tan-ah's heart with yearning.
Ke-ah-soit gave out such sighing,
and their glances stabbed each other
like the piercing of an arrow.

Through the forest glades they rambled
hand in hand he led her onward
through the meadow grass and flowers.
Ke-ah-soit would braid her black hair

while he told her of the deer skins,
and the furs of wolf and beaver,
he would one day lay before her.
Yan-tan-ah cast shy glances at him
and in halting half-confusion
told him how her fingers dreamed of
making moccasins with trimmings
for the swift feet of her lover.
He would wear them in the splendor
of Soparoievan, the council,
where the youths of other tribesmen
came bedecked in paint and feathers.

Once they ran into the forest
and sat down beside two saplings.
These were growing close together
with their interlacing branches
like the arms of two enfolded.
Ke-ah-soit twined their trunks together,
and so deftly left them fastened,
that no matter how he shook them
they would never part asunder.
"These," he said, "shall grow together,
and as one we shall behold them,
and their roots, the more extended,
shall defy all wind and weather."

"Thus our hearts are," said Yan-tah-ah,
"like the tree trunks twined together,
time shall see our lives so shapened,
as always to support each other."
Turning then she touched the stronger
of the tree trunks so enfolded,
"Ke-ah-soit," she sweetly named it,
then speaking softly to the other,
called it symbol of her love wish,
clinging always to her soul-mate.

He, one day in autumn's splendor,
led her to a pool so silent
that the mountains and the clear sky

on its placid face reflected.
There she left her lover sitting
while to further shore she wandered.
Looking back the maid was startled
at the clearness of his features
gazing at her from the water.
"My love's face," she cried out to him,
"from the pool is looking at me,
smiles are in his dark eyes lurking,
there is not a trace of anger."

"Ke-ah-soit," said her heart-friend,
with his maid is never angry,
"Anger is a straight line," said he,
"driving ever farther from me,
love's a circle all embracing,
here I send a message to you."
Then his brown foot touched the water
and the rings went rolling to her.
Back and forth they corresponded
'til their feet were wet with wooing.
Thus they played and thus he wooed her,
everything they turned to love song.

Un-nu-pit, the evil spirt,
looked and saw these favored children,
angered was his soul and jealous,
jealous of the love between them.
"I will spoil it," said the devil,
"I will put suspicion in them
that will make them quarrel together
and their lives shall be unhappy."

Un-nu-pit the land swept over
like a cold and chilling night wind,
and the eyes he touched turned glassy
for their vision was distorted.
When the lovers saw each other
in their hearts there came a question,
and the shadow of the devil
hanging always round about them

filled them with a dark suspicion
and their words became repellent.
Jealousy flamed in Yan-tan-ah
and the tears of red hot anger
filled her eyes and drowned her vision
'til her heart was sore with aching.

To the forest fled the maiden,
like a frightened deer she bounded,
while her bitter soul was saying,
"All my love is turned to hatred.
He shall never see me suffer,
nor shall hear my bitter soul cry."
Saying thus she hurried onward
ever farther in the forest.
Wounded pride was burning in her
and her heart was wet with weeping.

Weary from her aimless wandering
Yan-tan-ah sat down to rest her,
stopped to quell the doubts within her,
stopped to clarify her thinking.
Nervous fingers crushed her mantle,
plucked the fringes of her girdle,
while her aching feet she dangled
in a brooklet running by her.

Thither faithful Ke-ah-soit followed,
and tried to sit down by her.
Like a taut bow were her feelings
when she saw him coming near her.
She leaped across the brooklet
forbidding him to touch her.
Earnestly they pressed their quarrel,
vehemently she argued with him,
and ruthless were the accusations,
hurled in her impetuous onset.
Ke-ah-soit was much bewildered
at the fury of her passion.
For he vaguely grasped the meaning
of her sudden vengeful temper.

When Shinob, the love god, heard them,
all his soul was filled with sorrow.
Un-nu-pit, he knew, had broadcast
seeds of jealousy and anger
that in the hearts of men may fester
causing all they touch to suffer.
Shinob then said to doubting Tobats,
"I must go and be peace maker,
if they quarrel long in anger,
all their love will turn to hatred
and they will never come together."

And so the god Shinob came to them,
bid them cease at once their quarrel,
told them jealousy was like a distance
that very far apart would set them.
"Calm your jealous anger," said he,
"ere the waves of hate divide you
like a canyon deep and yawning
that you cannot speak together.
Love is a pain that does not hurt
in souls that hath a trusting feeling,
but jealous hearts may ache and fester
and love wounds are slow in healing.
Do not quarrel like little children,
but casting all suspicion from you,
come together and be happy,
forgetting all your thoughts of anger."

Still Yan-tan-ah would not listen,
but she seemed the more offended.
Long the maiden sat in silence,
and her face was dark and sullen.
When Ke-ah-soit pled with her,
she stamped her foot in anger,
and when the god of love spoke to her
she said to him, "I will not listen."

Once again the god talked with them,
told them of their silly foibles
and the danger of their rashness:

showed how their happiness was breaking
and their hearts were separating.
In sternness he rebuked the maiden
for her stubborn, willful anger.
"It was Un-nu-pit, the devil
who whispered evil to you."
But Yan-tan-ah turned her back
disdaining all his pleadings.
Then spoke the god, Shinob in warning,

"If you do not listen to me
all your life you will be sorry.
Jealousy will put a gulf between you
that you cannot come together.
Then your anger will be silenced
and your hearts will cry forever.
When other lovers see you
you shall be a warning to them
and the anguish of your sorrow
shall become tradition to them."
Still Ke-ah-soit sat on one bank
and Yan-tan-ah on the other.
When darkness fell upon them,
they were seated thus, and silent.

Through the night there came a shaking,
Tu-weap seemed to be dividing,
and there came the roar of many waters
rushing madly down between them.
When Ke-ah-soit thought of her in danger,
all his soul strength called out to her
but his voice was only mingled
with the roaring of the waters.

On her bank sat Yan-tan-ah
weeping, bitterly repentant.
How she wished that she had listened
to the warnings of the love god,
how she cried out her affection
to her lover through the darkness,
but the sullen waters swallowed

every word that passed between them,
and the winds swept madly outward
all their pleadings for forgiveness.

So, alas, when came the morning,
and the earth had stilled its shaking,
and the waters had receded,
and the wind had ceased its howling,
they beheld this awful chasm
that had opened out between them.
Ke-ah-soit waved wildly
to Yan-tan-ah in the distance,
and answering, she held her arms
extended widely to him.
Thus they sat and thus they perished
never once they left their places.

When Shinob again beheld them
all his soul was touched with pity.
Wishing them to be remembered,
to enduring stone he turned them.
They were left, forever sitting,
silent, mute, as now you see them.

* * *

"Now, my children," said Ats-man-aka, turning to Mah-seep and Chu-ara, "you have always loved each other, but today I heard your quarrel and the sharp words of my daughter. See this man-rock poised on this side and Yan-tan-ah in the distance: see the yawning gulf between them and their helplessness to bridge it? It is the warning of the love god and his symbol of the distance Un-nu-pit may put between you when you yield to jealous anger. Forget your temper," pled the old man, "and come together and be happy."

Saying thus the bow-man left them
And returned to stir his glue pot.

Silvestre Vélez de Escalante

The Domínguez-Escalante Journal

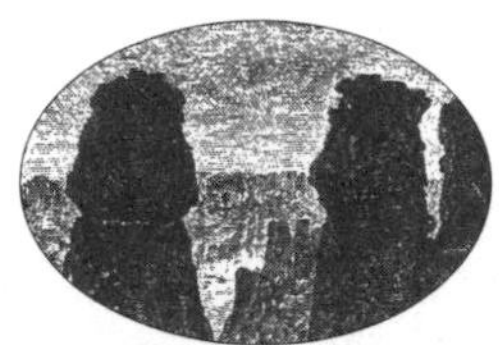

This section from the diary of Fray Silvestre Vélez de Escalante takes place between November 3 and 7, 1776, when the expedition had arrived in the vicinity of Glen Canyon long after its embarking from Santa Fe, New Mexico, on July 29 of the same year. Fray Escalante and Fray Francisco Domínguez were in search of a route through the canyonlands to the missions of California.

November 3.—On the 3rd we set out from San Diego, headed east-southeast, and after going two leagues came to the river a second time, that is, at the edge of the canyon[1] which here serves as its box channel. The descent to the river is very long, steep, rugged, and precipitous, consisting of such terrible rock embankments that two pack animals which descended the first one could not make it back, even without the equipment. Those who had come by here before had not informed us of this declivity, and here we learned that they had not found the ford either, nor in so many days made the necessary exploration of so small a space of terrain, for their having wasted the time looking for those Indians who live hereabouts, and accomplished nothing.

The river was very deep, although not as much as at Salsipuedes, but the horse herds had to swim for a long distance. The good thing about it is that it was not quicksand, either going in or getting out. The companions kept

---

From *The Domínguez-Escalante Journal: Their Expedition Through Colorado, Utah, Arizona, and New Mexico*, edited by Ted J. Warner, trans. by Fray Angelico Chavez (Salt Lake City: University of Utah Press, 1995).

1. Navajo Creek Canyon.

insisting that we should descend to the river, but since there was no way on the other side to go ahead after one crossed the river, except a deep and narrow canyon of another small one which joins it here—and since we had not learned if this one could be negotiated or not—we feared finding ourselves obliged (if we went down and crossed the river) to do the necessary backtracking which on this precipice would be extremely difficult. So as not to have to risk it, we halted above and sent the mixed-breed Juan Domingo to go across the river and find out if the said canyon had an exit, but if he did not find it this afternoon to return so that we might continue upstream along this side until we found the Indians' ford and trail.

After the latter was dispatched on foot, Lucrecio Muñiz said that if we let him he would also go bareback on a horse, taking along the things needed for making a fire and sending up smoke signals in case he found an exit, so that with this message we would try finding our way down and shorten the delay. We told him to go, but reminding him that we expected him back this afternoon, whether he found the exit or not. They did not return, and so we passed the night here without being able to water the horse herds while being so adjacent to the river. We named the place El Vado de los Chamas, or San Carlos.[2] Today two leagues[3] east-southeast.

November 4.—On the 4th, day broke without our learning about the two whom we had dispatched yesterday on the reconnaissance mentioned. The meat from the second horse had run out, we had not eaten a thing today, and so we breakfasted on toasted pads of low prickly pear cactus and gruel made from a tiny fruit[4] they brought from the river bank. This tiny fruit of itself has a good taste but, crushed and boiled in water the way we had it today, is very insipid. On seeing how late it was and that the two aforementioned ones did not show up, we ordered that an attempt be made to get the animal herd down to the river and on the bank to slaughter another horse. They got them down with great difficulty, some of the mounts injuring themselves because, when they lost a foothold on the big rocks, they rolled down a long distance.

A little before nightfall, the mixed-breed Juan Domingo returned, asserting that he had found no way out and that the other one, leaving the horse midway in the canyon, had kept on following some fresh Indian tracks. And so we decided to continue upstream until we found a good ford and passable terrain on one and the other side.

---

2. "The Hill of the Chamas," or "Saint Charles." The campsite was on the west rim of the canyon opposite the mouth of Navajo Creek. The site is now covered by Lake Powell.

3. About 5¼ miles.

4. Probably hackberries.

November 5.—On the 5th we left San Carlos, no matter if Lucrecio had failed to return, his brother Andrés remaining behind with orders to wait for him until evening, and for him to try to overtake us tonight. We went along this western side and over many ridges and gullies a league and a half to the north; we went down to a dry arroyo[5] and very high-walled canyon where there was a great deal of copper sulphate. In it we found a little-used trail; we followed it and by means of it came out of the canyon, passing over a brief shelf of soft [white?] rock, difficult but capable of improvement. We kept on going and, after we went a league and a quarter toward the north-northeast, found water, even though a little, and enough pasturage; and since it was almost dark, we halted close to a high mesa, naming the place Santa Francisca Romana.[6] Today three short leagues.[7]

Tonight it rained heavily here, and it snowed in some places. It was raining at daybreak and kept it up for some hours. About six in the morning Andrés Muñiz arrived, saying that his brother had not turned up. This news caused us plenty of worry, because he had been three days without provisions and no covering other than his shirt, since he had not even taken trousers along—for, even though he crossed the river on horseback, the horse swam for a long stretch and the water reached almost to the shoulders wherever it faltered. So when the mixed-breed mentioned decided to go and look for him for this reason, by following the tracks from where he saw him last, we sent him on his way with meat for provision and with orders to leave the mount behind if it could not get out of the canyon and to proceed on foot; and should he find him on the other side, for them to look along it for signs of us and to come after us—and if on this one, to try to overtake us as quickly as possible.

November 6.—On the 6th, after it had stopped raining, we left Santa Francisca and headed northeast, and after we had gone three leagues we were stopped for a long time by a strong blizzard and tempest consisting of rain and thick hailstones amid horrendous thunder claps and lightning flashes.[8] We recited the Virgin's Litany, for her to implore some relief for us, and God willed

---

5. Warm Creek. At the upper end of the trail out of Warm Creek to the east, researchers found a rock cairn marking the spot.

6. Near the base of Ramona Mesa, near the head of Cottonwood Wash, one of the tributaries of Warm Creek.

7. As they measured only "short leagues," this date they probably made something less than 7.5 miles.

8. They were in Gunsight Canyon, probably on the west bank of that gulch, when the storm broke with all its fury, sending a flash flood down the canyon and causing the party to stop until the storm and flood had cleared.

for the tempest to end. We continued east for half a league and halted near the river because it kept on raining and some rock cliffs blocked our way. We named the place San Vicente Ferrer.[9] Today three leagues and a half.[10]

Don Juan Pedro Cisneros went to see if the ford lay around here and came back to report having seen how very wide the river was hereabouts and that he did not think it was deep according to the current, but that we could get to it only through a nearby canyon. We sent two others to inspect it and to ford the river, and they came back saying that everything was difficult to negotiate. We did not give much credence to the latters' report, and so we decided to examine it ourselves next day along with Don Juan Pedro Cisneros. Before night came the mixed-breed arrived with the said Lucrecio.

November 7.—On the 7th we went out very early to inspect the canyon[11] and ford, taking along the two mixed-breeds, Felipe and Juan Domingo, so that they might ford the river on foot since they were good swimmers. In order to have the mounts led down to the canyon mentioned, it became necessary to cut steps with axes on a stone cliff for the space of three yards or a bit less.[12] Over the rest of it the horse herds were able to get across, although without pack or rider.

We got down to the canyon, and after going a mile we reached the river[13] and went along it downstream for about as far as two musket shots, now through the water, now along the edge, until we came to the widest part of its currents where the ford[14] appeared to be. One man waded in and found it all right, not having to swim at any place. We followed him on horseback,

---

9. The site was within a mile of the Colorado River just southeast of the base of Gunsight Butte on the west side of Padre Creek, but not in sight of either it or the Colorado.

10. Slightly over nine miles.

11. On the west rim of Glen Canyon overlooking the likely fording place.

12. Access to the floor of Padre Creek was over a steep sandstone slope which a man could negotiate without danger. However, lest the horses lose their footing and tumble to the canyon floor, the expedition hacked out some shallow footholds, or steps, for about ten feet in one of the most dangerous places, making it less hazardous for the animals. This used to be one of Utah's most historic sites. It is now covered with 550 feet of water from Lake Powell.

13. That is, the Colorado River. The distance was actually not more than a quarter of a mile.

14. This is located where a permanent sandbar was found at the base of the west canyon wall. Diagonally across from that bar was a similar one on the opposite side of the river. A ripple in the water surface indicated the shallowest point leading directly to that sandbar. It was evidently from this point that the camp gear was lowered over the cliff to the sandbar. The journal statement that the ford was a mile wide would have to mean from Padre Creek to the sandbar at the east side of the river. The water at the ripple was not more than three feet deep. The actual fording place probably changed slightly from time to time, depending on the shifting sandbar.

entering a little farther down, and in its middle two mounts which went ahead missed bottom and swam through a short channel. We held back, although with some peril, until the first one who crossed on foot came back from the other side to lead us, and we successfully passed over without the horses on which we were crossing ever having to swim.[15]

We notified the rest of the companions, who had stayed behind at San Vicente, to hoist with lassos and ropes—down a not very high cliff to the ford's bend—the equipment, saddles, and other effects and to bring the horse herd along the route we had come. They did it that way and finished crossing the river about five in the afternoon, praising God our Lord and firing off some muskets in demonstration of the great joy we all felt in having overcome so great a problem, one which had caused us so much labor and delay—even when the main cause of our having suffered so much, ever since we entered Parussi country, was our having no one to guide us through so much difficult terrain. For through the lack of expert help we made many detours, wasted time from so many days spent in a very small area, and suffered hunger and thirst.

And now that we had undergone all this, we got to know the best and most direct route where the water sources helped in the planning of average day's marches, and we kept on gathering reports about the others, especially when we stopped going south the day we left San Dónulo or Arroyo del Taray[16]—because, from this place, we could have gone to the bounteous water source that we found on the plain which came after; from here we could have conveniently reached another copious water source which lies some three leagues northeast of San Ángel. From this one to Santa Gertrudis; from here we could have gone three leagues, to halt in the same arroyo having sufficient water and pastures, gain as much distance as possible during the afternoon by heading northeast, and, by following the same direction and entirely avoiding the sierra, arrive next day at El Río de Santa Teresa, three or four leagues north of San Juan Capistrano; from this river to San Diego toward the east-southeast, and from this place to the ford without any special inconvenience while evading many detours, inclines, and bad stretches.

But God doubtless disposed that we obtained no guide, either as merciful chastisement for our faults or so that we could acquire some knowledge of

---

15. This marks the famous "Crossing of the Fathers." Most of the area traversed by the 1776 Spanish party now lies beneath the waters of Lake Powell. At the point where the padres crossed, the lake is now about 550 feet deep. Several research teams explored this region in 1938, 1950, and 1958, prior to the construction of the Glen Canyon Dam. See David E. Miller, "Discovery of Glen Canyon, 1776," *Utah Historical Quarterly*, 26 (1958): 221–37.

16. That is, October 15, 1776.

the peoples living hereabouts. May His most holy will be done in all things, and may His holy name be glorified.

The river's ford is very good. Here it must be a little more than a mile wide. Already here the rivers Navajó and Dolores flow joined together,[17] along with the rest which we have said in this diary enter either one or the other; and in all that we saw around here no settlement can be established along their banks, nor can one even go one good day's march downstream or upstream along either side with the hope of their waters being of service to the people and horse herd, because, besides the terrain being bad, the river flows through a very deep gorge. Everything else adjacent to the ford consists of very tall cliffs and precipices. Eight or ten leagues to the northeast of it rises a round mountain, high but small, which the Payuchis—who begin from here onward—call Tucane, meaning Black Mountain,[18] and the only one to be seen hereabouts. The river passes very close to it.

---

17. The Colorado River.

18. This high but small, round mountain, called Tucane by the Payuchis (Southern Paiute) and *cerro negro* by the padres, is known today as Navajo Mountain.

John Wesley Powell

From the Grand to the Little Colorado

This selection by 19th-century explorer J. W. Powell focuses on Marble Canyon. The entries date between August 5 and 12, 1869, during Powell's first expedition from Green River, Wyoming, on May 24, 1869, to the western edge of the Grand Canyon on September 1, 1869.

August 5.—With some feeling of anxiety we enter a new canyon this morning. We have learned to observe closely the texture of the rock. In softer strata we have a quiet river, in harder we find rapids and falls. Below us are the limestones and hard sandstones which we found in Cataract Canyon. This bodes toil and danger. Besides the texture of the rocks, there is another condition which affects the character of the channel, as we have found by experience. Where the strata are horizontal the river is often quiet, and, even though it may be very swift in places, no great obstacles are found. Where the rocks incline in the direction traveled, the river usually sweeps with great velocity, but still has few rapids and falls. But where the rocks dip up stream and the river cuts obliquely across the upturned formations, harder strata above and softer below, we have rapids and falls. Into hard rocks and into rocks dipping up stream we pass this morning and start on a long, rocky, mad rapid. On the left there is a vertical rock, and down by this cliff and around to the left we glide, tossed just enough by the waves to appreciate the rate at which we are traveling.

From *An Exploration of the Colorado and Its Canyons* by J. W. Powell (New York: Dover Publications, Inc., 1961).

The canyon is narrow, with vertical walls, which gradually grow higher. More rapids and falls are found. We come to one with a drop of sixteen feet, around which we make a portage, and then stop for dinner. Then a run of two miles, and another portage, long and difficult; then we camp for the night on a bank of sand.

August 6.—Canyon walls, still higher and higher, as we go down through strata. There is a steep talus at the foot of the cliff, and in some places the upper parts of the walls are terraced.

About ten o'clock we come to a place where the river occupies the entire channel and the walls are vertical from the water's edge. We see a fall below and row up against the cliff. There is a little shelf, or rather a horizontal crevice, a few feet over our heads. One man stands on the deck of the boat, another climbs on his shoulders, and then into the crevice. Then we pass him a line, and two or three others, with myself, follow; then we pass along the crevice until it becomes a shelf, as the upper part, or roof, is broken off. On this we walk for a short distance, slowly climbing all the way, until we reach a point where the shelf is broken off, and we can pass no farther. So we go back to the boat, cross the stream, and get some logs that have lodged in the rocks, bring them to our side, pass them along the crevice and shelf, and bridge over the broken place. Then we go on to a point over the falls, but do not obtain a satisfactory view. So we climb out to the top of the wall and walk along to find a point below the fall from which it can be seen. From this point it seems possible to let down our boats with lines to the head of the rapids, and then make a portage; so we return, row down by the side of the cliff as far as we dare, and fasten one of the boats to a rock. Then we let down another boat to the end of its line beyond the first, and the third boat to the end of its line below the second, which brings it to the head of the fall and under an overhanging rock. Then the upper boat, in obedience to a signal, lets go; we pull the line and catch the nearest boat as it comes, and then the last. The portage follows.

We go into camp early this afternoon at a place where it seems possible to climb out, and the evening is spent in "making observations for time."

August 7.—The almanac tells us that we are to have an eclipse of the sun to-day; so Captain [W. H.] Powell and myself start early, taking our instruments with us for the purpose of making observations on the eclipse to determine our longitude. Arriving at the summit, after four hours' hard climbing to attain 2,300 feet in height, we hurriedly build a platform of rocks on which to place our instruments, and quietly wait for the eclipse; but clouds come on and rain falls, and sun and moon are obscured.

Much disappointed, we start on our return to camp, but it is late and the clouds make the night very dark. We feel our way down among the rocks with great care for two or three hours, making slow progress indeed. At last we lose our way and dare proceed no farther. The rain comes down in torrents and we can find no shelter. We can neither climb up nor go down, and in the darkness dare not move about; so we sit and "weather out" the night.

August 8.—Daylight comes after a long, oh, how long! a night, and we soon reach camp. After breakfast we start again, and make two portages during the forenoon.

The limestone of this canyon is often polished, and makes a beautiful marble. Sometimes the rocks are of many colors—white, gray, pink, and purple, with saffron tints. It is with very great labor that we make progress, meeting with many obstructions, running rapids, letting down our boats with lines from rock to rock, and sometimes carrying boats and cargoes around bad places. We camp at night, just after a hard portage, under an overhanging wall, glad to find shelter from the rain. We have to search for some time to find a few sticks of driftwood, just sufficient to boil a cup of coffee.

The water sweeps rapidly in this elbow of river, and has cut its way under the rock, excavating a vast half-circular chamber, which, if utilized for a theater, would give sitting to 50,000 people. Objection might be raised against it, however, for at high water the floor is covered with a raging flood.

August 9.—And now the scenery is on a grand scale. The walls of the canyon, 2,500 feet high, are of marble, of many beautiful colors, often polished below by the waves, and sometimes far up the sides, where showers have washed the sands over the cliffs. At one place I have a walk for more than a mile on a marble pavement, all polished and fretted with strange devices and embossed in a thousand fantastic patterns. Through a cleft in the wall the sun shines on this pavement and it gleams in iridescent beauty.

I pass up into the cleft. It is very narrow, with a succession of pools standing at higher levels as I go back. The water in these pools is clear and cool, coming down from springs. Then I return to the pavement, which is but a terrace or bench, over which the river runs at its flood, but left bare at present. Along the pavement in many places are basins of clear water, in strange contrast to the red mud of the river. At length I come to the end of this marble terrace and take again to the boat.

Riding down a short distance, a beautiful view is presented. The river turns sharply to the east and seems inclosed by a wall set with a million brilliant gems. What can it mean? Every eye is engaged, every one wonders. On coming nearer we find fountains bursting from the rock high overhead, and the spray in the sunshine forms the gems which bedeck the wall. The rocks below the fountain are covered with mosses and ferns and many beautiful flowering plants. We name it Vasey's Paradise, in honor of the botanist who traveled with us last year.

We pass many side canyons to-day that are dark, gloomy passages back into the heart of the rocks that form the plateau through which this canyon is cut. It rains again this afternoon. Scarcely do the first drops fall when little rills run down the walls. As the storm comes on, the little rills increase in size, until great streams are formed. Although the walls of the canyon are chiefly limestone, the adjacent country is of red sandstone; and now the waters, loaded with these sands, come down in rivers of bright red mud, leaping over the walls in innumerable cascades. It is plain now how these walls are polished in many places.

At last the storm ceases and we go on. We have cut through the sandstones and limestones met in the upper part of the canyon, and through one great bed of marble a thousand feet in thickness. In this, great numbers of caves are hollowed out, and carvings are seen which suggest architectural forms, though on a scale so grand that architectural terms belittle them. As this great bed forms a distinctive feature of the canyon, we call it Marble Canyon.

It is a peculiar feature of these walls that many projections are set out into the river, as if the wall was buttressed for support. The walls themselves are half a mile high, and these buttresses are on a corresponding scale, jutting into the river scores of feet. In the recesses between these projections there are quiet bays, except at the foot of a rapid, when there are dancing eddies or whirlpools. Sometimes these alcoves have caves at the back, giving them the appearance of great depth. Then other caves are seen above, forming vast dome-shaped chambers. The walls and buttresses and chambers are all of marble.

The river is now quiet; the canyon wider. Above, when the river is at its flood, the waters gorge up, so that the difference between high and low water mark is often 50 or even 70 feet, but here high-water mark is not more than 20 feet above the present stage of the river. Sometimes there is a narrow flood plain between the water and the wall. Here we first discover mesquite shrubs,—small trees with finely divided leaves and pods, somewhat like the locust.

August 10.—Walls still higher; water swift again. We pass several broad, ragged canyons on our right, and up through these we catch glimpses of a forest-clad plateau, miles away to the west.

At two o'clock we reach the mouth of the Colorado Chiquito. This stream enters through a canyon on a scale quite as grand as that of the Colorado itself. It is a very small river and exceedingly muddy and saline. I walk up the stream three or four miles this afternoon, crossing and recrossing where I can easily wade it. Then I climb several hundred feet at one place, and can see for several miles up the chasm through which the river runs. On my way back I kill two rattlesnakes, and find on my arrival that another has been killed just at camp.

August 11.— We remain at this point to-day for the purpose of determining the latitude and longitude, measuring the height of the walls, drying our rations, and repairing our boats.

Captain Powell early in the morning takes a barometer and goes out to climb a point between the two rivers. I walk down the gorge to the left at the foot of the cliff, climb to a bench, and discover a trail, deeply worn in the rock. Where it crosses the side gulches in some places steps have been cut. I can see no evidence of its having been traveled for a long time. It was doubtless a path used by the people who inhabited this country anterior to the present Indian races—the people who built the communal houses of which mention has been made.

I return to camp about three o'clock and find that some of the men have discovered ruins and many fragments of pottery; also etchings and hieroglyphics on the rocks.

We find to-night, on comparing the readings of the barometers, that the walls are about 3,000 feet high—more than half a mile—an altitude difficult to appreciate from a mere statement of feet. The slope by which the ascent is made is not such a slope as is usually found in climbing a mountain, but one much more abrupt—often vertical for many hundreds of feet,—so that the impression is given that we are at great depths, and we look up to see but a little patch of sky.

Between the two streams, above the Colorado Chiquito, in some places the rocks are broken and shelving for 600 to 700 feet; then there is a sloping terrace, which can be climbed only by finding some way up a gulch; then another terrace, and back, still another cliff. The summit of the cliff is 3,000 feet above the river, as our barometers attest.

Our camp is below the Colorado Chiquito and on the eastern side of the canyon.

August 12.—The rocks above camp are rust-colored sandstones and conglomerates. Some are very hard; others quite soft. They all lie nearly horizontal, and the beds of softer material have been washed out, leaving the harder forming a series of shelves. Long lines of these are seen, of varying thickness, from one or two to twenty or thirty feet, and the spaces between have the same variability. This morning I spend two or three hours in climbing among these shelves, and then I pass above them and go up a long slope to the foot of the cliff and try to discover some way by which I can reach the top of the wall; but I find my progress cut off by an amphitheater. Then I wander away around to the left, up a little gulch and along benches, climbing from time to time, until I reach an altitude of nearly 2,000 feet and can get no higher. From this point I can look off to the west, up side canyons of the Colorado, and see the edge of a great plateau, from which streams run down into the Colorado, and deep gulches in the escarpment which faces us, continued by canyons, ragged and flaring and set with cliffs and towering crags, down to the river. I can see far up Marble Canyon to long lines of chocolate-colored cliffs, and above these the Vermilion Cliffs. I can see, also, up the Colorado Chiquito, through a very ragged and broken canyon, with sharp salients set out from the walls on either side, their points overlapping, so that a huge tooth of marble on one side seems to be set between two teeth on the opposite; and I can also get glimpses of walls standing away back from the river, while over my head are mural escarpments not possible to be scaled.

Cataract Canyon is 41 miles long. The walls are 1,300 feet high at its head, and they gradually increase in altitude to a point about halfway down, where they are 2,700 feet, and then decrease to 1,300 feet at the foot. Narrow Canyon is 9½ miles long, with walls 1,300 feet in height at the head and coming down to the water at the foot.

There is very little vegetation in this canyon or in the adjacent country. Just at the junction of the Grand and Green there are a number of hackberry trees; and along the entire length of Cataract Canyon the high-water line is marked by scattered trees of the same species. A few nut pines and cedars are found, and occasionally a redbud or Judas tree; but the general aspect of the canyons and of the adjacent country is that of naked rock.

The distance through Glen Canyon is 149 miles. Its walls vary in height from 200 to 300 to 1,600 feet. Marble Canyon is 65½ miles long. At its head it is 200 feet deep, and it steadily increases in depth to its foot, where its walls are 3,500 feet high.

Robert Brewster Stanton

Cataract Canyon from the Junction of the Green and Grand to Dandy Crossing

R. B. Stanton's Down the Colorado *is the account of a railway survey undertaken in 1889, which was published for the first time in 1965. The survey started in Green River Station, Utah, on May 25, 1889, and ended in disaster in Marble Canyon on July 10, 1889, where businessman and sponsor Frank Brown drowned.*

After establishing a true meridian, adjusting all instruments, and locating by triangulation the junction of the three rivers, we took up Kendrick's line, on the afternoon of May 30th., and carried it down about a mile on the left bank of the Colorado, into the head of Cataract Canyon, and walked leisurely up the River and crossed in our boats to camp. The next morning, leaving one of my men with the cook and his helper, for President Brown and his two guests to bring on the boats and camp outfit, and make camp for us below, we continued down the River bank, some four miles, with the survey, until 4:30 P.M., when, although we could have run a mile or two further, we turned back to find our boats before it became dark. We found them some distance up, at the head of the first bad rapid, and camp made on the opposite side of the River. Why over there I never found out, for, as Reynolds says in his published article: "We . . . had difficulty in finding room

---

among the rocks sufficient to spread our blankets,[1] while, on the survey side of the River—the left bank—there were, perhaps, one hundred acres of good, level land, and smooth water between.

It would be a great relief, if it were possible, for me to blot out remembrance of the two weeks following this evening of May 31st. . . . [but] I feel it my duty to put on record this account, taken from my note book written each day as the work progressed.

Our survey work had been all day on a broad almost level talus flat, and although we had seen the boats start from camp in the morning, and pass us about 11:30, we had not seen them again, and only learned of their troubles when, returning up River, we crossed to the new made camp on the right bank.

It was intended to reload the boats at the head of Cataract Canyon and no longer use our raft, but for some reason, after I left camp in the morning, this was not done. Feeling, as I did, a particular interest in the two Negro boys, Gibson and Richards, who had for years been servants in my family and nursed my children, I had told them from the very start, as they were towing the raft of zinc lined boxes, which would be a very difficult craft to handle in rough water, if they got into swift water, to pull to the nearest shore, tie up, and wait for assistance. On reaching camp that evening, I found that this was just what they had done when they first came down the River—had tied up the raft and their own boat, to the left bank in the eddy at the head of the rapid. They were then ordered from the camp, on the opposite side, to bring the raft across the River. Gibson had served fifteen years in the regular army, and knew the nature of an order. They started to obey, and were being drawn down towards the rapid, when, the River being shallow, they both jumped out into the water and struggled hard to save the raft, but the current was too strong, and finding they would be carried through the rapid—a very powerful one—they cut the rope to the raft and let it go. By quick and hard work they saved themselves from going over, and, getting in their boat, pulled to camp. No blame whatever could be attached to the men. We thought we had lost a large part of our food supplies. This proved, however, not to be the case, for we picked up the greater number of the boxes, later on, in the eddies below in perfect condition.

The next day, June 1st., we began our descent of that eighteen and a half mile stretch of raging, tumbling, foaming waters, that so appropriately have

---

1. Ethan A. Reynolds, "In the Whirlpools of the Grand Canyon of the Colorado," *The Cosmopolitan,* Vol. VIII (November, 1889), 29. "None of the first railway party ever saw the Grand Canyon, and Reynolds left the party at Lee's Ferry, sixty-five miles above the head of the Grand Canyon."—Stanton.

given their name to Cataract Canyon. Standing at the head of the first rapid of all, and looking over the tops of the high waves breaking among the angular boulders that filled the channel everywhere, I was forcibly reminded of the character of our brittle cedar boats. We were cautious at first. The survey work was dropped, and all hands spent the day getting our boats and supplies past the first three rapids. We portaged all supplies over the rocky talus and lined the boats down along the shore. All was successfully done, with but one or two exciting moments. As boat No. 3, "The Mary" was being lined down, with Hislop in it to ward it off the rocks, it was caught by a powerful wave, Hislop was carried into a whirlpool, and he and the boat were spun around like a top for several minutes, when suddenly, for no apparent reason, the River having shown what it could do, the boat was lifted up out of the vortex of the whirlpool, and shot into the eddy below, without the least damage. Hislop had lost his oars, which were recovered later, but Coe and Howard went out in another boat and brought him in. Tired out by our day's work we went into camp for our Sunday's rest.

Monday morning, we had our first experience in running real rapids on the Colorado. Having formed my opinion of the unsuitableness of the cedar boats, I can well remember my feelings, as I took my seat in boat No. 2, when, in a moment we were tumbling over the first fall and rolling over the great waves of Rapid No. 4, and on into Rapid No. 5. I tried to calculate how brittle cedar was, and how hard and sharp limestone boulders could be. The two rapids, however, were free from rocks, and the little fleet of six boats danced lightly over and through the waves, with no trouble except a good ducking for all of us.

In Cataract Canyon, which by river is forty-four and two-tenths miles long, this eighteen and a half mile stretch has a fall of 304 feet,[2] divided into fifty-seven rapids and roaring cataracts. It is almost one continuous rapid, being one of the three steepest portions of the Green and Colorado.

The three greatest descents on the two Rivers are as follows:

Lodore Canyon, 16 miles, 425 feet fall, average 26.56 ft. per mile. From Government Reports—and maps, and private data of 1912.

Cataract Canyon, 18½ miles, 304 ft. fall, average 16.43 ft. per mile, with a maximum fall of 55 ft. in two miles. From D.C.C. and P.R.R. Survey, 1889.

Grand Canyon, 10 miles, 165 ft. fall, average 16½ ft. per mile. From Government Maps of 1906, 1907 and 1908. Corrected in 1915.

---

2. "By the D.C.C.&P. Railroad levels."—Stanton.

As to which of these three is the most difficult to navigate with a boat is a matter of opinion, depending also upon the stage of water, and the time of year when it is undertaken. Major Powell had his greatest disaster in the Lodore,[3] we had ours in Cataract, and so did Best in 1891[4] with his heavy oak boats, but, later, [other] parties went through all three without any real disaster at all. When we were going through Cataract, the River was rising, though it had not gotten to its full high water stage, and that year, 1889, the rise did not reach its average height, so that most of the rapids were full of rocks above the water, and their sharp edges played havoc with our *thin cedar* boats. It was not any individual rapid, but the eighteen and a half miles of continuous boiling, tumbling waters among the rocks that wore them out, and so severely tried our powers of endurance.

To do no injustice to the events of this trying time, there would seem to be but one way, that is, by quoting, as far as possible, the record from my note books as written each day, and then giving such explanations as are necessary to make them clear.[5]

"Monday, June 3. Loaded up all boats and all hands got aboard & ran rapid just below camp [No. 8] and in fine style landing on left bank—I then took Bush, Hislop, Potter, Nims, Coe, Rigney & Terry & picked up [our survey] line. . . . Mr. Brown took rest of men to move boats down to next camp/ About noon we came up to [the] boats, & found Boat No. 5 'Colo.' had run against a rock & sunk . . . been under water one hour. Reynolds had Swam out and saved the boat, but almost every thing [in it] was lost. . . . Saved 2 Sax flour, black bag & medicine chest & some dried fruit. . . . [All hands] helped with boats till 2 P.M. [and then we resumed the survey, run-

---

3. One of Powell's boats was completely wrecked. Powell, *Exploration of the Colorado River*, 23–25.

4. A river-running venture under the leadership of James S. Best and under the auspices of the Colorado Grand Canyon Mining and Improvement Company. Stanton, "The River and the Canyon" (manuscript in the New York Public Library), II, 739–43. The manuscript is described in the Introduction.

5. Entries for June 3–6, 1889, Field Notes, Book A (manuscript in the New York Public Library). In this, as in subsequent quotations from his Field Notes, Stanton freely edits without notice; hence it is necessary to introduce editorial ellipses for the omissions he makes and brackets for the additions. Usually the words or passages in brackets represent a rearrangement or a different selection of words by Stanton, but they do not substantially change the meaning of the passages quoted from the Field Notes.

Also, in copying, Stanton supplies punctuation marks which are frequently lacking in his Field Notes. For the sake of accuracy these additions are deleted. For the sake of preserving the flavor of his original passages but at the same time increasing their readability, editorial virgules or slanting lines are introduced to supply needed punctuation.

ning two miles and] Quit work at 4 P.M. [to go up the River to find Camp. As no better progress had been made, it was decided that the next day the whole party should remain to portage the boats and supplies by the heavy rapids.] . . .

"Tuesday, June 4. . . . while we were finishing loading up Cook boat Brown Hughes & Reynolds [the two guests] start off in advance to run the rapid/ After going about ½ m their boat (No. 1 Ward) was Capsized in heaviest [part of the] rapid and all thrown out. They clung to boat & went down some half m. [farther] when they righted her—full of water—Still clung on [the air tight compartments keeping them up] & and were carried down about ½ mile when the eddy took them against [the] right bank at cliff. They scrambled out & stayed on rocks, all day—drying out clothes . . . [and remained there all night as they could not get up the River that day].

"Soon after this in swinging boat 5 [the 'Colorado'] around point—line broke. Sutherland in her & she was Swept about a mile down stream thro same rapid as above but went thro safely, shipped very little water & landed on Left shore. Sutherland quite frightened, but kept his head pulled in the loose line & only lost one oar. One Portage nearly all day/ In rapid No. 10 we swing around all the small boats safely (except 5) when the line of our Cook boat the Brown Betty, being swung round [a point] in the same manner . . . caught on rock under water & held her before she got into rapid. She was swinging into shore nicely when the line as mysteriously let go as it had caught, and let her down into the worst part of the rapid next the shore, and against a huge rock. She did not break at once but soon filled with water. Rigney tied a line around his body [while the men held the line] & jumped into the boat & unloaded her as far as possible—Hislop also went over & helped. We saved a part of the Cooks outfit, but lost all but seven of our plates, all spoons, . . . two camp kettles, the buckets, pans &c &c—Saved the three bake ovens, but only one Cover, the frying pans & cups & a few Sauce pans &c. Lost nearly all our grub in Cook's boat—Tried every way to save the boat but [jammed in under the rock with the whole powerful current beating against it,] she broke all up & was a total loss. After this accident we went into camp (No. 10) just 3,000 ft beyond Camp No. 9, tired and worn out. Having all of us been in the water some up to their necks *all day* Nearly every thing was wet . . . so we spread out our Supplies to dry & found many of them *Spoilt* by being wet & in the sun. Dried peaches Spoiling/Hominy so bad we had to throw it away & everything in very bad shape—The matter of Supplies till we get to the Dandy Crossing begins to look serious. Had a talk this evening with Hislop & Bush & proposed that Brown & his crew [the guests] take Terry & push on & get supplies at Dandy Crossing. They both said this met their approval & that they thought we would get along much better & faster if these men were out of camp. Talked to Several of the men & find a good deal of dissatisfaction among them as to the way Mr. Brown is managing the expedition & the way Hughes & Reynolds try to boss the handling of the boats. . . .

"Wednesday, June 5. . . . moved down river about a mile & camped . . . about center of large flat, one mile long by 1,000 ft wide at mouth of Side canyon coming in from East. . . . [Rapids] not so bad. . . . [The 'Mary' had bow badly broken—but all repaired on] reaching Camp—By the boats leaking *all* our provisions got wet again & I . . . Spread every thing out. . . & took stock . . . have still left about

4 weeks supply of flour,
3 weeks supply of bacon,
1 weeks supply of sugar
6 weeks supply of dried fruit &
6 to 8 weeks supply of coffee.
With enough Salt, pepper &c . . .

"As we started with 75 days supplies of everything this looks rather serious. I . . . went to Mr. Brown [who had come across the River from their stay under the cliff] & proposed that he . . . [and his men, with Terry,] go in advance to Dandy Crossing & get supplies ready for us. And we would push on as rapidly as possible [with the survey]. Telling him that the men were getting alarmed about our grub & I feared that when the men Saw their supplies were getting so low they would abandon the Survey—take what was left & go down river. He said he would think of it over night. . . .

"Thursday, June 6. Mr. Brown told me this morning he could not go down river with one boat, but proposed to divide the party & go down with Seven men to Dandy Crossing—get supplies for us & start new survey there, & leave us to catch up. I told him this would gain nothing except get supplies & would cripple the party and in my opinion would be unwise . . . [and the discussion ended.] Resumed Ry Survey at 6:30 [(a mile and a half above camp No. 11)]/ . . . Ran today over 5 miles. . . . stopped at 4:30 to go back to find boats/"

Just here it may be well to explain, that it would have been possible to make the survey through the Cataract and Narrow Canyons in ten days, if we had had a means of keeping our camp up with the work. For the greater part of the way the survey was a simple matter, over the broad flats and sloping talus, as shown in many of our photographs. In a few places, the cliffs rising up vertically from the water to some height, though not to the top of the canyon, cut off easy progress on foot; but, with a boat to cross the River in smooth water, it is possible to walk at low water time, dry shod, the whole length by crossing from side to side. It is true that in doing this one would have to leave the River in a number of places, and go along the ledges a hundred or so feet above the water, and, in one place at least, three hundred feet up, but the whole distance could be traveled in that manner.

It would not be possible while making such a survey to transport on the men's backs the necessary supplies for subsistence, but, in a final location survey, trails could be cheaply built so as to transport by burros all necessary supplies.[6] . . . easily good wagon roads can be built, through some of the difficult portions of Glen Canyon . . . we built some years later. I refer to this, at this time, to show why our survey work went by fits and starts, and how the handling of the brittle cedar boats was so slow and disastrous, without special, experienced boatmen to handle them, while we were on the survey work.

June 6th (continued). We found the boats "about 2 miles back & 2 m. below last camp [No. 12]. Water had been good to this point & they had come down without accident—except boats leak—more provisions—and cook's bedding thoroughly wet. . . .

"Friday, June 7. Resumed Survey. . . . [two miles below camp, and] Ran about 2½ miles. . . . 2:15 Hansbrough comes up with a bucket of bread, corn bread & bacon all worked into a mush by being under the river for an hour. We each took a hand full of this mixture & 'sopped' it up & Started back to camp which we found 2½ miles back at the point where we Started line this A.M. We learn that, while Bush & Hislop came down from Camp 12 to this point safely early this A.M., when rest of party came down, the cook boat was upset—lost *all* plates & . . . Reynolds [and Hughes had their boat] . . . sucked down . . . in whirlpool [which Reynolds described later in these words:]

> Just as we passed a jutting pinnacle of rock, we were unaccountably swept into a small but vicious whirlpool which was just behind it. Around and around we spun, and although I rowed with all my might, we drew steadily nearer the vortex. Finally my end of the boat began to sink, and Hughes's end to rise in the air. Finding we were going down, I let go of the oars, and hung on to the seat of the boat. I saw Hughes twirled around once or twice, and then the boat *seemed* to end straight up, and I went clean under the water together with half of the boat. I suppose that I was under but half a minute, though I found myself getting short for breath. The sensation was very queer, but there was a pleasant relief from the roar of the water. Suddenly, the

---

6. Stanton, "Availability of the Canyons of the Colorado River," *Transactions* of the American Society of Civil Engineers, Vol. XXVI (1892), 318–19—Stanton.

> vortex being choked, it released its grip, and the boat shot into the air. As I came up Hughes called to me to hold on. I called back, asking him if I was not holding on, and shook the water from my eyes just in time to see a huge wave roll over Hughes and give him a beautiful ducking. The boat did not capsize, and although we had lost an oar, we managed to paddle into the current, and soon reached shore. . . .[7]

". . . Sunday, June 9. . . . Mr. Brown's & Gibson's [the Cook's] *Birthday/* [Gibson was much chagrined that his stores would not permit him to make a birthday cake for Pres. Brown.]

"Monday, June 10. . . . [To-day we made] *one* long & *two* Short Port [ages, and lined down our boats a distance of one and one-quarter miles, over some very heavy rapids, without serious accident and] . . . Went into camp . . . [tired out] at 4:30/

"Just before this Brown & Hughes . . . attempted to push on over rapid No. 31—Line got caught in oar lock, swung boat No. 1 ["The Ward"] into Current. They could not hold her—& so she went down [over the rapid. In it was a new] . . . transit, 2 sax flour 1 keg Vinegar, 3 sax fruit, 1 sax beans &c, &c. Brown & Potter followed boat . . . [on shore] for 3 miles, but saw nothing of it. [It was found four days later practically uninjured.]

"On the way [they] found *one* of the *five* floats [zinc boxes of the raft], which were lost June 1st. It was buried in sand in eddy . . . & contained 2 sax flour, 2 cans tomatoes, soap 2 sax fruit, 1 sax meal, & some tobacco all in pretty good condition. . . .

"Tuesday, June 11. . . . Brown, Reynolds & Hughes [the two guests] Stayed in camp—all forenoon/ Made in all *five* portages today two very long & 3 short. . . . [Only two slight accidents to the brittle cedar planking of our boats.]

"Wednesday, June 12. (Reynolds) & Hughes start [up side Canyon] after resin for boats. All hands moving still further down river—but every one is so stiff and sore that but little progress can be made. . . . [Worked until noon, and then] went back to last camp for lunch because cook had *bean Soup* for us. . . . [In the afternoon the "Mary," No. 3, damaged] against a rock . . . losing our last coffee pot, all but nine cups, all our dried peaches and one sack of beans. . . . [We thought our cook would be in a bad humor with no coffee pot, but, with his characteristic cheerfulness, he simply said: 'Never mind sir; leave me a tomato can and a frying pan, and I'll get you a good

---

7. Reynolds, "In the Whirlpools of the Grand Canyon of the Colorado," *The Cosmopolitan*, Vol. VIII (November, 1889), 30–32. Italics by Stanton.

supper,' and he did. Later, Howard and his men had a similar accident with Boat No. 5, 'Colorado,' losing the last of our meat, some more fruit and beans;] Rather a bad disaster to wind up the day . . . [at camp No. 17, but] Potter . . . reports finding two more 'floats' intact . . . [containing] 2 sax flour, coffee, Syrup, 2 kegs pickles, 12 cans cond. milk. A [very] good find.

"Thursday, June 13. . . . Breakfast on Flap Jacks, Syrup & coffee/ [the engineer party walked back two miles and resumed the survey.] . . . Line today is the heaviest work we have yet encountered. . . . [Made camp, two miles, by 3:00 P.M., and, from 4:30 to 6:15, one and one-quarter miles farther. It is also the heaviest fall in the river, put down in the Government reports as] '75 ft fall in ¾ mile'. . .[but our levels show] only about 55 ft in *two miles* . . . [as the greatest fall in any mile distance.]"[8]

Other Dangers Beside Rapids

One personal incident, in Cataract Canyon, I will relate, as one time when, I am free to acknowledge, I was completely unnerved. Going over the rough rocky talus, stepping from boulder to boulder, I slipped and my right foot went down between two rocks. My foot was jammed in tight, and I lost my balance sideways, so that my whole weight was thrown against the strength of the bones of my right leg, resting against the top edge of the rock about one-quarter way below the knee. It was only a few seconds, but it seemed an hour while I was waiting to hear those bones snap. In that short time, I realized the whole situation; where we were, the height of the limestone cliffs, the distance to outside assistance, the heat of the summer, and that when those bones gave way—the end. Not a sudden blotting out of existence, that was not what I feared, but with a mangled leg, a sure, but lingering, death in that hot desolate canyon. I was utterly astonished that the bones could resist such a sudden strain, but they did not break. I regained my balance, and, extricating my foot, stood up, but then came the reaction and I fell limp upon the ground. In after months, we dashed in our boats at least one hundred times into the head of a rapid, with no certainty that we would be alive at its foot; that never affected me, but the memory of the moments, which seemed hours, of waiting for those bones to snap, and contemplating that *lingering death,* makes me shudder, even to this day.

Such work as we had in Cataract Canyon, with our frail boats, being thrown into the water bodily every day, and working in water almost up to ones arm pits for days at a time, guiding boats through the whirlpools and eddies, and,

---

8. Entries for June 6–7, 9–13, 1889, Field Notes, Book A.

when not thus engaged, carrying sacks of flour and greasy bacon on ones back, over boulders half as high as a house, is not the most pleasant class of engineering work to contemplate—except as a "backsight."

Hislop and I had another experience, at our Camp No. 17, which we never told of at the time, but which afterwards leaked out. Our instruments had had some pretty severe knocking about over the rocks, and after adjusting them, we decided to take that night another observation of the North Star, for a true meridian, to test the transit work. We were camped on a broad flat, cut by many small gulches, and in order not to carry the instrument out in the night, we set it up over a permanent hub in a little cove on the side of one of the gullies, before dark, and went to bed to wait for the proper time for our observation towards morning. We were up before 2:00 A.M., in plenty of time, and, with a lantern, wandered up and down that flat for an hour and a half, searched in and out of every gulch we could find, looked behind every rock—but nowhere could we find a transit.

The North Star had other business to attend to, and paid no attention to our misfortunes, but went on its way and was soon in a position to be of no service to us that night. The next morning, we slipped out and said nothing, to find where that transit had gone, and we discovered it, encircled by our footmarks in the sand where we had walked around it a half-dozen times—within twenty feet of it. We had lost a half night's sleep; lost our tempers as well, and had gotten no observation. We attempted to account for this by the peculiar shape of a bush near by, and seeing them together we thought the transit part of the bush—for we did not admit, even to ourselves, that we could not find it. The boys found us out later, and it was our treat, so we invited them all down to the (sand) bar and gave them a cup of River water at our expense.

In my note book I find:

"Thursday, June 13. . . . While in camp (17) at dinner I . . . took stock of all provision . . .

No meat
5# dried fruit
[150#] . . . flour . . .
2 weeks [supply] coffee
12 Cans Cond. milk
10# beans
6 cans Tomatoes
30# lard
2# baking powder
Salt, pepper &c.

. . . Sutherland found [to-day in a drift pile] ½ barrel ½ full white *lump sugar.*

This is pretty slim for sixteen men & will not last even with *short* allowance for Six days. Mr. Brown does not seem to grasp the Situation . . . but goes on as if we had two months Supplies in camp. He seemed much Surprised when I started out after dinner (4:30) to run more line & was thunderstruck when I suggested that he and the rest of the men [in camp] . . . bring down . . . [the rest of the boats. Nothing was done except our survey work,] but at dark all howled for Supper. This making *four* meals for . . . [our guests] today. . . . After supper . . . I took Brown aside and explained the Situation that we did not have Six days provisions in Camp, and if we went on as we were . . . we would all be hungry before we got . . . [to] Dandy Crossing. . . . I told him I would take 5 men . . . our share of the [grub and go ahead with the survey,] . . . and leave him 10 men to repair boats and overtake us. . . . [He consented,] & said if . . . I was able to go on & do as I thought best, . . . I then went to the [men, and] . . . will take Hislop, Coe, Rigney, Potter & Hansbrough.

"Friday, June 14. . . . At 9:00 A.M. . . . [we were ready to separate. My party] had 10 cakes of [light] bread . . . 12 inch in diam. & 1½ in. thick/ . . . [which] gave 1⅔ cakes to each man [in a cotton sack, some coffee and canned milk]. . . . We each stopped as we passed and took in our sacks some of the government Sugar . . . The keg was marked [on its end] thus, [the three dotted lines being so blurred that they could not be read:]

[We] Ran 3 miles . . . & camped [without blankets] in broad [open flat]. . . . Our rations being very short we lunched today on *three lumps sugar* and *plenty* of river water. For supper . . . [one-tenth of the amount of bread we had,] with a cup of hot water & Condensed milk. . . .

"Saturday, June 15. . . . Breakfast consisted of 1/6 of loaf bread 2 cups of coffee & one lump of sugar. . . . [With] 2 lumps sugar & *plenty* of water for lunch. . . . [With this we ran three and one-quarter miles, when we came to] an *almost* perpendicular cliff rising out of the water with a very swift rapid running at its base. . . . [Having no boat to cross the river, three of us started over to get a sight ahead. Made it easily, on a bench 300 ft. up. In a cove in the limestone, found a beautiful clear spring, with bright green shrubbery of many kinds growing around it. This was most refreshing, as we had not had a drink for many hours. We had gone farther than we supposed, and, on account of a bend in the cliff, could not see the instrument men. It being now 7 o'clock we could not return.]

"Sunday, June 16. . . . make another attempt to get along [under] the cliff . . . where the transitman can see us, but . . . [it could not be done] without a boat. . . . [and so we go] back over the cliff to join the other boys. . . . and go back to [get boat No. 1, the "Ward," the one lost six days ago, and which we had found.] . . . about 1 m. back [up the River, from the cliff we had crossed], met Howard & saw various things—bags blankets &c floating down river. Howard told us the whole party were about 2 ms up river, . . . that Bush and Hughes had lost the boat "Denver" . . . [in which] was Bush's transit, . . . [two sacks of flour, etc.] Meet whole party . . . about noon. They had come down from Camp #17 [four miles, over some of the worst of the rapids,] in the last day & a half, . . . making five portages on Saturday and three today. [To get material to repair the boats,] They had torn up [the most damaged one—] the "Mary" . . . This affected Brown very much [and brought tears to his eyes,] as the boat was named for his wife. . . . The men went over river & got Boat Ward No. 1 [lost June 10th]. Found it little damaged [so we still have four boats. All the party being together again we made camp No. 19.][9]

Prompt Action Necessary

I had a long talk with my old household servant, Gibson, who told me the real condition of affairs. There had been great grumbling. The men [were] threatening to take the boats and leave down the River for grub. It seemed to me that it was time for some vigorous action, and, without consultation with anyone, I took the responsibility upon myself. I ordered Gibson to cook at once everything there was in camp, and then sat down for a rest. We had supper on a large fish Hislop had caught. After supper, the cook and I divided all the food into sixteen equal parts, putting it in separate piles on a log. Each pile consisted of one and one-half cakes of bread, twelve inches in diameter and one inch thick, without baking powder or salt, one can of condensed milk, a little coffee, and hand full of beans. I then called President

9. Entries for June 13–16, 1889, Field Notes, Book A.

Brown and all the men up to the log, and told them there was all there was left, that each man must take his share and care for it himself. That I had determined to remain with that amount of food, and finish the survey out of the canyon (twenty-seven miles) with as many men as would stay with me. This seemed to stagger most of the men. President Brown was particular to say he would not ask me to remain, nor would he ask any one to stay and work without enough to eat, but, if we did stay, he would hurry back supplies to us even if he had to carry a sack of flour on his shoulders up the River. It was arranged that he should go ahead, with one boat and a few men, and send back supplies from Dandy Crossing, some thirty seven miles down the River.

Separation of the Party

The next morning, I learned from Hislop that the men had had a conference, and nearly all had determined to go out at once to try to induce all the men to leave, so as to prevent me from staying, in order to place upon me the responsibility of quitting the survey. I was determined to remain, knowing that if we abandoned the survey then, we could not return to it, and feeling sure we could carry on the work to Dandy Crossing with what food we had. I did not intend to leave without an effort to complete the work if men enough would remain to assist me.

At such times, men's real characters come to the surface. I said to Hislop: "Well, Hislop, what are you going to do?" Straightening up his six feet two, and stiffening his Scottish backbone, he said: "Mr. Stanton, I came down here as your assistant engineer, to obey your orders. I am here, sir!" I spoke to the two Negro men, Gibson and Richards. They both said they would stay with me, and then C. W. Potter came without my asking and volunteered to remain.

The other men tried in every way to persuade Potter to go. It had no effect, for Potter was one of the most faithful, plucky, and determined little men I ever knew. They then attacked Gibson, thinking they could reach me through my personal servant. They tried to frighten him, by telling him we would all starve, and Gibson answered, with that true loyalty which I had known so long: "No, sir! If Mr. Stanton stays here and starves to death, I stay and starve to death with him." They also sent Hansbrough, my old foreman from Idaho, to plead with me not to stay. His effort was on account of his personal feeling for me, and he proved it by demanding later that he be one of the crew to bring us back food, which came the next week.

Of all the men who left me at that time, I have felt most kindly towards Hansbrough, for his efforts to save me from what he felt was sure destruction in the rapids, or, worse than that, starvation. It was not a pleasant prospect, for not far below where we were camped we had found, that day, a human skeleton, among the timbers of a drift pile—ghastly suggestion of what might be our fate. It was but a month after, when, not I, but Hansbrough himself sank beneath the muddy waters in Marble Canyon never to rise again. Six months later, as I helped to bury his bleached bones in the sands beside a marble cliff, I thought of his kind and earnest efforts to save me from such a last resting place.

On the morning of June 17th., we separated, the eleven men taking three boats, and leaving us one. In the first rapid, they had a slight accident and lost the "grub sacks" of three of the men, and then they threw everything away—blankets, clothes, and everything else, except their remaining grub. This was the last rapid, No. 57, of the 18½ mile tumble of Cataract Canyon. They soon turned a bend in the River, and we saw them no more for days to come.

Just how long it took President Brown and his men to reach Dandy Crossing, I do not know, but they arrived pretty well starved out. This incident was related to me afterwards. The Hites, with true frontier hospitality, at once set to work cooking dinner. The table in the little cabin, . . . was too small for the whole party to sit at, at one time. Part of them ate at the first table, among whom was the hungriest one of the outfit, the one man I had known as such, all the way from Green River. This man ate as long, and as fast, as the rest, and, when the second table was ready, went in again and ate as long as the second meal lasted. When the third batch was called, he tried it for the third time, but here he failed and gave himself away.

Food for the hungry man is common property in such a barren country, and I may relate here how one man invited himself to dinner, at my cabin in Colorado, in 1897. We were camped at Tickaboo. We had just finished our dinner, when a stranger rode up and, without even saying "Howdy," exclaimed, as he alighted: "I'm good and damned hungry!" That was all. We soon filled him up, though there was a large cavity to fill, for he had been without food for two days, and I did not blame him for his emphatic language. This man became one of my best friends, in Utah, for the next four years.

The Work of Our Party of Five

Our small party, with the one boat, triangulated around the cliff, and camped (No. 20) on the opposite bank of the River, at the foot of rapid No. 57. This cliff was the first Vertical one, more than forty or fifty feet high, that we had seen. It was perhaps 500 feet high, and *seemed* perpendicular from the water, but in reality had small benches along it, one of which, 300 feet up, we had traveled over twice in the last two days; and, above the 500 feet height, the walls benched back in easy benches to the top.

This is the only point where any such height of vertical walls is found in Cataract Canyon, and this is not one-half mile long nor is it straight. A sketch made in my note book at the time shows the cross section of the canyon at this point, as it appeared from Camp No. 20.

On this part of the survey we had no photograph instruments with us. . . .

Even with this form, it is remarkable what an effect such a narrow gorge has upon one in looking up through it, especially when lying in bed. At first it is perfectly natural in shape, but, as you look, the walls seem to close in upon you, especially from the top, and, if one will let his imagination run riot with his thoughts, he can easily *feel* the cliffs closing in upon him and hanging over his head. It was of this section, at a point a little farther down, that Major Powell wrote . . . "the canyon is very tortuous, so that we can see but a few hundred feet ahead; the walls tower over us, often overhanging *so as to almost shut out the light.*"[10] The rock of this part of the Canyon is hard flinty limestone.

I find in my topography book the following notes, made during the survey, of the section just below the cliff at Camp No. 20, in short distances covering about three miles. "Over hanging cliffs both sides, water fills canyon, *with benches above* beginning from 40 to 100 ft. above River, and continuing to top," "Over hanging cliff, 40 to 50 ft. high, with talus slope below." "Second bench, 40 to 50 ft. wide, extends for three quarters mile, 40 to 100 feet above the River," the narrowest part from wall to wall being from 250 to 300 ft. wide, at the bottom. With these notes, and the evidence of the U.S. Geological Survey maps, made in after years, made largely, if not entirely, from the notes of the work of 1871 and '72, I rewrite what I stated in 1889—There is not a stretch of the River, one-half mile in length, where the direct rays of the sun do not shine on the water, at some time of the day, during some season of the year. And in this part of the Canyon, the cliffs do not over hang more than 10 to 30 feet and that only in points, and are only 50, 100, or 300 feet high, (the latter in one place) where they approach the vertical, and then bench back, by narrow and broader benches, to the top. The Canyon is about 1,800 feet deep, and the walls at the top are from *3,500 feet to one mile apart.* Rather a difficult place, I should think, *to "shut out the light!"*

Making our survey, with only one boat, in the narrow part of the Canyon, where the walls in points were vertical next to the river—even if only for fifty or one hundred feet up—was a risky operation. At one point, with the transit on a little sand pile at the mouth of a small side canyon, with vertical walls

---

10. Powell, Exploration of the Colorado River, 67.—Stanton. Italics by Stanton.

above and below us, the three boys went ahead in the boat to set a point a half-mile beyond, expecting to return for us, while Hislop and I remained to take the sight. The water was smooth, but, when the boys below tried to row upstream to us, they found the current was so strong in the narrow, confined channel, that they could make no progress. Hislop and I climbed up the little side gulch, and along the cliff on a bench a hundred feet above the River, and, after a hard scramble down, finally reached the boat.

We were now below all but one of the rapids of Cataract Canyon, and the water was much less powerful, having much less fall. We made good progress with our survey, except being hindered by having only one boat. At one point it was necessary to triangulate a cliff, about one hundred feet high, where the water filled the canyon from wall to wall. With five men, instruments, etc. in our boat, it was a very dangerous operation. We were fearful we would have to give up the work. It being late, we ran the rapid at that point to find a camping place. Everyone was sad with the possible prospect of having to abandon the survey. Drifting down about half a mile, we came to a good camping ground, and, at the same time rounding a point, we saw what seemed to be open country ahead, with the setting sun shining in all its splendor of color on the marble cliffs beyond. It was such a glorious sight, after being for days in the narrow canyon, that it inspired everyone, and Potter and the negro boys spoke up first, and said: "We'll go back in the morning and bring down the survey," which, of course, we did.

How it Affected the Men

Before going farther, I wish to give credit and due praise to the four men who voluntarily remained with me on this particularly arduous piece of work. They were of the stuff that heroes are made of. They had, with the exception of Hislop, no professional pride at stake. For six days in all we toiled on, continuing the survey at the rate of four miles a day, with one small piece of bread, a little coffee and milk for our morning and evening meal, and three lumps of sugar and as much of the River water as we wished at noon. Under such circumstances the true nobleness of men's character [is] either shown in bright colors, or entirely lost. The men worked on without a murmur, carrying the survey over the rocks and cliffs on the side of the canyon and handling the boat through the rapids of the River. At night, when they [lay] down upon the sand to sleep, after a meal that was nine-tenths water and hope, and one-tenth bread and coffee, it was without a complaint. The deprivation did not of course affect all alike. Hislop and I cared little. It was not the first time that each of us had gone days with little or nothing to eat, and kept at our work. Potter, I think, deserves most praise. He started out in the morning cheerful and willing, and worked without flinching all day; but he was working upon his determination and nerve, for as soon as we stopped for camp, and the boat was tied up, he fell on the ground a total wreck. Each night I would mix him a cup of milk and water with a few spoons full of brandy (a small bottle of which I saved from the devastation, by our guests, of our medicine chest) and make him drink it, before he could sit up and eat his supper of three ounces of bread and coffee. After a night's sleep he was as ready and willing to push on as he was the day before. Richards, though perfectly willing, could not stand the loss of food as well as his Negro brother, and Gibson, unselfish fellow that he was, would each time divide his scanty meal and make Richards eat half of it.

It is but justice to say here that Nims, the photographer, was willing to stay with us, but, having only one boat, it was impossible to let him. Gibson took it upon himself to find some wild game to help out our scanty store, and was up by daylight wandering up the side canyons and over the cliffs with his rifle. He had no cooking to do now, but he never as much as had one shot. We put our fishing lines out every night, baited with lizards, but never a fish.

Our work was all earnest labor and much of it sad toil. One afternoon, as we were coming in our boat to camp, our cook spied, sitting on a rock down the River—not three, but only one black crow. The work was stopped, the boat was landed, and the whole railroad interest of the country stood still for the while. The cook crept out upon the sand bar with his Winchester. Our hearts beat quick in joyous expectation. Crack! went the rifle, and behind the rock fell the crow. Into the boat we jumped, and as we floated down the River, our cook grew eloquent on the supper he was going to prepare. Broiled crow, baked crow, and stewed crow with plenty of gravy! We stopped on the little sand bar on which he was, there he lay—our luscious supper—behind the rock. But, just as Gibson went to pick him up, he raised his wings and gracefully flew away. Poor fellow, he had only one leg broken, and we had lost our supper. It is said that blessings brighten as they take their flight. As that one black crow soared far above us into the light of the setting sun, he looked as large as a Rhode Island turkey.

It was on June 20th, in this narrow part of Cataract Canyon, that I discovered the inscription on the wall of "D. Julien"[11] . . . In the afternoon, we

11. "For myself, I claim to have discovered but few things in all of the Canyons through which we traveled in 1889 and '90. One of these few new things, that I did find, was an inscription on the left hand wall near the lower end of Cataract Canyon, recording the adventure of another early explorer of the Canyons this time of the Colorado itself. This was first seen on June 20th, 1889." Stanton, "The River and the Canyon," I, 135.

came to the half-mile chute of water so graphically described by Major Powell in his Report . . . but the water was undoubtedly much higher than when he was there, and, with only one boat, we were obliged to use great caution. Portaging the boat, etc. over the head of the rapid, and then running our survey line down to where the current beat up against a sixty foot marble wall, we took a bearing to a rock down the River, and set up a driftwood stick, twenty-eight feet high, with cross arms nailed at every foot, for a stadia rod. Hislop and Potter then ran the rapid in beautiful style.

The description of this rapid, referred to above, is so true as given by Major Powell, that I take the liberty of quoting it:

> We made two portages this morning, one of them very long. During the afternoon we run a chute, more than half a mile in length, narrow and rapid. The chute has a floor of marble; the rocks dip in the direction in which we are going, and the fall of the stream conforms to the inclination of the beds; so we float on water that is gliding down an inclined plane. At the foot of the chute, the river turns sharply to the right, and the water rolls up against a rock which, from above, seems to stand directly athwart its course. As we approach it, we pull with all power to the right, but it seems impossible to avoid being carried headlong against the cliff, and we are carried up high on the waves—not against the rocks, for the rebounding water strikes us, and we are beaten back, and pass on with safety, except that we get a good drenching.[12]

Thus on this 20th. of June, our party of five with our one little frail boat, made exactly the same two portages, "one of them very long," that were made on July 28th, '69 twenty years before . . . ran five other rapids, crossed the River ten times, for angle points to triangulate around cliffs where the water filled the whole gorge, besides rowing up stream three-quarters of a mile, and made four and a half miles of railroad survey, doing all instrument work, and sketching complete contour topography; which I think is a pretty fair answer to criticism referred to [above] . . . that we "seldom attempted to cross the river . . . never entering the boats at all except where absolutely necessary, [and] Thus they were greatly hampered in their movements."[13]

For additional description and comments on this inscription dated 1836, see Stanton, "Availability of the Canyons of the Colorado River," *Transactions* of the American Society of Civil Engineers, Vol. XXVI (1892), 284–85.

12. Powell, *Exploration of the Colorado River,* 66.

13. Dellenbaugh, *The Romance of the Colorado River,* 351.

Provisions Reach Us From Below

Our provisions being so very valuable just now, we did not trust them to the boat, but we carried the grub, and all instruments, over the cliff past the rapid, which filled the canyon from wall to wall. At 6:30 this evening, as we were coming down the hill, we met Howard, Coe, and Hansbrough, who had come up the River from Dandy Crossing, with plenty of supplies, through Narrow Canyon to a point some four miles above Millecrag Bend. Our only trouble now was not to eat too much at our first supper. Two of the men forgot the necessity to be careful, and were made very sick, but Hislop and I ate two griddle cakes, drank one cup of coffee, and went to bed well satisfied with our supper and the work of the past week.

Now having two boats, and all the heavy rapids of Cataract Canyon being behind us, we skipped along, making six to eight miles of survey each day, at the cost of some exertion, however, for a plentiful supply of food made us tired, listless, and sleepy. We reached Dandy Crossing at the mouth of Trachyte Creek the evening of June 24th, having rested the day before, over Sunday, at the lower end of Narrow Canyon, at a number of magnificent sulphur springs—hot ones at one side of the river, and cold ones on the other.

In the afternoon of Sunday, President Brown came up from Dandy Crossing and congratulated us on our bringing the survey successfully through.

The distance through Cataract Canyon is forty-four and two-tenths miles, and Narrow Canyon, eight and three-tenths miles. *By our survey*, which, on the broad flats, cut off as much distance as possible, these distances were—Cataract, 39.585 miles and Narrow, 7.575 miles, with the fall of the River in this distance of our survey of 47.16 miles, of 355 feet, having at one point the extreme fall of 55 feet in two miles.[14]

14. "In [Table 1 page 226] . . . will be found the tabulated results of this work of the first railroad division on the Colorado, and also that from Grand Junction, Colorado, to the head of the River, together with the other divisions extending to the Gulf of California."—Stanton.

John C. Van Dyke

The Silent River

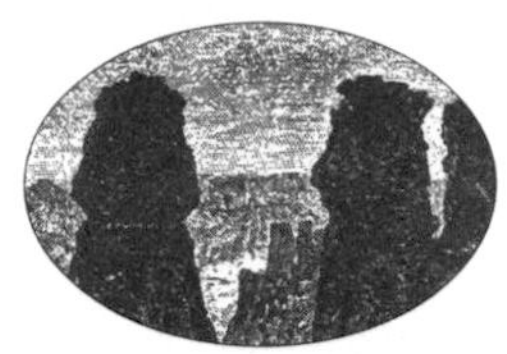

The Colorado River itself is the center of attention in this excerpt from explorer J. C. Van Dyke's Desert. *Other chapters in the volume focus on the plants, animals, and vivid landscapes of the arid desert of the American Southwest.*

The career of the Colorado, from its rise in the Wind River Mountains in Wyoming to its final disappearance in the Gulf of California, seems almost tragic in its swift transitions. It starts out so cheerily upon its course; it is so clear and pure, so sparkling with sunshine and spirit. It dashes down mountain valleys, gurgles under bowlders, swirls over waterfalls, flashes through ravines and gorges. With its sweep and glide and its silvery laugh it seems to lead a merry life. But too soon it plunges into precipitous canyons and enters upon its fierce struggle with the encompassing rock. Now it boils and foams, leaps and strikes, thunders and shatters. For hundreds of miles it wears and worries and undermines the rock to its destruction. During the long centuries it has cut down into the crust of the earth five thousand feet. But ever the stout walls keep casting it back, keep churning it into bubbles, beating it into froth. At last, its canyon course run, exhausted and helpless, it is pushed through the escarpments, thrust out upon the desert, to find its way to the sea as best it can. Its spirit is broken, its vivacity is extinguished, its color is deepened to a dark red—the trail of blood that leads up to the death. Wearily now it drifts across the desert without a ripple, without a moan. Like a wounded snake it

---

From *The Desert* by John C. Van Dyke (New York: Charles Scribner's Sons, 1901).

drags its length far down the long wastes of sand to where the blue waves are flashing on the California Gulf. And there it meets—obliteration.

After the clash and roar of the conflict in the canyons how impressive seems the stillness of the desert, how appalling the unbroken silence of the lower river! Day after day it moves seaward, but without a sound. You start at its banks to find no waves, no wash upon gravel beaches, no rush of water over shoals. Instead of the soothing murmur of breaking falls there is at times the boil of currents from below—waters flung up sullenly and soon flattened into drifting nothingness by their own weight.

And how heavily the stream moves! Its load of silt is gradually settling to the bottom, yet still the water seems to drag upon the shores. Every reef of sand, every island of mud, every overhanging willow or cottonwood or handful of arrow-weed holds out a restraining hand. But slowly, patiently, winding about obstructions, cutting out new channels, creeping where it may not run, the bubbleless water works its way to the sea. The night-winds steal along its shores and pass in and out among its sedges, but there are no whispering voices; and the stars emerge and shine upon the flat floor of water, but there is no lustre. The drear desolation of it! The blare of morning sunlight does not lift the pall, nor the waving illusions of the mirage break the stillness. The Silent River moves on carrying desolation with it; and at every step the waters grow darker, darker with the stain of red—red the hue of decay.

It was not through paucity of imagination that the old Spaniards gave the name—Colorado.[1] During the first fifty years after its discovery the river was christened many times, but the name that finally clung to it was the one that gave accurate and truthful description. You may see on the face of the globe numerous muddy Missouris, blue Rhones, and yellow Tibers; but there is only one red river and that the Colorado. It is not exactly an earthy red, not the color of shale and clay mixed; but the red of peroxide of iron and copper, the *sang-du-boeuf* red of oriental ceramics, the deep insistent red of things time-worn beyond memory. And there is more than a veneer about the color. It has a depth that seems luminous and yet is sadly deceptive. You do not see below the surface no matter how long you gaze into it. As well try to see through a stratum of porphyry as through that water to the bottom of the river.

To call it a river of blood would be exaggeration, and yet the truth lies in the exaggeration. As one walks along its crumbling banks there is the thought of that other river that changed its hue under the outstretched rod of the

1. Colorado is said to be the Spanish translation of the Piman name *buqui aquimuti*, according to the late Dr. Elliot Coues; but the Spanish word was so obviously used to denote the red color of the stream, that any translation from the Indian would seem superfluous.

prophet. How weird indeed must have been the ensanguined flow of the Nile, with its little waves breaking in crests of pink foam! How strange the shores where the receding waters left upon sand and rock a bordering line of scarlet froth! But the Colorado is not quite like that—not so ghastly, not so unearthly. It may suggest at times the heavy welling flow of thickening blood which the sands at every step are trying to drink up; but this is suggestion only, not realization. It seems to hint at blood, and under starlight to resemble it; but the resemblance is more apparent than real. The Colorado is a red river but not a scarlet one.

It may be thought odd that the river should change so radically from the clear blue-green of its fountain-head to the opaque red of its desert stream, but rivers when they go wandering down to the sea usually leave their mountain purity behind them. The Colorado rushing through a thousand miles of canyons, cuts and carries seaward with it red sands of shale, granite, and porphyry, red rustings of iron, red grits of carnelian, agate and garnet. All the tributaries come bearing their tokens of red copper, and with the rains the whole red surface of the watershed apparently washes into the smaller creeks and thus into the valleys. When the river reaches the desert carrying its burden of silt, it no longer knows the bowlder-bed, the rocky shores, the breaking waterfalls that clarify a stream. And there are no large pools where the water can rest while the silt settles to the bottom. Besides, the desert itself at times pours into the river an even deeper red than the canyons. And it does this not through arroyos alone, but also by a wide surface drainage.

Often the slope of the desert to the river is gradual for many miles—sometimes like the top of a huge table slightly tilted from the horizontal. When the edge of the table is reached the mesa begins to break into terraces (often cut through by small gullies), and the final descent is not unlike the steps of a Roman circus leading down into the arena. During cloud-bursts the waters pour down these steps with great fury and the river simply acts as a catch-basin for all the running color of the desert.

The "bottom" lands, forming the immediate banks of the river, are the silt deposits of former years. Often they are several miles in width and are usually covered with arrow-weed, willows, alders, and cottonwoods. The growth is dense if not tall and often forms an almost impenetrable jungle through which are scattered little openings where grass and flowers grow and Indians build reed wickiups and raise melons and corn in season. The desert terraces on either side (sometimes there is a row of sand-dunes) come down to meet these "bottom" lands, and the line where the one leaves off and the other begins is drawn as with the sharp edge of a knife. Seen from the distant mountain tops the river moves between two long ribbons of green, and the borders are the gray and gold mesas of the desert.

Afloat and drifting down between these lines of green your attention is perhaps not at first attracted by the water. You are interested in the thickets of alders and the occasional bursts of white and yellow flowers from among the bushes. They are very commonplace bushes, very ordinary flowers; but how lovely they look as they seem to drift by the boat! How silent again are these clumps of alder and willow! There may be linnets and sparrows among them but they do not make their presence obtrusive in song. A hawk wheels along over the arrow-weed looking for quail, but his wings cut the air without noise. How deathly still everything seems! The water wears into the soft banks, the banks keep sloughing into the stream, but again you hear no splashing fall.

And the water itself is just as soundless. There is never a sunken rock to make a little gurgle, never a strip of gravel beach where a wave could charm you with its play. The best of oars breaks the air with a jar, but breaks no bubbles on the water. You look long at the stream and fall to wondering if there can be any life in it. What besides a polywog or a bullhead could live there? Obviously, and in fact—nothing. Perhaps there are otter and beaver living along the pockets in the banks? Yes; there were otter and beaver here at one time, but they are very scarce to-day. But there are wild fowl? Yes; in the spring and fall the geese and ducks follow the river in their flights, but they do not like the red water. What proof? Because they do not stop long in any one place. They swing into a bayou or slough late at night and go out at early dawn. They do not love the stream, but wild fowl on their migratory flights must have water, and this river is the only one between the Rockies and the Pacific that runs north and south.

The blue herons and the bitterns do not mind the red mud or the red water, in fact they rather like it; but they were always solitary people of the sedge. They prowl about the marshes alone and the swish of oars drives them into the air with a guttural "Quowk." And there are snipe here, bands of them, flashing their wings in the sun as they wheel over the red waters or trip along the muddy banks singly or in pairs. They are quite at home on the bars and bayou flats, but it seems not a very happy home for them—that is judging by the absence of snipe talk. The little teeter flies ahead of you from point to point, but makes no twitter, the yellow-leg seldom sounds his mellow three-note call, and the kill-deer, even though you shoot at him, will not cry "Kill-deer!" "Kill-deer!"

It may be the season when birds are mute, or it may merely happen so far to-day, or it may be that the silence of the river and the desert is an oppressive influence; but certainly you have never seen bird-life so hopelessly sad. Even the kingfisher, swinging down in a blue line from a dead limb and skimming the water, makes none of that rattling clatter that you knew so well when you were a child by a New England mill-stream. And what does a kingfisher on such a river as this? If it were filled with fish he could not see them through that thick water.

The voiceless river! From the canyon to the sea it flows through deserts, and ever the seal of silence is upon it. Even the scant life of its borders is dumb—birds with no note, animals with no cry, human beings with no voice. And so forsaken! The largest river west of the mountains and yet the least known. There are miles upon miles of mesas stretching upward from the stream that no feet have ever trodden, and that possess not a vestige of life of any kind. And along its banks the same tale is told. You float for days and meet with no traces of humanity. When they do appear it is but to emphasize the solitude. An Indian wickiup on the bank, an Indian town; yes, a white man's town, what impression do they make upon the desert and its river? You drift by Yuma and wonder what it is doing there. Had it been built in the middle of the Pacific on a barren rock it could not be more isolated, more hopelessly "at sea."

After the river crosses the border-line of Mexico it grows broader and flatter than ever. And still the color seems to deepen. For all its suggestion of blood it is not an unlovely color. On the contrary, that deep red contrasted with the green of the banks and the blue of the sky, makes a very beautiful color harmony. They are hues of depth and substance—hues that comport excellently well with the character of the river itself. And never a river had more character than the Colorado. You may not fancy the solitude of the stream nor its suggestive coloring, but you cannot deny its majesty and its nobility. It has not now the babble of the brook nor the swift rush of the canyon water; rather the quiet dignity that is above conflict, beyond gayety. It has grown old, it is nearing its end; but nothing could be calmer, simpler, more sublime, than the drift of it down into the delta basin.

The mountains are receding on every side, the desert is flattening to meet the sea, and the ocean tides are rising to meet the river. Half human in its dissolution, the river begins to break joint by joint. The change has been gradually taking place for miles and now manifests itself positively. The bottom lands widen, many channels or side-sloughs open upon the stream, and the water is distributed into the mouths of the delta. There is a break in the volume and mass—a disintegration of forces. And by divers ways, devious and slow, the crippled streams well out to the Gulf and never come together again.

It is not so when the river is at its height with spring freshets. Then the stream is swollen beyond its banks. All the bottom lands for miles across, up to the very terraces of the mesas, are covered; and the red flood moves like an ocean current, vast in width, ponderous in weight, irresistible in strength.

All things that can be uprooted or wrenched away, move with it. Nothing can check or stop it now. It is the Grand Canyon river once more, free, mighty, dangerous even in its death-throes.

And now at the full and the change of the moon, when the Gulf waters come in like a tidal wave, and the waters of the north meet the waters of the south, there is a mighty conflict of opposing forces. The famous "bore" of the river-mouth is the result. When the forces first meet there is a slow push-up of the water which rises in the shape of a ridge or wedge. The sea-water gradually proves itself the greater and the stronger body, and the ridge breaks into a crest and pitches forward with a roar. The undercut of the river sweeps away the footing of the tide, so to speak, and flings the top of the wave violently forward. The red river rushes under, the blue tide rushes over. There is the flash and dash of parti-colored foam of the crests, the flinging of jets of spray high in air, the long roll of waves breaking not upon a beach, but upon the back of the river, and the shaking of the ground as though an earthquake were passing. After it is all done with and gone, with no trace of wave or foam remaining, miles away down the Gulf the red river slowly rises in little streams through the blue to the surface. There it spreads fan-like over the top of the sea, and finally mingles with and is lost in the greater body.

The river is no more. It has gone down to its blue tomb in the Gulf—the fairest tomb that ever river knew. Something of serenity in the Gulf waters, something of the monumental in the bordering mountains, something of the unknown and the undiscovered over all, make it a fit resting-place for the majestic Colorado. The lonely stream that so shunned contact with man, that dug its bed thousands of feet in the depths of pathless canyons, and trailed its length across trackless deserts, sought out instinctively a point of disappearance far from the madding crowd. The blue waters of the Gulf, the beaches of shell, the red, red mountains standing with their feet in the sea, are still far removed from civilization's touch. There are no towns or roads or people by those shores, there are no ships upon those seas, there are no dust and smoke of factories in those skies. The Indians are there as undisturbed as in the days of Coronado, and the white man is coming but has not yet arrived. The sun still shines on unknown bays and unexplored peaks. Therefore is there silence—something of the hush of the deserts and the river that flows between.

Frederick S. Dellenbaugh

A Wonderland of Crags and Pinnacles

F. S. Dellenbaugh's Canyon Voyage *is a record of J. W. Powell's second exploration of the Colorado River with Dellenbaugh as his photographer and artist. The expedition left Green River, Wyoming, on May 21, 1871, and arrived in Cataract Canyon by mid-September of the same year.*

We were on the threshold of what the Major had previously named Cataract Canyon, because the declivity within it is so great and the water descends with such tremendous velocity and continuity that he thought the term rapid failed to interpret the conditions. The addition of the almost equal volume of the Grand—indeed it was now a little greater owing to extra heavy rains along its course—doubled the depth and velocity of the river till it swirled on into the new canyon before us with a fierce, threatening intensity, sapping the flat sand-bank on which our camp was laid and rapidly eating it away. Large masses with a sudden splash would drop out of sight and dissolve like sugar in a cup of tea. We were obliged to be on the watch lest the moorings of the boats should be loosened, allowing them to sweep pell-mell before us down the gorge. The long ropes were carried back to their limit and made fast to stakes driven deep into the hard sand. Jack and I became dissatisfied with the position of our boat and dropped it down two or three hundred yards to a place where the conditions were better, and camped by it. There were a few small cottonwoods against the cliff behind the sand-bank, but

---

From *Canyon Voyage* by Frederick S. Dellenbaugh (New York: G. P. Putnam's Sons, 1908).

they were too far off to be reached by our lines, and the ground beneath them was too irregular and rocky for a camp. These trees, with the hackberry trees across the river and numerous stramonium bushes in full blossom, composed the chief vegetation of this extraordinary locality. No more remote place existed at that time within the United States—no place more difficult of access. Macomb in his reconnaissance in 1859 had tried hard to arrive here, but he got no nearer than the edge of the plateau about thirty miles up Grand River.

It was necessary that we should secure topographic notes and observations from the summit, and we scanned the surroundings for the most promising place for exit. The Major was sure we could make a successful ascent to the upper regions by way of a narrow cleft on the right or west some distance back up the Green, which he had noted as we came along; so in the morning of Saturday, September 16th, he and Jack, Beaman, Clem, Jones, and I rowed up in the *Cañonita*, the current being slow along the west bank, and started up the crevice, dragging the cumbrous photographic outfit along. Prof. remained below for observations for time. The cleft was filled with fallen rocks, and we had no trouble mounting, except that the photographic boxes were like lead and the straps across one's chest made breathing difficult. The climb was tiring, but there was no obstacle, and we presently emerged on the surface of the country 1300 feet above the river and 5160 above the sea. Here was revealed a wide cyclorama that was astounding. Nothing was in sight but barren sandstone, red, yellow, brown, grey, carved into an amazing multitude of towers, buttes, spires, pinnacles, some of them several hundred feet high, and all shimmering under a dazzling sun. It was a marvellous mighty desert of bare rock, chiselled by the ages out of the foundations of the globe; fantastic, extraordinary, antediluvian, labyrinthian, and slashed in all directions by crevices; crevices wide, crevices narrow, crevices medium, some shallow, some dropping till a falling stone clanked resounding into the far hollow depths. Scarcely could we travel a hundred yards but we were compelled to leap some deep, dark crack. Often they were so wide a running jump was necessary, and at times the smooth rock sloped on both sides toward the crevice rather steeply. Once the Major came sliding down a bare slope till at a point where he caught sight of the edge of a sombre fissure just where he must land. He could not see its width; he could not return, and there he hung. Luckily I was where by another path I could quickly reach the rock below, and I saw that the crevice was not six inches wide, and I shouted the joyful news. Steward had not come up with us, but had succeeded in ascending through a narrow crevice below camp. He soon arrived within speaking distance, but there he was foiled by a crack too wide to jump, and he had to remain a stranger to us the rest of the day. At a little distance back from the brink these crevices were not so numerous nor so wide, and there we discovered a series of extremely pretty "parks" lost amidst the million turreted rocks. I made a pencil sketch looking out into this Sinav-to-weap, as the Major called it from information obtained from the Utes.[1] Beaman secured a number of photographs, but not all that were desired, and, as we did not have rations for stopping on the summit, we went back to camp and made the climb again the next day. Fortunately the recent rains had filled many hollows in the bare rock, forming pockets of delicious, pure water, where we could drink, but on a hot and dry summer's day travelling here would be intolerable, if not impossible. Fragments of arrow-heads, chips of chalcedony, and quantities of potsherds scattered around proved that our ancient Shinumos had known the region well. Doubtless some of their old trails would lead to large and deep water-pockets. There are pot-holes in this bare sandstone of enormous size, often several feet in depth and of similar diameter, which become filled with rain-water that lasts a long time. The Shinumos had numerous dwellings all through this country, with trails leading from place to place, highways and byways.

The following day the Major and Jones climbed out on the side opposite camp, that is on the east side, where they found an old trail and evidences of camping during the summer just closed, probably by the Utes. That night, Jones, in attempting to enter our boat in the moonlight, stepped on the corner of the hatch of the middle cabin, which was not on securely; it tipped, and he was thrown in such a way as to severely injure his leg below the knee. This was the first mishap thus far to any one of the party.

The Major entertained some idea of making a boat trip up the Grand, but he abandoned it, and we prepared for the work ahead. The rations, which were now fallen to poverty bulk, were carefully overhauled and evenly distributed among the boats, so that the wrecking of any one would not deprive us of more than a portion of each article. The amount for daily use was also determined; of the bacon we were to have at a meal only half the usual quantity. We knew Cataract Canyon was rough, but by this time we were in excellent training and thoroughly competent for the kind of navigation required; ready for anything that strong boats like ours could live through. At ten o'clock on Tuesday, September 19th, the cabins were all packed, the life preservers were inflated, and casting off from Camp 62 we were borne down with the swift current. The water was muddy, of a coffee-and-cream colour, and the river was falling. Not far below our camp we saw a beaten trail coming down a singular canyon on the left or east side, showing again that the

---

1. The pencil sketches I made on this trip were taken to Washington, but I do not know what became of them.

natives understood the way in to the Junction.[2] We knew it was not far to rapids, as we had seen two heavy ones from the brink above, and we soon heard the familiar roar of plunging water, a sound which had been absent since the end of Gray Canyon. Presently we were bearing down on the first one, looking for the way to pass it. On landing at the head it was seen to be a rather rough place, and it was deemed advisable to avoid running it. The boats were carefully let down by lines and we went on. In a short distance we reached a second rapid, where we decided to repeat the operation that took us past the other, but these two let-downs consumed much time and gave us hard work. The water was cold, we were wet and hungry, and when we arrived at a third that was more forbidding than the ones above we halted for dinner at its beginning. The muddy water boomed and plunged over innumerable rocks—a mad, irresistible flood. So great was the declivity of the river bed that boulders were rolled along under water with a sound like distant thunder. We had noticed this also in Lodore, but in Cataract it was more common. The rumbling was particularly noticeable if one were standing in the water, as we so continually were. After dinner the boats were lowered past the rapid, but we had no respite, for presently we came upon another big one, then another, and another, and then still another, all following quickly and giving us plenty of extremely hard work, for we would not risk the boats in any of them. When these were behind us we went on a distance and came to one that we ran, and then, wet through and shivering till our teeth chattered, as well as being hungry and tired, every one was glad to hear the decision to go into camp when we arrived at the top of another very ugly pair of them. The canyon having a north and south trend and it being autumn, the sun disappeared early so far as we were concerned; the shadows were deep, the mountain air was penetrating. As soon as possible our soaking river garments were thrown off, the dry clothing from the rubber bags was put on, the limited bacon was sending its fragrance into the troubled air, the bread took on a nice deep brown in the Dutch oven, the coffee's aromatic steam drifted from the fire, and warm and comfortable we sat down to the welcome though meagre meal. The rule was three little strips of bacon, a chunk of bread about the size of one's fist, and coffee without stint for each man three times a day. Sugar was a scarce article, and I learned to like coffee without it so well that I have never taken it with sugar since. The "Tirtaan Aigles" needed now all the muscle and energy they could command, and an early hour found every man sound asleep. The record for

2. As mentioned in a previous footnote, the name D. Julien—1836, was later found near this point and in two other places. All these inscriptions appear to be on the same side of the river, the east, and at accessible places.

the first day in Cataract Canyon was nine miles, with eight bad rapids or cataracts, as they might properly be called, and out of the eight we ran but one.[3] The river was about 250 feet wide.

The Major decided the next morning that he would try to get out on the right, and he took me with him. We had no great trouble in reaching the plateau at an elevation of eighteen hundred feet above the river, where we could see an immense area of unknown country. The broken and pinnacled character was not so marked as it had been at the Junction, but it was still a strange, barren land. We expected to find water-pockets on the top, and we had carried with us only one quart of canteen water. While the Major was taking notes from the summit of a butte, I made a zealous search for water, but not a drop could I find; every hole was dry. The sun burned down from a clear sky that melted black into eternal space. The yellow sand threw the hot rays upward, and so also did the smooth bare rock. No bird, no bee, no thing of life could be seen. I came to a whitish cliff upon which I thought there might be water-pockets, and I mounted by a steep slope of broken stones. Suddenly, almost within touch, I saw before me a golden yellow rattlesnake gliding upward in the direction I was going along the cliff wall. I killed it with a stone, and cut off the rattles and continued my reconnaissance. At length I gave up the search. By the time I had returned to the foot of the butte on which the Major was making his observations, the heat had exhausted me till I was obliged to rest a few moments before ascending the sixty feet to where he was. I had carried the canteen all the time, and the water in it was hot from exposure to the sun. The Major bade me rest while he made a little fire, and by the aid of a can and ground coffee we had brought he made a strong decoction with the whole quart. This gave us two cups apiece, and we had some bread to go with it. The effect was magical. My fatigue vanished. I felt equal to anything, and we began the return.

The Major having no right arm, he sometimes got in a difficult situation when climbing, if his right side came against a smooth surface where there was nothing opposite. We had learned to go down by the same route followed up, because otherwise one is never sure of arriving at the bottom, as a ledge half-way down might compel a return to the summit. We remembered that at one point there was no way for him to hold on, the cliff being smooth on the right, while on the left was empty air, with a sheer drop of several

---

3. The next party to pass through this canyon was the Brown Expedition, conducting a survey for the Denver, Colorado Canyon, and Pacific Railway in 1889. At the first rapid they lost a raft, with almost all their provisions, and they had much trouble. See *The Romance of the Colorado River*, Chapter xiv. Another expedition in 1891—the Best Expedition—was wrecked here.

hundred feet. The footing too was narrow. I climbed down first, and, bracing myself below with my back to the abyss, I was able to plant my right foot securely in such a manner that my right knee formed a solid step for him at the critical moment. On this improvised step he placed his left foot, and in a twinkling had made the passage in safety.

During our absence the men below had been at work. Camp was moved down the river some three quarters of a mile, while the boats had been lowered past the ugly pair of rapids, and were moored at the camp below the second. In one the current had "got the bulge," as we called it, on the men on the line; that is, the powerful current had hit the bow in such a way that the boat took the diagonal of forces and travelled up and out into the river. For the men it was either let go or be pulled in. They let go, and the boat dashed down with her cargo on board. Fortune was on our side. She went through without injury and shot into an eddy below. With all speed the men rushed down, and Jack, plunging in, swam to her and got on before she could take a fresh start. It was a narrow escape, but it taught a lesson that was not forgotten. Prof. had succeeded in getting some observations, and all was well. It was bean day, too, according to our calendar, and all hands had a treat.

By eight o'clock the next morning, Thursday, September 21st, we were on the way again, with the boats "close reefed," as it were, for trouble, but one, two, three and one half miles slid easily behind. Then, as if to make up for this bit of leniency, six rapids came in close succession, though they were of a kind that we could safely run, and all the boats went flying through them without a mishap of any kind. The next was a plunger so mixed up with rocks that we made a let-down and again proceeded a short distance before we were halted by one more of the same sort, though we were able to run the lower portion of it. A little below this we met a friendly drop, and whizzed through its rush and roar in triumph. But there was nothing triumphant about the one which followed, so far as our work was concerned. We manoeuvred past it with much difficulty only to find ourselves upon two more bad ones. Bad as they were, they were nevertheless runable, and away we dashed with breakneck speed, certainly not less than twenty miles an hour, down both of them, to land on the left immediately at the beginning of a great and forbidding descent. These let-downs were difficult, often requiring all hands to each boat, except the Major, whose one-armed condition made it too hard for him to assist in the midst of rocks and rushing water, where one had to be very nimble and leap and balance with exactness. Two good arms were barely sufficient. Sometimes, in order to pass the gigantic boulders that stretched far off from the shore, the boat had to be shot around and hauled in below, an operation requiring skill, strength, and celerity.

The walls, very craggy at the top, increased in altitude till they were now about sixteen hundred feet, separated from each other by one third of a mile. The flaring character of the upper miles of the canyon began to change to a narrower gorge, the cliffs showing a nearer approach to verticality. At the head of the forbidding plunge we had our slice of bacon, with bread and coffee, and then we fought our way down alongside amongst immense boulders and roaring water. It was an exceedingly hard place to vanquish, and required two and a half hours of the most violent exertions to accomplish it. All were necessary to handle each boat. Hardly had we passed beyond the turmoil of its fierce opposition than we fell upon another scarcely less antagonistic, but yet apparently so free from rocks that the Major concluded it could be run. At the outset our boat struck a concealed rock, and for a moment it seemed that we might capsize, but luckily she righted, swung free, and swept down with no further trouble. The *Nell* struck the same rock and so did the *Cañonita,* but neither was injured or even halted. These boats were somewhat lighter than ours, having one man less in each, and therefore did not hit the rock so hard. The boats were now heavy from being water-soaked, for the paint was gone from the bottoms. This would have made no difference in any ordinary waters, but it did here, where we were obliged to lift them so constantly.

This was an extremely rough and wet day's work, and the moment the great cliffs cut off the warmth of the direct sun we were thrown suddenly from summer to winter, and our saturated clothing, uncomfortably cool in sunlight, became icy with the evaporation and the cold shadow-air. We turned blue, and no matter how firmly I tried to shut my teeth they rattled like a pair of castanets. Though it was only half-past three, the Major decided to camp as soon as he saw this effect, much as we had need to push on. We landed on the right, and were soon revived by dry clothes and a big fire of driftwood. We had made during the day a total distance of a trifle less than seven miles, one and three quarters since dinner. There were fourteen rapids and cataracts, nine of which we ran, on a river about two hundred feet wide. We had sand to sleep on, but all around us were rocks, rocks, rocks, with the mighty bounding cliffs lifting up to the sky. Our books for the time being were not disturbed, but Whittier's lines, read further up, seemed here exactly appropriate to the Colorado:

> Hurrying down to its grave, the sea,
> And slow through the rock its pathway hewing!
> Far down, through the mist of the falling river,
> Which rises up like an incense ever,
> The splintered points of the crags are seen,

With water howling and vexed between,
While the scooping whirl of the pool beneath
Seems an open throat, with its granite teeth!

It was not long before the blankets were taken from the rubber bags and spread on the sand, and the rapids, the rocks, and all our troubles were forgotten.

The next day was almost a repetition of the preceding one. We began by running a graceful little rapid, just beyond which we came to a very bad place. The river was narrow and deep, with a high velocity, and the channel was filled with enormous rocks. Two hours of the hardest kind of work in and out of the water, climbing over gigantic boulders along the bank, lifting the boats and sliding them on driftwood skids, tugging, pulling, shoving every minute with might and main put us at the bottom. No sooner were we past this one than we engaged in a similar battle with another of the same nature, and below it we stopped for dinner, amidst some huge boulders under a hackberry tree, near another roarer. One of these cataracts had a fall of not less than twenty feet in six hundred, which gave the water terrific force and violence. The canyon walls closed in more and more and ran up to two thousand feet, apparently nearly vertical as one looked up at them, but there was always plenty of space for landings and camps. Opposite the noon camp we could see to a height beyond of at least three thousand feet. We were in the heart of another great plateau. After noon we attacked the very bad rapid beside whose head we had eaten, and it was half-past three when we had finished it. The boats had been considerably pounded and there was a hole in the *Dean*, and a plank sprung in the *Nell* so that her middle cabin was half full of water. The iron strip on the *Dean's* keel was breaking off. Repairs were imperative, and on the right, near the beginning of one of the worst falls we had yet seen, we went into camp for the rest of the day. With false ribs made from oars we strengthened the boats and put them in condition for another day's hammering. It seemed as if we must have gone this day quite a long distance, but on footing up it was found to be no more than a mile and a quarter. Darkness now fell early and big driftwood fires made the evenings cheerful. There was a vast amount of driftwood in tremendous piles, trees, limbs, boughs, railroad ties; a great mixture of all kinds, some of it lying full fifty feet above the present level of the river. There were large and small tree-trunks battered and limbless, the ends pounded to a spongy mass of splinters. Our bright fires enabled us to read, or to write up notes and diaries. I think each one but the Major and Andy kept a diary and faithfully wrote it up. Jack occasionally gave us a song or two from the repertory already described, and Steward did not forget the mouth-organ, but through the hardest part of Cataract Canyon we were usually tired enough to take to our blankets early.

In the morning we began the day by running a little rapid between our camp and the big one that we saw from there, and then we had to exert some careful engineering to pass below by means of the lines. This accomplished we found a repetition of the same kind of work necessary almost immediately, at the next rapid. In places we had to lift the boats out and slide them along on driftwood skids. These rapids were largely formed by enormous rocks which had fallen from the cliffs, and over, around, and between these it was necessary to manoeuvre the boats by lines to avoid the furious waters of the outer river. After dinner we arrived at a descent which at first glance seemed as bad as anything we had met in the morning but an examination showed a prospect of a successful run through it. The fall was nearly twenty feet in about as many yards. The Major and Prof. examined it long and carefully. A successful run would take two minutes, while a let-down would occupy us for at least two hours and it had some difficult points. They hesitated about running the place, for they would not take a risk that was not necessary, but finally they concluded it could be safely accomplished, and we pulled the *Dean* as quickly as possible into the middle of the river and swung down into it. On both sides the water was hammered to foam amidst great boulders and the roar as usual was deafening. Just through the centre was a clean, clear chute followed by a long tail of waves breaking and snapping like some demon's jaws. As we struck into them they swept over us like combers on the beach in a great storm. It seemed to me here and at other similar places that we went through some of the waves like a needle and jumped to the top of others, to balance half-length out of water for an instant before diving to another trough. Being in the very bow the waves, it appeared to me, sometimes completely submerged me and almost took my breath away with the sudden impact. At any rate it was lively work, with a current of fifteen or eighteen miles an hour. Beaman had stationed himself where he could get a negative of us ploughing through these breakers, but his wet-plates were too slow and he had no success. After this came a place which permitted no such jaunty treatment. It was in fact three or four rapids following each other so closely that, though some might be successfully run, the last was not safe, and no landing could be made at its head, so a very long let-down was obligatory; but it was an easy one, for each crew could take its own boat down without help from the others. Then, tired, wet, and cold as usual, we landed on the left in a little cove where there was a sandy beach for our Camp 67. We had made less than four miles, in which distance there were six rapids, only two of which we ran. At another stage of water the number and character of these rapids would be changed; some would be easier at higher water, some harder, and the same would be true of lower water. Rapids also change their character from time to time as rocks are shifted along the bottom and more rocks fall from the cliffs or are brought in by side floods. The walls were now about two thousand feet, of limestone, with a reddish stain, and they were so near together that the sun shone to the bottom only during the middle hours of the day in September.

It was now September 24th; a bright and beautiful Sunday broke, the sky above clear and tranquil, the river below foaming and fuming between the ragged walls in one continuous rapid with merely variations of descent. In three quarters of a mile we arrived before the greatest portion of the declivity, where, though there seemed to be a clear chute, we did not consider it advisable to make the run because of conditions following; neither could we make a regular let-down or a portage. The least risky method was to carry a line down and when all was ready start the boat in at the top alone. In this way when she had gone through, the men on the line below were able to bring her up and haul her in before reaching the next bad plunge. There was no quiet river anywhere; nothing but rushing, swirling, plunging water and rocks. We got past the bad spot successfully and went on making one let-down after another for about four miles, when we halted at noon for the rest of the day, well satisfied with our progress though in distance it appeared so slight. The afternoon was spent in repairing boats, working up notes, and taking observations. The cliffs were now some 2500 feet in height, ragged and broken on their faces, but close together, the narrowest deep chasm we had seen. It was truly a terrible place, with the fierce river, the giant walls, and the separation from any known path to the outer world. I thought of the Major's first trip, when it was not known what kind of waters were here. Vertical and impassable falls might easily have barred his way and cataracts behind prevented return, so that here in a death trap they would have been compelled to plunge into the river or wait for starvation. Happily he had encountered no such conditions.

An interesting feature of this canyon was the manner in which huge masses of rock lying in the river had been ground into each other by the force of the current. One block of sandstone, weighing not less than six hundred tons, being thirty or forty feet long by twenty feet square, had been oscillated till the limestone boulders on which it rested had ground into it at least two feet, fitting closely. Another enormous piece was slowly and regularly rocking as the furious current beat upon it, and one could feel the movement distinctly. A good night's sleep made all of us fresh again, and we began the Monday early. Some worked on the boats, while Beaman and Clem went up "Gypsum" Canyon, as Steward named it, for views, and the Major and I climbed out for topographic observations. We reached an altitude above camp of 3135 feet at a point seven or eight miles back from the brink. The view in all directions was beyond words to describe. Mountains and mountains, canyons, cliffs, pinnacles, buttes surrounded us as far as we could see, and the range was extensive. The Sierra La Sal, the Sierra Abajo, and other short ranges lay blue in the distance, while comparatively near in the southwest rose the five beautiful peaks just beyond the mouth of the Dirty Devil, composing the unknown range before mentioned. At noon we made coffee, had lunch, and then went on. It was four o'clock by the time we concluded to start back, and darkness overtook us before we were fairly down the cliffs, but there was a bright moon, and by its aid we reached camp.

At half-past eight in the morning of September 26th we were again working our way down the torrential river. Anybody who tries to go through here in any haphazard fashion will surely come to grief. It is a passage that can safely be made only with the most extreme caution. The walls grew straighter, and they grew higher till the gorge assumed proportions that seemed to me the acme of the stupendous and magnificent. The scenery may not have been beautiful in the sense that an Alpine lake is beautiful, but in the exhibition of the power and majesty of nature it was sublime. There was the same general barrenness: only a few hackberry trees, willows, and a cottonwood or two along the margin of the river made up the vegetation. Our first task was a difficult let-down, which we accomplished safely, to find that we could run two rapids following it and half of another, landing then to complete it by a let-down. Then came a very sharp drop that we ran, which put us before another easy one, that was followed by a difficult bit of navigation through a bad descent, after which we stopped for dinner on the right at the head of another rapid. The cliffs now on both sides were about 2800 feet, one quarter mile wide at top, and in places striking me as being perpendicular, especially in the outer curve of the bends. The boats seemed to be scarcely more than chips on the sweeping current and we not worth mentioning. During the afternoon we halted a number of times for Beaman to make photographs, but the proportions were almost too great for any camera. The foreground parts are always magnified, while the distances are diminished, till the view is not that which the eye perceives. Before stopping for the night we ran three more rapids, and camped on the right on a sand-bank at the head of another forbidding place. The record for the whole day was six and three quarter miles, with ten runs and two let-downs. At one bad place the *Nell* got too far over and laboured so heavily in the enormous billows that Cap., who pulled the bow oars, was completely lost to sight and the boat was filled with water. Only about thirty degrees of sky were visible as one looked directly up from our camp. A pretty canyon came in near camp, and some of us took a walk up its narrow way.

In the morning Beaman made some pictures, and it was eleven o'clock before we resumed our navigation. Our first work was a let-down, which took an hour, and about a mile below we stopped for dinner on the left. Then we continued, making eight miles more, in which distance we ran six rapids and made two line-portages. The last rapid was a bad one, and there we made one of the portages, camping at its foot on the left bank. The walls began to diminish in height and the river was less precipitous, as is apparent from the progress we were able to make. September 28th we began by running two rapids immediately below camp, and the *Nell* remained at the foot of the second to signal Beaman in the *Cañonita,* as he had stayed behind to take some views. Another mile brought us to a rather bad place, the right having a vertical cliff about 2700 feet high, but the left was composed of boulders spread over a wide stretch, so that an excellent footing was offered. The Major and Prof. concluded to climb out here, instead of a point farther down called Millecrag Bend, and, appointing Steward master of the let-down which was necessary, they left us. It was dinner-time when we got the boats below to a safe cove, and we were quite ready for the meal which Andy meanwhile had been cooking. A beautiful little brook came down a narrow canyon on the left, and it was up this stream that the Major went for a mile and a half and then climbed on the side. They were obliged to give it up and come back to the bottom. By this time it was too late to make another attempt, so they turned their backs on "Failure Creek," and, returning to us, said we would go on as soon as we had eaten the supper which Andy was preparing. They would climb out at Millecrag Bend. Andy had cooked a mess of beans, about the last we had, and what we did not eat we put on board in the kettle, which had a tight cover. The Major's manner for a day or two had been rather moody, and when Prof. intimated to me that we would have a lively time before we saw another camp, I knew some difficult passage ahead was on his mind; some place which had given him trouble on the first trip.

About five o'clock we were ready; everything was made snug and tight on the boats, nothing being left out of the cabins but a camp kettle in each standing-room for bailing, and we cast off. Each man had his life-preserver where he could get it quickly, and the Major put his on, for with only one arm he could not do this readily in case of necessity. The current was swift. We were carried rapidly down to where the gorge narrowed up with walls vertical on each side for a height of fifty to one hundred feet. We soon dashed through a small rough rapid. A splash of water over our bow dampened my clothes and made the air feel chilly. The canyon was growing dim with the evening light. High above our heads some lazy clouds were flecked with the sunset glow. Not far below the small rapid we saw before us a complicated situation at the prevailing stage of water, and immediately landed on the left, where there was footing to reconnoitre. A considerable fall was divided by a rocky island, a low mass that would be submerged with two or three feet more water, and the river plunging down on each side boiled against the cliffs. Between us and the island the stream was studded by immense boulders which had dropped from the cliffs and almost like pinnacles stood above the surface. One view was enough to show that on this stage of water we could not safely run either side of the cataract; indeed destruction would surely have rewarded any attempt. The right-hand channel from the foot of the island swept powerfully across to meet the left-hand one and together they boomed along the base of the left-hand cliffs before swinging sharply to the right with the trend of the chasm in that direction. There was no choice of a course. The only way was to manoeuvre between the great boulders and keep in the dividing line of the current till a landing could be effected on the head of the island between the two falls. The difficulty was to avoid being drawn to either side. Our boat went first and we succeeded, under the Major's quick eye and fine judgment, in easily following the proposed course till the *Dean* began to bump on the rocks some twenty yards above the exposed part of the island. I tested the depth of water here with an oar as Jack pulled slowly along, the current being quite slack in the dividing line, and as soon as practicable we jumped overboard and guided our craft safely to the island. Prof. in the *Nell* was equally precise, and as he came in we waded out to catch his boat; but the *Cañonita* passed on the wrong side of one of the pinnacles and, caught in the left current, came near making a run of it down that side, which would have resulted disastrously. Luckily they were able to extricate themselves and Beaman steered in to us. Had the water been only high enough to prevent landing on this island we would have been in a bad trap, but had it been so high as to make navigation down the centre possible the rapid might perhaps have been run safely.

We were now on the island, with darkness falling, and the problem was to get off. While Prof. and the Major went down to the foot to make a plan we sat in the diminishing light and waited. It was decided to pull the boats down the right-hand side of the island as far as the foot of the worst part of the right-hand rapid, and from there cut out into the tail of waves, pulling through as quickly as we could to avoid contact with the base of the left wall along which the current dashed. We must pull fast enough to get across in the very short time it would take the river to sweep us down to the crucial point. The gorge by this time was quite sombre; even the clouds above were losing their evening colour. We must act quickly. Our boat as usual made the first trial. As we shot out, Jack and I bent to our oars with every muscle we possessed, the boat headed slightly upstream, and in a few seconds we were flying along the base of the cliffs, and so close that our starboard oars had to be quickly unshipped to prevent their being broken. In a few seconds more we were able to get out into the middle, and then we halted in an eddy to wait for the other boats. They came on successfully and in the gloaming we continued down the canyon looking for a place to camp, our hearts much lightened with our triumph over the difficult rapid. Before long night was full upon us and our wet clothes made us shiver. About a mile below a warning roar dead ahead told us to make land at once, for it would be far from prudent to attack a rapid in the dark. Fortunately there was here room to camp on some rocks and sand on the right. Scarcely had we become settled than a tornado broke over the canyon and we were enveloped in a blinding whirl of rain and sand. Each man clung to his blankets to prevent their departure and waited for the wind to pass, which it did in less than ten minutes. The storm-clouds were shattered and up the gorge, directly east from our position, from behind a thousand needle-like spires that serrated the top of the cliffs, the moon like a globe of dazzling silver rolled up with serene majesty, flooding the canyon with a bright radiance. No moon-rise could have been more dramatic. The storm-clouds were edged with light and the wet cliffs sparkled and glittered as if set with jewels. Even the rapid below was resplendent and silvery, the leaping waves and the spray scintillating under the lustrous glare.

Morning brought a continuation of the rain, which fell in a deluge, driving us to the shelter of a projecting ledge, from which comparatively dry retreat we watched the rain cascades that soon began their display. Everywhere they came plunging over the walls, all sizes, and varying their volume with every variation in the downpour. Some dropped a thousand feet to vanish in spray; others were broken into many falls. By half-past eight we were able to proceed, running the rapid without any trouble, but a wave drenched me so that all my efforts to keep out of the rain went for nothing. By ten o'clock we had run four more rapids, and arrived at the place the Major had named Millecrag Bend, from the multitude of ragged pinnacles into which the cliffs broke. On the left we camped to permit the Major and Prof. to make their prospective climb to the top. A large canyon entered from the left, terminating Cataract Canyon, which we credited with forty-one miles, and in which I counted sixty-two rapids and cataracts, enough to give any set of boatmen all the work they could desire. The Major and Prof. reached the summit at an altitude of fifteen hundred feet. They had a wide view over the unknown country, and saw mountains to the west with snow on their summits. Snow in the canyons would not have surprised us now, for the nights were cold and we had warmth only in the middle of the day. Near our camp some caves were discovered, twenty feet deep and nearly six feet in height, which had once been occupied by natives. Walls had been laid across the entrances, and inside were corncobs and other evidences usual in this region, now so well known. Pottery fragments were also abundant. Another thing we found in the caves and also in other places was a species of small scorpion. These venomous creatures were always ready to strike, and somehow one got into Andy's shoe, and when he put on the shoe he was bitten. No serious result seemed to follow, but his general health was not so good after this for a long time. He put tobacco on the wound and let it go. This was the second accident to a member of the party, which now had been out four months.

The last day of September found us up before daylight, and as soon as breakfast was eaten, a small matter these days both in preparation and consumption, we pulled away, intending to reach the mouth of the Dirty Devil as soon as possible. The morning was decidedly autumnal, and when we arrived at a small rapid, where we had to get overboard to help the boats, nothing ever came harder than this cold bath, though it was confined to our legs. Presently we saw a clear little rivulet coming in on the left, and we ran up to that shore to examine it, hoping it was drinkable. Like the first party, we were on the lookout for better water to drink than the muddy Colorado. The rivulet proved to be sulphurous and also hot, the temperature being about 91 F. We could not drink it, but we warmed our feet by standing in the water. The walls of this new canyon at their highest were about thirteen hundred feet, and so close together and straight that the Major named it Narrow Canyon. Its length is about nine miles. Through half of the next rapid we made a let-down, running the remainder, and then, running two more below which were easy, we could see through to the end of the canyon, and the picture framed by the precipices was beautiful. The world seemed suddenly to open out before us, and in the middle of it, clear and strong against a sky of azure, accented by the daylight moon, stood the Unknown Mountains, weird and silent in their untrodden mystery. By this token we knew that the river of the Satanic name was near, and we had scarcely emerged from Narrow Canyon, and noted the low bluffs of homogeneous red sandstone which took the place of the high cliffs, when we perceived a sluggish stream about 150 feet wide flowing through the barren sandstone on our right. Landing on its west bank, we instantly agreed with Jack Sumner when on the first trip he had proclaimed it a "Dirty Devil." Muddy, alkaline, undrinkable, it slipped along between the low walls of smooth sandstone to add its volume to that of the Colorado. Near us were the remains of the Major's camp-fire of the other voyage, and there Steward found a jack-knife lost at that time. At the Major's request he gave it to him as a souvenir.

Our rising had been so early and our progress from Millecrag Bend so easy that when our camp was established the hour was only nine o'clock, giving us still a whole day. The Major and Prof. started off on an old Indian trail to see if there was a way in to this place for horses, Cap. took observations for time, and the others occupied themselves in various ways, Andy counting the rations still left in our larder.

That night around our camp-fire we felt especially contented, for Cataract and Narrow canyons were behind, and never would we be called upon to battle with their rapids again. The descent from the mouth of Green River was 415 feet, most of it in the middle stretch of Cataract Canyon.

Frank Waters

Its Delta

In The Colorado *Frank Waters captures his impressions of the physical aspects of the river from its headwaters in snow country to its terminus at the Gulf of California. "Its Delta" appears in part one, "Its Background"; parts two, three, and four of the book concern the people of the Colorado River Basin, future engineering projects, and poetic landscapes of the Grand Canyon itself.*

It has often struck me how parallel the course of my own life has run with the Colorado. I could no more write an autobiography without the river than I have been able in this to ignore its fellow traveler. We were both born in the high Colorado Rockies. Progressively in childhood and youth we made our way back down the peaks and mountains. Meandering back and forth across mesa and plateau our lives assumed their permanent color, our tempers set. On the desert below we both were harnessed to work for the first time. And the last part of this vast background that I saw, like the river, was its Mexican delta.

Comprising about 2,000 square miles, it extended north and south from the international boundary to the gulf, and east and west from the Sonoran mesa on the mainland to the Cocopah mountains in the peninsula of Lower California.

It was a strange subworld of the Colorado Pyramid.

On the Sonoran side of the river a few ranchers ran cattle and horses on the dry bottomlands. At the upper end, in Mexicali Valley, was the largest

---

single area in the world devoted exclusively to the cultivation of cotton. But below this, from the bajadas of the Cocopah Mountains to the west bank of the Colorado, it was a strange, wild terra incognita to all but a few nomadic groups of Cocopah Indians.

It was desert. Mountains. Chaparral. Swamps. Lakes—dry and wet and salt. A crazy quilt of waterways: 600 miles of canals; a dozen channels of the river itself, the Alamo, Abejas, Boat Slough, Rio Paredones, Rio Nuevo, the Pescadero and the Hardy. At low water dry stinking bottomlands, salt-encrusted sinks, alkali flats, tidal flats and geysers of hot mud. At high water a vast bayou.

Flanking the Cocopah Range on the west lay the great Macuata Basin, Laguna Salada, connected with the tidal flats of the lower river at its southern tip. Some 50 miles long, 10 miles wide, and only 12 feet above sea level, it was a vast dry lake bordered by sand dunes. But containing hot springs as queer as the mud volcanoes near Volcano Lake across the range.

Abounding with game, the tule lands about the head of tidewater were full of small wild hogs, descendants of domesticated swine brought in years ago. Wild burros in herds of twenty or more traveled back and forth between water holes. On the highflanking sierras appeared small chamois called "amagoquio" by the Indians. Preying on these were the animals "not unlike the African leopard" which the Patties had noticed a century ago. They might have been the "chimbi," a mountain wildcat with a short tail and beautiful fur, or the lion called "chimbicá," held sacred by the Indians. Larger and more ferocious, it decapitated its victim and after drinking its blood buried the carcass for later eating. Mountain sheep, small deer, fox, rabbits, skunk, muskrats and beaver were common. In the thick chaparral fluttered wild pigeon, quail, doves and occasionally a scrawny turkey. Strange birds with stranger names, "cenzontli" perhaps in Aztec, and "pajaro chollero" in Spanish, the latter suspiciously like an ordinary woodpecker. Buzzards and vultures, hawks, owls and eagles. And above all, the boundless flocks of waterfowl—ducks, geese, herons, coots, wrens, sea gulls and pelicans.

It was all one vast contradiction. A jigsaw puzzle confusing as the Mojave Maze. And solved only by the few, shy and decadent Cocopah Indians retreating farther and farther into extinction. One month you might ride on horseback to one of their crude ramadas that a month later you would paddle to in a dugout canoe.

Through this strange wild delta there were no railroads and few roads. The blooming Border district of Mexicali was as effectively isolated as if it had been a desert island. It was barred on the north by the United States boundary with its customs duties and all the regulation red tape of immigration and international trade. On the west it was separated from the open

Pacific port of Ensenada and the town of Tijuana by a tall range of jagged picachos. Due south the peninsula of Lower California extended in an almost unbroken wilderness. And south and east it was separated from the lower mainland of Mexico by the gulf.

Yet into the Mexican half of the Colorado delta as into the American struggled thousands of new settlers. For the most part these were peons and enterprising young businessmen from Mexico, and Chinese laborers imported by powerful Chinese merchants of San Francisco organized to operate in Mexico under great companies with huge capitalization like the "Compania Chino Mercantil Mexicana." Overland and by water they fought their way northward up from the gulf coasts, and each route bore witness to their tragic struggles. "El Desierto de los Chinos" is still a local name given to a grim stretch of desert where a large company of Chinese laborers perished of thirst. The fate of another group of Mexican peons which attempted the water route is equally tragic.

In November, 1922, the little 36-ton steamer *Topolobampo* chugged out of the beautiful bay of Guaymas on the gulf coast of Sonora, Mexico. She had been named for the bay not far south and was crowded with 125 peons and their families bound for the cottonfields of the Mexicali valley. Little by little the tiny overloaded steamer crept up the coast to the head of the gulf and entered the mouth of the Colorado. At dusk on the night of November 18th the captain ordered the steamer stopped in mid-channel near La Bomba. A small tide was coming in. Two heavy steel hawsers were thrown out to anchor the ship securely on the bar. Tossing lightly on the muddy river, crew and passengers dropped off to sleep.

Near midnight everyone on board was awakened by a terrifying roar. It sounded like a gigantic waterfall booming downriver. Terrified, the passengers rushed to the deck. Clearly in the moonlight they saw traveling upriver with the speed of an express train an immense wall of water nearly fifteen feet high. There was hardly time for a single frightened cry. The wave caught the *Topolobampo* squarely abeam, snapped the hawsers like threads, and rolled the ship over like a log.

Only 39 passengers survived. Days later they were still being dragged out from the mud flats nude, half insane from thirst, blistered by the sun, and raw from predatory swarms of insects. Of the 86 drowned, only 21 bodies were ever recovered. It was one of the worst disasters in the 400-year history of the Colorado, and like Ulloa's first experience it attested the ferocity of the river's phenomenal bores.

But if there were a highway through the delta, Hardy's channel of the Colorado, dangerous as it was, offered the only one available. For several years a courageous and enterprising gentleman named Arnulfo Liera provided the only passage. Under the imposing ownership of his "Compañia de Navegacion del Golfo de California, S.A.," a small steamer ran down the river from El Mayor and La Bomba to Santa Rosalia on the gulf coast of Lower California, and thence across to the port of Guaymas on the mainland of Mexico. Early one August three years after the loss of the *Topolobampo*, Señor Liera suggested I make the trip for a pleasant paseo.

Like all things Mexican, the steamer ran by God rather than by schedule. Señor Liera was in no hurry. He waited until he had scraped together a full cargo and a few passengers before dispatching the boat. So every few days I dropped in to see him. Things were progressing nicely. The boat was almost ready to leave. There were already two more passengers sitting on the floor of his office. Two Polish emigrants bound for Mexico City, a man and his wife with innumerable bundles, a case of beer and a caged parrot.

A week later things looked even better. A few green hides to be picked up downriver were being brought by muleback down from the sierras. The two Poles were still waiting, now spread out on the floor of the adobe warehouse on a tattered quilt. A few more days passed. This time Señor Liera was most cheerful. There had been a spell of unseasonable weather. The heat had cracked a seam in the boat, which had to be recalked. Cómo no? Those few hides were still coming down the trail. I saw the two Poles. Unkempt, the man unshaved, they were on their knees sprinkling the bedraggled parrot with water through the battered bars of its cage.

Two days later we were ready to start. Señor Liera was beaming. The office was full of more passengers—peons and their families who were returning to their homeland villages in Mexico. The two Poles were frantic. In broken, almost unintelligible Spanish the man kept asking if there was time for one last drink of cold beer at the corner cantina. "No entiendo, no entiendo," he wailed. The woman began to sob. She wanted to go to the toilet and there wasn't time. There wasn't time.

Next morning at dawn, loaded in an old truck, we started. The voyage had begun.

The Lower River

Unpainted, repellent and inexpressively dirty, the *Rio Colorado* hugged broadside the slimy adobe bank. A small, old steamer of perhaps fifty tons, her 50-foot length was held against the current by a line snagged round a tree. Forward and stern the narrow decks were clear. In the center, divided by a passage wide enough for the open hatchway, were two small deckhouses, each just big enough to hold eight bunks. On the other side of one, protruding toward the rail, was a tiny galley. On the opposite side of the other was the excusado, backed up against the tall smoke-stack of rusty iron.

Sitting under the tree, I looked for something reassuring about her. There was nothing. I doubted if there was a place on the whole craft to hang my hat. Not only had our own truck been crowded, but another had arrived an hour later to add still more peons to the crowd on the bank. Hour after hour we kept waiting.

It was early morning, but already the heat was so stifling that it seemed to weigh the bright stillness flooding the bare rock hills, the narrow bank and the unbroken solitude of the river's bend. Above us in the sullen cloudless sky hung a hawk motionless as if stuck like a fly to paper. Yards downstream a huddle of wooden shacks and an empty corral were wedged between the water and the up-thrust wall of rock. From these filed cargadores, each carrying a heavy green cattle hide bundled with twine. Sweat rolled down their muscular torsos, cutting through the layer of dust raised by their naked feet. Each man trod precariously the narrow plank to the hatch, let fall his hide into the hold, and slouched back down the trail.

Beside me sat the two forlorn Poles dipping water from the river to splash on the parrot. Its bright feathers were dull and bedraggled. It lay on its back with its beak open, one claw raised overhead to grasp the cage. Diseased and panting, it was a pitiful sight until you noticed its eyes. Round, open and clear, they stared back with a satisfied look at once contemptuous and supremely indifferent to the anxious administrations of its benefactors—the look of a spoiled and pampered child.

On the other side lounged a young mestizo named Jimenez. He had made his fortune—nearly two hundred pesos, he confided, and was going back to his village to lord it over his family and home folks. One by one he took off his high buttoned coat which revealed a striped silk shirt, his yellow paper shoes, florid necktie, and stiff straw hat, and then rolled up the legs of his pleated trousers. Lying on his back with one leg upflung, and taking a swig of tequila from time to time like a child at bottle, he looked exactly like the parrot.

Behind us some forty peons squatted with immemorial patience in the blazing sun. The men dark faced and handsome, their strong muscular bodies hidden by shapeless denim. The women meek and submissive as nuns in the folds of their black cotton rebozos. Not a child whimpered.

The smell of hides increased as the hold was gradually filled. Twelve hundred! Señor Liera counted off the last with a broad grin. Immediately the cloud of green riverflies hovering over the landing and the corral swarmed to the boat. Meekly we followed them on board. The two Poles, grabbing up bundles and parrot cage and beer, rushed for the two corner bunks in the rear deckhouse, where at last, completely worn out, they lay throughout the voyage. Jimenez, blind drunk, collapsed beside them. In an instant all bunks filled. The rest of the peons stolidly settled on the stern deck—an immense octopus with dozens of heads, arms and legs.

Suddenly all throats raised a single cry. A huge tree was slowly swirling round the bend upon the boat. At once there answered a calm voice in Spanish. The half dozen cargadores who constituted the crew leapt forward to the rail and with long poles pushed the trunk safely offside. That voice, slow and authoritative, was the only inspiring thing about the *Rio Colorado*. It showed she had a master.

He had been tipped back in his chair against the tiny wheelhouse, asleep in the sun, and now stood imperturbably watching the trunk floating by. He was a full-blooded Cocopah nearly six feet six inches tall and so massively built he appeared fat. The tail of a sweaty blue work shirt hung over his beltless dungarees. His feet were bare, but on his enormous head perched a small white uniform cap. This single and ludicrous badge of authority was unnecessary. Command showed in his face. It was almost black, hairless, with the great nose of initiative and a bony protruding ridge of observation across his lower forehead. Under this his bright black Indian eyes shone hard and steady as a snake's.

A whistle blew. Señor Liera, his truck drivers and a group of horsemen and mule drivers from the corral gathered on the bank. The capitán jerked a bell cord, and the *Rio Colorado* shook with the life of her engines. The plank was drawn on. The line was loosed. Immediately the boat swung offshore; that slow stream masked a current. And when I looked back the clutter of shacks and the group of watchers were no more than a diminutive splotch receding around the bend.

Old, foul with hides and reeking in the blazing sun like a garbage tug, the *Rio Colorado* crawled swiftly downstream. A thin breeze blew in our faces and carried some of the stench behind. I stood on the sloping foredeck, watching the slow red river uncurling like a sluggish serpent ahead. There is always something appallingly monotonous to me in a trip by water; a forlorn sense of sameness and an aloofness from the land that one who prefers burro-back to all other means of travel cannot abide. You will not find it going down the Colorado, perhaps because the river is so inalienably a part of its shores. The chaparral became more and more dense. Shadows of willows darkened the cool glades on each side. Lagoons crept under the overhanging foliage and reappeared between limbs in an aspect of serene and unbroken placidity. Innumerable flocks of cranes and herons floated like spotless white blankets on the muddy brown surface of the river, refusing to be disturbed until we were almost upon them. Then abruptly and silently they rose as if someone had grasped the edge of their feathery blanket and shook it over our heads. And borne forward along that serene and remote watercourse in an attitude of complacent calm, it was as if the doubtful virtues of all our obscure and meaningless lives had been recognized and rewarded with a benign and earthly peace.

The capitán sat backed against the wheelhouse, his bare feet braced against a coil of anchor chain. In this position of easy vigilance he was staring fixedly at the river. From time to time and without turning his head, he murmured a soft command to the boy at the wheel inside. Obedient to his will the *Rio Colorado* veered from midstream into a placid pool gleaming like a plate of bright copper or swung slowly toward the thickets of the opposite shore. Since childhood he had known the river well. He sat there as if it were no more than a brown skein running through his great hands for him to inspect for the slightest flaw. In his hands too he held in bondage our own tangled pasts, the meaningless perplexities of our complex lives.

We were still in this thick twilight jungle when supper was served. Crew and passengers alike stood in line at the galley for a tin plate filled with beans, fried pork, a slice of goat cheese, hard biscuits which exploded with tiny puffs of flour when broken, and a cup of bitter reddish coffee. Darkness fell suddenly. Save for a small riding light on the masthead, the *Rio Colorado* was indistinguishable from the chaparral on each side.

An hour later we stopped and dropped anchor. Immediately silence and heat and mosquitoes settled down upon us. To ward off the latter the peons on the stern deck lighted their charcoal braziers, and in their ruddy glow dropped off to sleep. The bunks of the deckhouses were already filled with the Poles, Jimenez and their lucky companions. On the foredeck the capitán was spread out with the crew around him. Among them on the hard flooring and with my hat for a pillow I lay down. The cry of a night bird rose from the marshes. We slept.

Past midnight a bell sounded. A child awakened by the rattle of the anchor chain set up a plaintive cry. The engines began, and again we slipped downstream in ghostly gray moonlight.

By dawn the peace of night was dispelled. The river had grown to twice its width and reflected a sullen muddy aspect that changed our wholesome mood. Trees and chaparral had vanished. There was nothing but a flat expanse of barren tidal plain stretching toward the gaunt dry hills faintly rising on the horizon. Across this the river wound drunkenly and gracefully in great curves and loops as if it had lost its way. As it straightened, more and more bars appeared. We crept along slowly, like a fat beetle crawling down a dusty road.

Near noon we dropped anchor again. The day dragged by and still the *Rio Colorado* did not move from her mooring fifty feet from shore. For what were we waiting? Only the capitán knew. But impassive and unmoving, perhaps asleep, he lay there as if oblivious of heat, sun, flies and our own impatience. The river, slow, indifferent and majestic, crept by us as though we, heirs to power over all the living earth and its stubborn elements, were no more than an insignificant and unmoving speck upon its muddy surface. It did not know us; and we, with resentful, sun-glazed eyes, stared back upon the river.

For three days and four nights we lay as if frozen in time and abandoned to the capricious stubbornness of that massive Indian. Perhaps fifty people crowded on a flat board surface 50 feet long and 20 feet wide, anchored in the middle of a muddy river flowing through a flat sandy plain, and exposed to the glaring desert sun of August. Psychologists assert that a dream exists no longer than a second in a sleeper's mind, and only the most foolish of us deny that a man may live longer in the stress of a single hour than during a year of easy life. So those interminable days on the *Rio Colorado* comprise a period which remains timeless and immeasurable, like a fragment of life curiously detached from the moving stream of years.

Lackadaisically each morning at sunrise the mongrel crew scrubbed the deck and wiped off the rail. The rest of the day they lay in every torpid shadow on the boat. The two Poles never ventured out of their bunks, exemplifying by their patience a belief in the invincibility of time to remedy all ills. Jimenez was a bore. Running out of tequila he would lie awake at night, then reach out and jerk a feather from their parrot. At its squawk the Poles would awake, curse and plead, then finally pass over to him a bottle of their treasured warm beer. The peons on the stern crouched patiently under their canvas flaps, their naked feet sluffing to and from the water cask wearing a trail into the planks. Courteous and soft spoken, they never passed without murmuring "Permiso, Yanqui" or a slow "Con su permiso, señor."

The fried pork gave out. Thereafter we ate beans, cheese and biscuits three times daily. The uncovered metal water casks developed a thick green scum from beneath which we dipped stale and tepid drinking water. The toilet became a horror against whose rusty back we burned our own whenever the engines were running. The hatch was opened to let in air to the hides, and the sun circling overhead drew from the hold a stench that made us dizzy by midday. I would have given anything for a bar of soap and a toothbrush, but my duffelbag had been thrown in the hold and could not be found.

Not a soul on board spoke English, and this with my incomplete Spanish set me apart in the unenviable position of a solitary white Yanqui in the midst of an alien race. The two Poles were curiously self-isolated with their diseased and pampered parrot. Jimenez with his pathetic illusion of superiority derived from the money hidden in his waist was separated from the ill-kempt crew of Mexicans; and with the crew from the horde of peons by a greater gulf—the impassable breach between the mestizo and the Indian. Between the capitán and crew and passengers alike lay an intangible barrier composed of authority, race and his own temperament. He was a man who would have been alone in any crowd. So that jammed together as we were, and weighted down by the same miseries, we were at once a world isolated in space and time, and a dozen worlds.

Feliz alone expressed our common humanity. He was a little shirtless fellow about eight years old, the eldest of four children of one of the señoras nesting on the stern deck, and was working his passage. Next to the capitán he assumed all the responsibilities of the *Rio Colorado*. If he had not, they would have been thrust upon him. For two hours, three times a day, he washed tin plates and scrubbed greasy pots in a wooden tub in the narrow passage outside the galley. The filthy ill-tempered cook compelled him to haul his own water buckets up the side of the boat, an almost impossible feat. Once at the lurch of the steamer he almost went overboard, a diminutive weight hanging grimly to the end of his line. Luckily the capitán was passing by and caught him by the heels. Thereafter Feliz substituted a tin pail for the heavy bucket. Between times he did chores for the crew, waited on the capitán, carried water to the peons and coffee to Jimenez. Answering to the call of "muchacho!—muchacho!" he was kept on the jump day and night. The only time I ever caught him loafing he was munching on one of the hard floury biscuits with the rapidity and ferocity of a squirrel. His precocious little face, always unwashed and sharpened with hunger, already had assumed the solemn gravity of a peon. Yet throughout he maintained an unsmiling good nature. Invulnerable to jests and curses, denying pity for his lot with a subtle self-reliance, he always carried about him a staunch reassurance that he found the world agreeable enough without rest or play.

Restless, anxious and bored, suffering heat, sun, mosquitoes and the stench of hides, we continued to watch with dull glazed eyes the chocolate river oozing past. Only the nights seemed real. Under the moon the river took on an aspect of serenity and mellowed age, and its broad gentle windings seemed like a road that had been long abandoned. Far out midstream a fish rose leaping, and its splash might have been a tuft of dust. Forgetting each day as we had forgotten the others, yet unreasonably hopeful of the morrow, we lay uncovered on the hard decks. And steadily, hour after hour, a boy sitting on a water cask kept taking soundings of the river. We heard the splash of lead, its bump against the rail, and in a moment his soft voice rising into the night. "Cinco brazas, capitán."—"Cuatro y media."—"Cuatro!"—"Seis, capitán."

The massive Indian was still awake and waiting. One night it came. The river rose rapidly. The *Rio Colorado* jerked at her anchor chain. The capitán stirred for the first time. The anchor was brought up and the engines started, though we did not move. Greasy lanterns were lit, and in their dim flicker the crew lounged restlessly, rolling cigarettes. Far downstream sounded a low resounding boom. Swiftly it advanced upstream upon us, clearly visible in the moonlight: a wall of water some four feet high sweeping round the bend. The *Rio Colorado*, unfettered and with engines running, met it squarely. She went nose down until her decks were washed and came up with a dizzy roll streaming torrents from every passageway.

The capitán seemed pleased at her ducking. Wet to the knees, he stood listening to the receding roar as if oblivious to the commotion on board. It was punctuated by the blasts of a raucous siren which turned out to be the squawking parrot. People poured from the flooded deckhouse. Foremost came the two Poles carrying the parrot. Its cage had been sitting on the floor beside their bunk; the flood had dunked it thoroughly; and now, indignant at having been doused instead of sprinkled, the bedraggled lump of feathers was screaming with rage. Jimenez clung to his stiff straw hat, his money belt and yellow paper shoes—all that would differentiate him as a pompous man of fortune among his simple villagers at home. Feliz, eyes scared to twice their size, still munched absent-mindedly at a biscuit as though his unconscious hunger would accept nothing short of drowning as a surcease from its task. Only the peons made no sound. With peasant stolidity they endured water as they had endured sun, secure in the unrelenting justice of their fate. But we, frightened into an abject mass clinging to door-posts, deck rails and bunks, shivered in abysmal misery wringing out our clothes, and waited for the sun.

Impassively the capitán ordered the crew to drop sounding line and anchor again. The engines were stilled. Again we lay waiting in the river.

What we had experienced was one of the tide bores of the Colorado. And what we had escaped, due to the capitán's caution in waiting far up the channel until its full force was spent, was the fate of the *Topolobampo* three years before.

A bore is simply a tidal wave which rushes up between the narrow converging shores of a river in a high and advancing wall of water opposing in turbulent conflict the current of the river itself. Such bores are encountered in but few river mouths in the world. The Hangchow Bore at the mouth of the Tsientang in China, and the Shat El Arab where the Tigris and Euphrates unite to flow into the Gulf of Persia are notable examples. Bore waves rising from 6 to 9 feet high are known at the mouths of the Severn in England, the Seine in France, and the Hugli in India; waves 15 feet high have been known in the Amazon. Of all these the bores of the Colorado are perhaps the most phenomenal. For here the tidal variation of the Gulf of California ranges from 22 feet to a high of 32 feet, rhythmically generating tremendous waves that sweep up the river for 37 miles.

Opposed to this is the phenomenal force of the Colorado itself. Perhaps the heaviest silt-laden river in the world, it sweeps down into the gulf at the rate of 200,000 cubic feet per second.

Always strange, terrifying and dangerous, thc tremendous conflicts of these opposing forces vary in season with the flood, high- and low-water discharges of the river; with the monthly phases of the moon which control the ascending tides of the gulf; and with the distance upriver from the mouth. Yet from Ulloa's first experience in 1539 to the disaster of the *Topolobampo* in 1922, every boatman who has witnessed the bores has attested their ferocity.

We had been lucky; it was August and the river was at its summer low; also the tide of the full moon was past its peak. But our huge, taciturn capitán was taking no chances. With an eye on the waning moon and an ear cocked to his boy's cry of diminishing soundings, he lounged patiently on the still-anchored *Rio Colorado.*

* * *

The river fell eight feet, ten. We awoke one morning in what seemed a different channel. The flat edge of the plain was now a steep, muddy bank rising above our heads. Downstream the river parted to each side of a sand bar already drying in the sun.

But the capitán could not be hurried; it was almost noon before we started. The sound of the engines warming up and the boat's vibration shook us alive. With something of a shock we remembered we were on a boat and had a destination. Imperceptibly, strangely enough, the *Rio Colorado* began moving past the bar toward La Bomba.

The histories of most great rivers are written in the cities at their mouths. Paris, London, Buenos Aires, New Orleans—they are all no more than what the Seine, the Thames, La Plata and the Mississippi have made them. But it is a singular characteristic of the Colorado that it has no city at its mouth. Like all the others it was the first known highway into a new and unknown wilderness; for three centuries it was the clearest trail into the deep hinterland of our America; and its mouth was the only portal. Strategically located at the head of an immense gulf, it could have commanded the dominance of a peninsular province and its motherland shore, the trade of two countries and one of the greatest fishing grounds in the world. Yet only La Bomba remains as a monument to what might have been the first and greatest city in the New World. It lacked only the one thing that would have made its development possible, a rich, accessible hinterland instead of a terrifying desert.

A dreary, sun-struck huddle of deserted shacks, a crumbling loading pier—no more than this, it slips past without a hail. It is not even a remote little fishing village like San Luis Gonzaga, a watering place like El Doctoro, a boat landing like El Mayor. It is simply an Almayer's Folly that today has no name upon a map. Here for four hundred years or more Cocopah dugout canoes, Spanish galleons, Hardy's *Bruja*, all the early American steamboats and Mexican fishing boats have stopped. And so today it persistently exists in the memory of every man who has ever run the lower river, one of the most familiar names throughout the gulf. And yet as if by some strange miscalculation of fate, it remains a site that has missed a resplendent destiny by a hair.

Slowly we nosed past it into the broad highway of the sea. Almost two kilometros wide, the river kept spreading out. What was river, gulf, tidal plain, mud flats and fields of alkali and salt no one could distinguish in the blazing sea of heat waves shimmering in the sun. For here at its mouth the Colorado, gorged with silt, is as much land as water. Looking down over the rail we seemed to be afloat in what resembled a vast settling basin or a vat of ore concentrates red as burnished copper.

Such areas of extreme sedimentation have given rise to many strange phenomena. On June 16, 1819, at Cutch, India, one of the strangest occurred in the Indus delta. Without warning 2,000 square miles of land suddenly sank beneath the sea. The shock of this tremendous displacement spread throughout an area within a radius of 1,000 miles. The town of Bhooj collapsed in ruins. At Ahmedabad, 200 miles away, the famous mosque built 450 years before was shaken to pieces. To the northwest the Denodur Volcano erupted. As the shock subsided, the sea rushed in, inundating miles of land. Then suddenly and mysteriously the "Ullah Bund," or the "Mountain of God," lifted bodily out of the level plain.

Little wonder that men fell on their knees, though powerless in prayer to stop, control or even understand this manifestation of a mysterious power that in an instant could wipe out cities, alter history and forever change the face of the land.

And yet what had taken place was simple enough even to the most ignorant. Like man, the earth but trembled on the scales of God. When one area went down beneath the sea another rose to maintain the balance. It is the perpetual, recurring history of islands and mountain peaks, of continents themselves. "Isostatic equilibrium," Grandfather's old phrase; it holds as true at the mouth of the Colorado as it did on a high peak above timberline at its source.

From this has evolved the Subsidence Theory, which holds simply that the sinking of land at the mouths of rivers is due to the enormous weight of the deltas breaking through the crust of the earth.

According to this, the great earthquake of Lisbon in 1775, at Cutch in 1819 and at Cachar, India, on the Ganges, and at Charleston in 1886 were all caused by the subsidence of delta areas. Even the San Francisco earthquake of 1906 was aided by the subsidence of the heavy silt deposits of the Columbia River brought southward by the drift of coast currents in the Pacific.

Consider the Colorado delta, about which J. O. Turle, a geographical engineer, collected in 1928 some amazing facts for his study. It is one of the greatest accumulations of silt in the world. The whole area south of Imperial and Coachella valleys to the gulf is but a vast delta bar built up by the Colorado's deposition of silt. The river has gouged out of the Grand Cañon alone 350 cubic miles of rock, which has been deposited at its mouth. And still every day it carries through the Grand Cañon an average of one million tons of sand, equivalent to 80,000 railroad carloads, to pour on top of them.

A subsidence of less than 50 feet of this enormous weight would cause the gulf to rush up into Imperial Valley and cover the whole Colorado Desert—a catastrophe beside which the flooding of the river itself would seem trivial. What are the prospects?

It is true that areas of sedimentation occur near the mouths of all large rivers. Yet in almost all cases tidewaters sweeping along the seacoast carry away the silt, distributing it equally over the ocean floor. The Gulf of California, narrow and landlocked, offers no such release. Furthermore, the rate of subsidence of these areas at the mouths of rivers is nearly proportional to the ratio of their drainage area to the area of their deposition. This average ratio is 16 to 1. That of the Colorado—draining 246,000 square miles and depositing upon less than 1,000 square miles—is 250 to 1, the highest in the world. Also in the former average, the usual rate of subsidence is from 2 to 4 feet each hundred years, whereas at the mouth of the Colorado it is 44 feet.

The proof of a pudding is in the eating. What about the theory? The answer, according to Mr. Turle, was obvious to geological engineers and laymen alike. Hardly a month went by without a minor earthquake in Imperial Valley rattling windows and cracking another cornice of the Barbara Worth Hotel. A few years later he could have offered another proof with the serious earthquake of Long Beach and Los Angeles. A map of the great rift faults of Southern California, the San Andreas rift fault north of Yuma, the Salton Sink blocks, and others converging at San Gorgonio Pass show that all were ready to go under weight. Unless—as had been pointed out—an immense dam of some kind was built to stop the deposition of silt at the mouth of the Colorado.

But to us on board the *Rio Colorado* that fantastic project seemed as hazy as the far-off volcanic sierras floating on the horizon. We were more interested in the water content of this strange area than in its discoloring silt. It was still as thick and dark as chocolate as far as we could see. But somewhere in this vast dark upper end of the gulf there was a strange white circle of clear, fresh water bubbling up through silt and salt water. In it, completely marooned, so to speak, lived a school of strange fish found nowhere else in either river or gulf. Now these fish, breeding at such a rate as soon to overpopulate their tiny pool, had developed a peculiar custom. The females were ferocious, bullheaded and much stronger than the males. So each year, as the spawning season passed, these amazons would draw up in battle array and rush upon the males. Wriggling, butting with their bullheads like great stags and slashing with their teeth, they would force the unneeded males out of the circle where they would be choked in silt, drowned in salt water or burned to death in the lagoons on either side.

For also in the mouth of the river were two lagoons of reddish water of such a caustic quality and so malignant that a mere drop on any part of a human body creates blisters and burns into the bone like acid if not wiped off. This was probably caused by a bituminous mineral on the beds of the lagoons, which has often eaten up the anchors of fishing boats by its corrosive action.

It was the ingeniero of the *Rio Colorado* who vouched for both these tales. He had just come up from his boiling engines down below, and stood reeking with sweat and grime. He was a talkative fellow. Born in a remote fishing village along the gulf, he still talked of fish. Besides his engines they were all he knew or cared about. All the grease and oil in which he seemed invariably clothed, as if in the raiment of his new calling, never obscured the imagined smell of fish about him. Even his long drooping mustaches seemed perpetually awiggle as he talked.

"This gulf, señor, is a garden of fish. They sprout here faster and thicker than corn on the hillsides." And his greasy arms, sweeping in generous, careless arcs over the water, seemed to mark off those pastures of the sea as a ranchero on a hilltop marks off his crops and herds. He was particularly enthusiastic over the totoaba which he called the "crow." Of steel-blue color, and weighing up to 165 pounds, the totoaba breed in greatest numbers in the mouth of the Colorado which they enter for alimentation in the shallower water. Fishing for them is not much sport; once hooked they are pulled in like a cow on a halter. Only their size impresses a visiting Yanqui, and the poor fisherfolk are always glad to get them for the "buche," or bladder, which can be sold. There was also el lobo marino—the sea wolf; the atun; the delicious dorado, a gold finch; the palometa, a perch with four blue lines running across its back; the huachinango; the pez-gallo, or flying fish; the barge tarpon with two white mustaches hanging from its pouting lower lip; the mammals cochinillo and tintorera, which change colors when dying; the valuable shark whose fins were sold to the Chinese in Mexicali; together with tortoises, sea hogs and water eels.

The ingeniero's voice ran on. Then after a lurch to the rail to point out a flash in a trough, he recalled sadly, "But I, señor, I am but an engineer," and clattered back down the steps into the hold.

The *Rio Colorado* kept nosing into the gulf, plunging uneasily in choppy waves that gradually cleared of silt. Suddenly we noticed that they were blue, bright blue. We were out of the river, past the islands at its mouth, and abroad in the open sea.

Slowly our little vapor crawled down the desolate coast of the peninsula. Caught between the great blue sea and the jagged, black, volcanic sierras of the shore, she seemed to have shrunk perceptibly. But only to increase the stature of her massive Indian master. The capitán had come to be my best friend on board. Day and night he lay beside me in his habitual posture of watchful ease. He was as familiar with the gulf as with the river, and his eyes did not miss a point or cape. And those sharp, barren outcroppings of rock, imprinted as indelibly upon his mind as upon the horizon, seemed like symbols of his life's corners, like cryptic sign posts of his domain. The *Rio Colorado* was his life and its horizons his chosen world. Sure of it, certain of himself, he carried an air of unmarred self-content.

Toward evening a squall blew up. The Sea of Cortez has always been known for its rough passage. Luckily we were too early for El Cordonazo de Francisco, that hurricane which invariably occurs on the saint's day of San Francisco and is dreaded throughout the gulf. Nevertheless, we crept into a small bay. Instantly the boat ceased pitching and lay so quiet in the darkness I must have fallen asleep. Near midnight I was roused by the capitán's hand laid lightly on my shoulder. For what I never knew. He did not speak or turn around, but remained staring fixedly across the still water.

The moon was up, and over that remote and placid pool it gleamed silver as the shield of Cortez himself. In it, in profound silence, slept the *Rio Colorado* enclosed by a great half circle of somber cliffs. There was no movement of the boat, but we could hear the resonant thunder of high waves against the rocks and with it the low undertone of wind rushing by the entrance of the bay. I have always remembered it and that touch upon my shoulder. But what could you say to a man like that?

Next morning we put out again, stung by a fine spray blowing across decks. We were in a storm. The capitán said so. To a landsman a storm at sea carries the reasonable expectation of something awe-inspiring and magnificent. Yet there was nothing to see. The sea was merely choppy, the waves breaking into tiny whorls of white spume like hillocks of prairie grass stirred by the wind.

Among them the *Rio Colorado* staggered like a locoed cow. Between jerky pitchings over their crests she lay wallowing from side to side in the troughs. Only occasionally did she meet a wave head-to with any drive at all, and then the surge, just deep enough to be disagreeable, drained down the dirty decks. We might have been in a rowboat for all our feeling toward that 50-foot steamer. For not once had the *Rio Colorado* proved to us her superiority over her medium. Frightened equally by river and sea she seemed a trespasser fleeing for a port to hide in. True, she had kept afloat, but any log might have done the same, and we had long given up the feeling of going anywhere. Imprisoned on that miserable craft we could only adjust our lives to hopeless bondage until our time was up.

The first of several huge swells caught us at an angle. All morning we had been keeping our internal equilibrium only by an effort of our wills. That swell caught us off guard. One by one we gave up the ghost and lay weak and sweaty on the planks. Four of the crew crawled into the lifeboat, where they collapsed retching over its sides upon the deck. Even the capitán retreated to sit behind the boy at the wheel, refusing even coffee. Certainly the wet foredeck was no place to spend the night. I went to the stern deck. One of the women had built a tiny fire in a charcoal brazier, and its flicker revealed a shapeless, intertwined mass of naked, shivering children, women and men spread out upon the flooring and convulsing at every lurch. The terrible stench drove me to the deckhouse. It was worse.

Things in that 12-foot cube were indescribable and unbearable. In bunks scarcely wide enough for one person, two and even three lay together like limp bundles of rags. The floor was a solid mass of peons who had crawled in to escape the flying spray. Upon these, those in the upper bunks vomited at will.

The night dragged by. Another day passed. The pitching of the boat had ceased but still we could not eat. The huge pot of beans, untouched for two days, stood in the passageway crawling with maggots. The water casks were filthy with algae as if the water had been dipped up from a marsh. Tin cups and plates littered the *Rio Colorado* from bow to stern. Her decks were slimy and encrusted with salt. We and she needed a hose more than anything else, but weak and dizzy, we shivered the instant the sun went down. Yet the engines going at top speed had so heated the rusty side of the smokestack forming the back wall of the excusado that it could not even be approached. The *Rio Colorado* was not a squeamish place. We were all reduced to our common humanity at last, an integrated whole.

In this immense and haunting delirium I saw Jiminez staggering out on deck. He had mashed his stiff straw hat. His silk shirt, slept in for a week, was stripped of buttons and hung tail out over his pleated trousers. They were splotched with vomit. Then I saw his sick, anguished face. It had turned a bright yellow, even to the whites of his eyes: yellow jaundice. And seeing him I knew I was looking at a mirror.

He staggered to the rail and retched. Instantly from the surface of the water heaved a dark slimy body that resolved for an instant in a row of gleaming teeth. Sharks. All day they followed us down the coast, a row of thin knife-edge fins cutting the blue.

But we were moving. Out of the gray watery plain rose La Isla Angel de la Guarda. Between it and the Bahia de Los Angeles we crept down through the channel of Sal-si-puede—Get-out-if-you-can—to the island of San Lorenzo. Eastward loomed the island of San Esteban and still farther, as if it were the mainland, rose the brown rock walls of Tiburon, the last home of cannibals.

Still we kept moving under a bright and merciless sun, kept moving across a sea that was as hard and smooth as a plate of stainless steel. But drawing closer to shore to see the jutting bare brown cliffs. Punta San Juan Bautista, Punta Trinidad, Punta Baja . . .

"Cabo Virgenes, señor. We are here."

It was the capitán who had spoken. He had put on another shirt, tail in for once, an enormous pair of bright yellow shoes with glass buttons and "bull-dog" toes, and his ludicrous marine cap.

The engines slowed. High upon the scorched hills stood a huddle of board shacks. A little farther and we saw a long breakwater, a rattletrap jetty and a single palm. The engines stopped and immediately a torpid silence embalmed the boat. "Santa Rosalia, amigo. . . . Señor Yanqui, we are here!" the capitán nudged me again. I thought I had best be getting with him down into a boat. Perhaps there would be a comfortable toilet, a bar of soap and a tooth-brush on shore.

Two evenings later we left Santa Rosalia. It was still merely a French concession of the Boleo Mining Company: a great smelter and a group of aloof living quarters on top of the hill, and below it a tiny plaza surrounded by the squalid adobes of native Mexican workers, formerly Yaqui slaves brought across the gulf from Sonora.

The *Rio Colorado* had been cleaned up considerably and the other passengers, with fresh water and food, looked better. Jimenez, skin and eyes more sickly yellow than ever, had put on a new silk shirt without removing its price and size tags. Little Feliz was contentedly munching on a banana. The two Poles at last had ventured from their bunks, and even the parrot had perked up. They were all gathered on the foredeck about a new passenger sitting—of all things—in a deck chair. She was a Frenchwoman about sixty years old who had come from Marseilles in time for the birth of her grandson. The father, she said, was employed by the Boleo Company and still had two years to serve.

The *Rio Colorado* slid quietly eastward across the glazed, deep-blue expanse of gulf. Dark came on. All night long we could see the vivid flashes of sheet lightning over the Sonora highland nearly a hundred kilometros away. And then, awakening suddenly to what it meant, we saw a faint dark blur of hills. Guaymas!

In the ghostly darkness of early morning we entered the outer harbor. Not only to me and the capitán is that landlocked harbor the most beautiful in the world. We seemed lost in a maze of hills; then suddenly, magically, they fell away. We were sliding across a buckler of smooth steel studded with the bolts of tiny islands. We passed a small packet standing under a load of sail. We crawled, black and brutish and still stinking, past a pleasure schooner spotless white, with a sheer as trim and lovely as a lady's waist. That was a ship! Yet what could she do an hour up the Colorado? Somehow for the first time the *Rio Colorado* seemed other than what she was, humble and courageous, forever familiar and ineffably dear.

Offside a voice eerie in the early morning cried out and was answered by our capitán. A rampart of hills rose up and blocked our passage. The engines stopped. Waiting for daylight we washed from buckets hauled up the side. The capitán put on his shoes again and got out his papers. Jimenez nervously wrapped round his throat a new silk scarf.

Gradually the darkness thinned to a sullen gray and suddenly it was light. Those hills were green. Vivid green! Imagine green hills! The sierras of Mexico. And below them the tall towers of a cathedral, a row of palms, a long embarcadero. Home! For still and always Mexico remains the spiritual mother of that vast wild province of the north, the wilderness basin of the Colorado. It seemed suddenly, for no other reason one could rationalize, that after four hundred years we had at last returned home. And with the first shaft of the sun clearing the sierras and striking into the stainless bright blue of the bay, a boat put out to us from shore.

T. H. Watkins

The River Runners

This selection by T. H. Watkins appears in part three of his book The Grand Canyon, *an anthology which includes contributions by Roderick Nash, William E. Brown, Jr., and Wallace Stegner, among others. Earlier parts of the book concentrate on pre-Columbian times and the Spanish conquest of the Colorado River Basin.*

For most of the pilgrims who have come to the Colorado and its canyons during the past century, the experience has been a limited one, though even in its limitations enough to jar the sensibilities into disbelief, as Dutton suggested. To stand on the rim, north or south, is for most people in itself the outside dimension of experience; others take to the trails to enlarge even the boundary, but this is as far as most of the pilgrims go. There are some, however, who feel a need to cross the boundary itself, to enter an older, deeper experience by stepping from the world of human time to the geologic time of the still canyons and the river that made them.

These are the river-runners, a stalwart and fast-growing breed of men and women—and children—who make their own kind of pilgrimage throughout each summer to Lees Ferry on the Colorado, where they enter Galloway boats, Nevills boats, custom-designed wooden, aluminum, and fiberglass boats, neoprene rafts, canoes, and kayaks for the often violent, sometimes dangerous and to most of them utterly beautiful ten-day, 300-mile run through the Grand Canyon to Lake Mead. In the summer of 1968, 3,609

From *The Grand Colorado* by T. H. Watkins (Palo Alto: American West Publishing, 1969).

river enthusiasts tumbled down this still-wild stretch of the Colorado, reliving, for a time, the lonely pioneering explorations of John Wesley Powell and exulting in an intimacy with the river, the Canyon, and all the profound forces they represent—experiencing a "oneness with the Canyon," as one of them has described it.

River-running on the Colorado, like the more sedate forms of Grand Canyon–watching, is a comparatively recent recreational development. For John Wesley Powell and those who came after him for more than a generation, the tumbling journey down the Colorado was a necessity—and while it cannot be denied that such men sought and found adventure in it, few of them would have cared to describe the trip as a form of recreation. As the Grand Canyon began to fall into the ken of the tourist, however, there were some who took to the river for nothing more practical than the sheer adventure of it—a challenge, delight, and beauty of a kind that most people would never know.

The first purely recreational trip down the river was undertaken in September of 1909 by Ohio manufacturer Julius F. Stone. Accompanied by Nathaniel Galloway, a trapper who had run much of the river in search of pelts, and equipped with Galloway's specially-designed "cockpit" boats, Stone left Green River City, Wyoming (Powell's starting point), on September 12 and arrived at Needles, California, on November 19. The pair made it through without a single upset, an accomplishment rarely matched and one that may be attributable to Galloway's innovation in river-running: instead of taking rapids bow first, as Powell had done, Galloway ran them stern first, so that he could see where he was going. The method was adopted by nearly all who followed him.

In the winter of 1911, one of the most renowned of all the river trips was undertaken by a pair of brothers with a hunger for challenges and an instinct for publicity. Ellsworth and Emery Kolb arrived at the Grand Canyon in 1902, bought a small photographic studio in Williams, Arizona, and moved it to the head of the Bright Angel Trail. There they made a transient living by photographing people about to descend the trail to the canyon floor, an event that most visitors understandably felt should be immortalized. The brothers went after immortality themselves when they decided to run the Colorado from Green River City, Wyoming, to Needles, California, and record the trip on motion-picture film for the first time. They left Green River City on September 8, 1911, equipped with Galloway boats and thousands of feet of film. After a month-long rest during November at their Grand Canyon home, they arrived at Needles on January 18, 1912.

They had not been so fortunate as Stone and Galloway. They had upset several times, once losing a great deal of photographic equipment, and more than once had been forced to make extensive repairs on the boats. Moreover, Emery took ill during part of the trip, which increased Ellsworth's work load to grueling proportions. For all its problems, however, the journey was a resounding success, for the brothers had let nothing stop them from taking movies and still photographs of everything they could document—the running of rapids, the scenery, the repairing of boats, and camp life—compiling one of the most complete photographic records of the river system ever produced. Emery took the films and photographs on a profitable lecture tour of the East, while Ellsworth after making a quick trip from Needles to the Gulf of California in 1913 to round out the journey, sat down and wrote *Through the Grand Canyon from Wyoming to Mexico*, which—even though inaccurately titled—has since become a classic among river-running enthusiasts. Ten years later, Emery went through the Canyon again as chief boatman of the United States Geological Survey's exploration expedition.

Perhaps the most deliberately unnecessary and faintly ludicrous of all the early river trips was that organized and conducted by Clyde Eddy in the spring of 1927. Eddy, a member of the Explorer's Club of New York, had offered in newspaper advertisements "A fine opportunity for geology students, or young members of teaching faculties, to do field work in virgin territory," and received more than one hundred applications. From these, he selected eleven—eight college boys, one cameraman, one member of the American Museum of Natural History, and one identified simply as Parley Galloway of southeastern Utah, presumably a relative of Nathaniel Galloway. All but Galloway were totally inexperienced in river-running, and all were motivated by what moved Eddy himself—the *idea* of running a river. A thirteenth member, a tramp that Eddy picked up at Green River, Utah, joined them before departure; his motivations have been lost to history. To reinforce the curious logic of the expedition, Eddy brought along a bear cub and a dog as mascots, companions, or whatever. On June 27, 1927, the three boats—the *Powell*, the *Dellenbaugh*, and the *Coronado*—pushed off into the Green River.

The ambitious expedition soon learned that it was no light matter to run the Colorado River. By the time the group had fought its way to Lees Ferry, four men—the tramp, the cameraman, and two college boys—had had enough. Somehow, the remaining nine, as well as the bear cub and the dog, made it through to Needles after six cruel weeks. Eddy, following in the footsteps of the Kolb brothers, promptly set down the adventure in a book: *Down the World's Most Dangerous River*, which sold well enough to justify a British printing.

Surely the saddest of all the river trips in the years before it became a yearly pastime for thousands was the honeymoon journey of Mr. and Mrs. Glen R. Hyde in the fall of 1928. Why they decided to do such a thing on their honeymoon is beyond immagination, but the two of them set off from Green River, Utah, in October, carried in a scow of Hyde's own design, featuring sweep oars at each end. The odd boat served them well for the first part of the trip, and less than a month after their departure they arrived at Bright Angel Creek. There, they debarked and climbed up to the South Rim to ask Emery Kolb about the river below Bright Angel Creek. Kolb tried to talk them into using life preservers for the rest of the trip, but Hyde waved off the possibility of trouble. Mrs. Hyde, however, might have had her doubts, for Kolb reported that shortly before their departure she looked down at her muddy, water-soaked boots and remarked, "I wonder if I shall ever wear pretty shoes again."

They were never seen again. When it became obvious that their long silence signified something more than normal delays, search for them began. All that was ever found was the boat, partially swamped but otherwise undamaged. Kolb speculated that Mrs. Hyde had been swept into a rapid while holding the boat's line, and that Hyde had drowned attempting to save her.

The monolith of Boulder Dam put an end to the possibility of river journeys from the Green to the lower Colorado, but it did not appreciably detract from this aspect of the river's wild appeal. All during the 1930's adventurers of one kind or another ran both the upper and lower reaches of the river. By 1939, it was even possible to buy a ticket for a trip down the Colorado, for by then Norman D. Nevills had organized Mexican Hat Expeditions, Inc., the first commercial river-running operation on the Colorado. Until his death in 1949, Nevills led annual trips down the river in an improved, wider version of the boat designed by Nathanial Galloway at the turn of the century. His business was purchased by James P. Rigg, Jr., John B. Rigg, and J. Frank Wright, and by 1950 it had several competitors, including the "Woman of the River," Mrs. Georgia White, whose neoprene raft trips down the Colorado surely have made her one of the most unusual career women in history.

By the mid-1960's, several hundred people a year were riding the river. By then, of course, the trip was a short one, since Flaming Gorge Dam, Glen Canyon Dam, and all the dams strung along the lower river reduced the length of wild water to a mere 279 miles between Lees Ferry and Lake Mead. Even this water was not truly wild, for, as one river-runner complained gently, "the river's level is no longer controlled by the snow melt in the Rockies, but by the Bureau of Reclamation. This introduced an element of uncertainty:

we could never be sure that we would not wake up one morning and find insufficient water to float our boats. . . ."

Still, the trip is a magic one, for the canyons of the river remain a genuine challenge, and their beauty a constant delight. In 1969, more than five thousand adventurers will course down the river. For those who might wonder why they do it, the answer can only be a paraphrase of the reason given by mountain-climbers: because the river and the canyons are there. Listen to one of them, Haldane Holstrom, writing finish to his solo journey of 1937, for nothing he says has changed: "I find I have already had my reward, in the doing of the thing. The stars, the cliffs and canyons, the roar of the rapids, the moon, the uncertainty and worry, the relief when through each one . . . the campfires at night . . . the real respect and friendship of rivermen I met. . . .

"This may be my last camp where the roar of the rapids is echoed from the cliffs around and I can look at the stars and moon only through a narrow slit in the earth.

"The river and the canyons have been kind to me. . . ."

John McPhee

Encounters with an Archdruid

This selection describes a now legendary float trip shared by antagonistic passengers, conservationist David Brower and dam builder Floyd E. Dominy. Preceding it are profiles by author McPhee which trace their lives from boyhood to their positions as Sierra Club President and Commissioner of the Bureau of Reclamation, respectively.

Mile 130. The water is smooth here, and will be smooth for three hundred yards, and then we are going through another rapid. The temperature is a little over ninety, and the air is so dry that the rapid will feel good. Dominy and Brower are drinking beer. They have settled into a kind of routine: once a day they tear each other in half and the rest of the time they are pals.

Dominy is wearing a blue yachting cap with gold braid, and above its visor in gold letters are the words "Lake Powell." His skin is rouge brown. His nose is peeling. He wears moccasins, and a frayed cotton shirt in dark, indeterminate tartan, and long trousers secured by half a pound of silver buckle. He has with him a couple of small bags and a big leather briefcase on which is painted the great seal of the Bureau of Reclamation—snow-capped mountains, a reservoir, a dam, and irrigated fields, all within the framing shape of a big drop of water. Dominy has been discoursing on the multiple advantages of hydroelectric power, its immediacy ("When you want it, you just throw a switch") and its innocence of pollution.

"Come on now, Dave, be honest," he said. "From a conservationist's point of view, what is the best source of electric power?"

"Flashlight batteries," Brower said.

Brower is also wearing an old tartan shirt, basically orange, and faded. He wears shorts and sneakers. The skin of his legs and face is bright red. Working indoors and all but around the clock, he has been too long away from the sun. He protects his head with a handkerchief knotted at the corners and soaked in the river, but his King Lear billowing white hair is probably protection enough. He travels light. A miniature duffelbag, eight inches in diameter and a foot long—standard gear for the river—contains all that he has with him, most notably his Sierra Club cup, without which he would be incomplete.

Dominy and Brower are both showing off a little. These organized expeditions carry about a dozen people per raft, and by now the others are thoroughly aware of the biases of the conservationist and the Commissioner. The people are mainly from Arizona and Nevada—schoolteachers, a few students, others from the U.S. Public Health Service. On the whole, I would say that Dominy so far has the edge with them. Brower is shy and quiet. Dominy is full of Irish pub chatter and has a grin as wide as the river.

Cans of beer are known as sandwiches in this red, dry, wilderness world. No one questions this, or asks the reason. They just call out "Sandwich, please!" and a can of Coors comes flying through the air. They catch the beer and drink it, and they put the aluminum tongues inside the cans. I threw a tongue in the river and was booed by everyone. No detritus whatever is left in the canyon. Used cans, bottles—all such things—are put in sacks and go with the raft all the way. The beer hangs in the water in a burlap bag from the rear of the raft, with Cokes and Frescas. The bag is hauled onto the raft before a heavy rapid but rides through the lighter ones.

The raft consists of, among other things, two neoprene bananas ten yards long. These pontoons, lashed to a central rubber barge, give the over-all rig both lateral and longitudinal flexibility. The river sometimes leaps straight up through the raft, but that is a mark of stability rather than imminent disaster. The raft is informal and extremely plastic. Its lack of rigidity makes it safe.

This is isolation wilderness: two or three trails in two hundred miles, otherwise no way out but down the river with the raft. Having seen the canyon from this perspective, I would not much want to experience it another way. Once in a rare while, we glimpse the rims. They are a mile above us and, in places, twelve miles apart. All the flat shelves of color beneath them return the eye by steps to the earliest beginnings of the world—from the high white limestones and maroon Hermit Shales of Permian time to the red sandstones that formed when the first reptiles lived and the vermillion cliffs that stood contemporary with the earliest trees. This Redwall Limestone, five hundred feet thick, is so vulnerable to the infiltrations of groundwater that it has been shaped, in the seas of air between the canyon rims, into red towers and red buttes, pillars, caverns, arches, and caves. The groundwater runs for hundreds of miles between the layers of that apparently bone-dry desert rock and bursts out into the canyon in stepped cascades or ribbon falls. We are looking at such a waterfall right now, veiling away from the Redwall, high above us. There is green limestone behind the waterfall, and pink limestone that was pressed into being by the crushing weight of the ocean at the exact time the ocean itself was first giving up life—amphibious life—to dry land. Beneath the pink and green limestones are green-gray shales and dark-brown sandstones—Bright Angel Shale, Tapeats Sandstone—that formed under the fathoms that held the first general abundance of marine life. Tapeats Sea was the sea that compressed the rock that was cut by the river to create the canyon. The Tapeats Sandstone is the earliest rock from the Paleozoic Era, and beneath it the mind is drawn back to the center of things, the center of the canyon, the cutting plane, the Colorado. Flanked by its Bass Limestones, its Hotauta Conglomerates, its Vishnu Schists and Zoroaster Granites, it races in white water through a pre-Cambrian here and now. The river has worked its way down the stillness of original time.

Brower braces his legs and grips one of the safety ropes that run along the pontoons. He says, "How good it is to hear a living river! You can almost hear it cutting."

Dominy pulls his Lake Powell hat down firmly around his ears. He has heard this sort of thing before. Brower is suggesting that the Colorado is even now making an ever deeper and grander Grand Canyon, and what sacrilege it would be to dam the river and stop that hallowed process. Dominy says, "I think most people agree, Dave, that it wasn't a river of this magnitude that cut the Grand Canyon."

Brower is too interested in the coming rapid to respond. In this corridor of calm, we can hear the rapid ahead. Rapids and waterfalls ordinarily take shape when rivers cut against resistant rock and then come to a kind of rock that gives way more easily. This is not the case in the Grand Canyon, where rapids occur beside the mouths of tributary creeks. Although these little streams may be dry much of the year, they are so steep that when they run they are able to fling considerable debris into the Colorado—sand, gravel, stones, rocks, boulders. The debris forms dams, and water rises upstream. The river is unusually quiet there—a lakelike quiet—and then it flows over the debris, falling suddenly, pounding and crashing through the boulders. These are the rapids of the Grand Canyon, and there are a hundred and sixty-one of them. Some have appeared quite suddenly. In 1966, an extraordinarily heavy rain fell in a small area of the north rim, and a flash flood went down Crystal Creek, dumping hundreds of tons of rock into the river at Mile 99. This instantly created the Crystal Rapids, one of the major drops in the Colorado. In rare instances—such as the rapid we are now approaching—the river has exposed resistant pre-Cambrian rock that contributes something to the precipitousness of the flow of white water. The roar is quite close now. The standing waves look like blocks of cement. Dominy emits a cowboy's yell. My notes go into a rubber bag that is tied with a string. This is the Bedrock Rapid.

We went through it with a slow dive and climb and a lot of splattering water. We undulated. The raft assumed the form of the rapid. We got very wet. And now, five minutes later, we are as dry and warm as if we were wearing fresh clothes straight out of a dryer. And we are drinking sandwiches.

We have a map that is seven inches high and fifty feet long. It is rolled in a scroll and is a meticulously hand-done contemporary and historical portrait of the Colorado River in the Grand Canyon. River miles are measured from the point, just south of the Utah line, where the Paria River flows into the Colorado—the place geologists regard as the beginning of the Grand Canyon. As the map rolls by, it records who died where. "Peter Hansbrough, one of two men drowned, Mile 24, Tanner Wash Rapids, 1889. . . . Bert Loper upset, not seen again, Mile 24, 1949. . . . Scout found and buried in talus, Mile 43, 1951. . . . Roemer drowned in Mile 89, 1948." The first known run of the river was in 1869, and the second shortly thereafter—both the expeditions of Major John Wesley Powell—and even by 1946 only about a hundred people had ever been through the canyon by river. With the introduction of neoprene rafts—surplus from the Second World War—the figure expanded. Five hundred a year were going through by the middle nineteen-sixties, and the number is now in the low thousands.

"As long as people keep on taking out everything that they bring in, they're not going to hurt the Grand Canyon," Brower says. "Rule No. 1 is 'Leave nothing—not even a dam.'"

Dominy does not hear that. He is busy telling a pretty young gym teacher from Phoenix that he played sixty minutes a game as captain of the ice-hockey team at the University of Wyoming. "I liked the speed. I liked the body contact. I developed shots the defense couldn't fathom."

Dominy is in his sixtieth year and is planning an early retirement, but he looks fifty, and it is not at all difficult to imagine him on a solo dash down the ice, slamming the Denver Maroons into pulp against the boards and breaking free to slap the winning shot into the nets. He once did exactly that. He has the guts he says he has, and I think he is proving it now, here on the Colorado. He may be an athlete, but he can't swim. He can't swim one stroke. He couldn't swim across a goldfish pond. And at this moment it is time for us to put things away and pull ourselves together, because although we are scarcely dry from the Bedrock Rapid, the crescendoing noise we hear is Deubendorff, an officially designated "heavy rapid," one of the thirteen roughest in the canyon. Brower goes quiet before a rapid, and he is silent now. He says he is not much of a swimmer, either. We all have life vests on, but they feel as if they would be about as effective against these rapids as they would be against bullets. That is not true, though. Once in a great while, these rafts turn over, and when they do the people all end up bobbing in the calmer water at the foot of the rapid like a hatful of spilled corks. Riding a rigid boat, Seymour Deubendorff was claimed by this rapid on the Galloway-Stone expedition, in 1909. This we learn from our map. Looking ahead, we see two steep grooves, a hundred and fifty yards apart, that have been cut into the south wall of the river gorge. They are called Galloway Canyon and Stone Canyon, and the streams in them are not running now, but each has thrown enough debris into the river to make a major rapid, and together they have produced Deubendorff. Directly in front of us, a mile ahead and high against the sky, is a broad and beautiful Redwall mesa. The river disappears around a corner to the left of it. Meanwhile, the big, uncompromising mesa seems to suggest a full and absolute stop, as if we were about to crash into a flight, for spread below it in the immediate foreground is a prairie of white water.

There is a sense of acceleration in the last fifty yards. The water is like glass right up to where the tumult begins. Everything is lashed down. People even take hats and handkerchiefs off their heads and tie them to the raft. Everyone has both hands on safety ropes—everyone but Dominy. He giggles. He gives a rodeo yell. With ten smooth yards remaining, he lights a cigar.

There is something quite deceptive in the sense of acceleration that comes just before a rapid. The word "rapid" itself is, in a way, a misnomer. It refers only to the speed of the white water relative to the speed of the smooth water that leads into and away from the rapid. The white water is faster, but it is hardly "rapid." The Colorado, smooth, flows about seven miles per hour, and, white, it goes perhaps fifteen or, at its whitest and wildest, twenty miles per hour—not very rapid by the standards of the twentieth century. Force of suggestion creates a false expectation. The mere appearance of the river going over those boulders—the smoky spray, the scissoring waves—is enough to imply a rush to fatality, and this endorses the word used to describe it. You feel as if you were about to be sucked into some sort of invisible pneumatic tube and shot like a bullet into the dim beyond. But the white water, though faster than the rest of the river, is categorically slow. Running the rapids in the Colorado is a series of brief experiences, because the rapids themselves are short. In them, with the raft folding and bending—sudden hills of water filling the immediate skyline—things happen in slow motion. The projector of your own existence slows way down, and you dive as in a dream, and gradually rise, and fall again. The raft shudders across the ridgelines of water cordilleras to crash softly into the valleys beyond. Space and time in there are something other than they are out here. Tents of water form overhead, to break apart to rags. Elapsed stopwatch time has no meaning at all.

Dominy emerged from Deubendorff the hero of the expedition to date. Deubendorff, with two creeks spitting boulders into it, is a long rapid for a Grand Canyon rapid—about three hundred yards. From top to bottom, through it all, Dominy kept his cigar aglow. This feat was something like, say, a bumblebee's flying through a field of waving wheat at shock level and never once being touched. Dominy's shirt was soaked. His trousers were soaked. But all the way down the rapid the red glow of that cigar picked its way through the flying water from pocket to pocket of air. Actually, he was lucky, and he knew it. "Lucky Dominy," he said when he moved into quiet water. "That's why they call me Lucky Dominy." The whole raftload of people gave him an organized cheer. And he veiled his face in fresh smoke.

We have now moved under and by the big mesa. Brower watched it silently for a long time, and then softly, almost to himself, he quoted Edith Warner: "'This is a day when life and the world seem to be standing still—only time and the river flowing past the mesas.'"

Wild burros stand on a ledge and look at us from above, right. All burros are on the right, all bighorns on the left. Who knows why? We have entered the beauty of afternoon light. It sharpens the colors and polishes the air.

Brower says, "Notice that light up the line now, Floyd. Look how nice it is on the barrel cactus."

"Gorgeous," says Dominy.

The river is in shadow, and we have stopped for the night where a waterfall arcs out from a sandstone cliff. This is Deer Creek Falls, and it is so high that its shafts of plunging water are wrapped in mist where they strike a deep pool near the edge of the river. The campsite is on the opposite bank. Brower has half filled his Sierra Club cup with water and is using it as a level with which to gauge the height of the falls. His measuring rod is his own height at eye level. Sighting across the cup, he has painstakingly climbed a talus slope behind us, adding numbers as he climbed, and he is now a small figure among the talus boulders at the level of the lip of the waterfall across the river. He calls down that the waterfall is a hundred and sixty feet high. With the raft as a ferry, we crossed the river an hour or so ago and stood in the cool mist where the waterfall whips the air into wind. We went on to climb to the top of the fall and to walk above the stream through the gorge of Deer Creek. The creek had cut a deep, crenellated groove in the sandstone, and for several hundred yards, within this groove, we moved along a serpentine ledge high above the water, which made a great deal of sound below, within the narrow walls of the cut. Brower walked along the ledge—it was sometimes only a foot wide—as if he were hurrying along a sidewalk. At the beginning, the ledge was perhaps fifty feet above the foaming creek, and gradually, up the gorge, the ledge and the creek bed came closer together. Brower just strode along, oblivious of the giddy height. In that strange world between walls of rock, a butterfly flickered by, and he watched it with interest while his feet moved surely forward, never slowing. "Viceroy," he said.

I am afraid of places like that, and my legs were so frozen that I couldn't feel the ledge underfoot. I suggested that we stop and wait for Dominy, who had started later and had said he would catch up. This would obviously provide a good rest, because where Dominy comes from the narrowest ledge is at least three hundred miles wide, and I thought if he was still coming along this one he was probably on his hands and knees. Just then, he came walking around a shoulder of the rock face, balanced above the gorge, whistling. We moved on. Where the ledge met the creek bed, the walls of the gorge widened out and the creek flowed in clear, cascading pools among cactus flowers and mariposa lilies under stands of cottonwood. A scene like that in a context of unending dry red rock is unbelievable, a palpable mirage. Brower walked in the stream and, after a while, stopped to absorb his surroundings. Dominy, some yards behind, had an enamelled cup with him, and he dipped it into the stream. Lifting it to his lips, he said, "Now I'll have a drink of water that has washed Dave Brower's feet."

The water was cold and very clear. Brower scooped some for himself, in his Sierra Club cup. "Any kind of water in country like this is good, but especially when man isn't hogging it for his own use," he said.

Watercress grew around the plunge pools of the short cascades—watercress, growing in cool water, surrounded by thousands of square miles of baking desert rock. Brower took a small bunch in his hand. Bugs were crawling all over it, and he carefully selected leaves and ate them, leaving the bugs behind. "I don't mind sharing my cress with them," he said. "I hope they don't mind sharing it with me."

Brower's snack appealed to Dominy. He waded into the same pool, picked two handfuls of cress, and ate them happily, bugs and all. "Paradise," he said, looking around. "Paradise."

Half obscured in the stream under a bed of cress was the distinctive shimmer of a Budweiser can. Brower picked it up, poured the water out of it, and put it in his pocket.

"When people come in, you can't win," Dominy said, and Brower looked at him with both approval and perplexity.

Inside Dominy's big leather briefcase is a bottle of Jim Beam, and now, at the campsite, in the twilight, with the sun far gone over the rimrocks, we are going to have our quotidian ration—and Dominy is a generous man. After dinner, if patterns hold, he and Brower will square off for battle, but they are at this moment united in anticipation of the bourbon. Big steaks are ready for broiling over the coals of a driftwood fire. There is calm in the canyon. The Commissioner steps to the river's edge and dips a half cup of water, over which he pours his whiskey. "I'm the nation's waterboy," he says. "I need water with my bourbon."

Over the drinks, he tells us that he once taught a German shepherd to climb a ladder. We believe him. He further reminisces about early camping trips with his wife, Alice. They were in their teens when they married. He was state Master Counsellor for the Order of DeMolay, and she was the Queen of Job's Daughters. They had married secretly, and she went with him to the University of Wyoming. "We lived on beans and love," he said. "Our recreation was camping. We went up into the Snowy Range and into the Laramie Peak country, where there was nothing but rattlesnakes, ticks, and us. We used to haul wood down from the mountains to burn for heat in the winter."

Jerry Sanderson, the river guide who has organized this expedition, calls out that dinner is ready. He has cooked an entire sirloin steak for each person. We eat from large plastic trays—the property of Sanderson. Brower regularly ignores the stack of trays, and now, when his turn comes, he steps forward to receive his food in his Sierra Club cup. Sanderson, a lean, trim, weathered man, handsome and steady, has seen a lot on this river. And now a man with wild white hair and pink legs is holding out a four-inch cup to receive a three-pound steak. Very well. There is no rapid that can make Sanderson's eyes bat, so why should this? He drapes the steak over the cup. The steak covers the cup like a sun hat. Brower begins to hack at the edges with a knife. Brower in wilderness eats from nothing but his Sierra Club cup.

10 P.M. The moon has moved out in brilliance over the canyon rim. Brower and Dominy are asleep. Dominy snores. Just before he began to snore, he looked at the moon and said, "What's the point of going there? If it were made of gold, we couldn't afford to go get it. Twenty-three billion dollars for landings on the moon. I can't justify or understand that. One, yes. Half a dozen, no. Every time they light a roman candle at Cape Canaveral, they knock four hundred million off other projects, like water storage."

Tonight's fight was about siltation. When Brower finished his steak, he looked across the river at the flying plume of Deer Creek Falls and announced to all in earshot that Commissioner Dominy wished to fill that scene with mud, covering the riverbed and the banks where we sat, and filling the inner gorge of the Colorado right up to within fifty feet of the top of the waterfall.

"That's God-damned nonsense," Dominy said.

Brower explained quietly that rivers carry silt, and that silt has to go somewhere if men build dams. Silt first drops and settles where the river flows into still water at the heads of reservoirs, he said. Gradually, it not only fills the reservoir but also accumulates upstream from the headwaters, and that might one day be the story here at Deer Creek Falls, for Dominy wanted to create a reservoir that would begin only seven miles downstream from our campsite.

"They said Hoover Dam was going to silt up Lake Mead in thirty years," Dominy said. "For thirty years, Lake Mead caught all the God-damned silt in the Colorado River, and Hoover has not been impaired."

"No, but when Mead is low there are forty miles of silt flats at its upper end, and they're getting bigger."

"Not appreciably. Not with Lake Powell three hundred miles upstream."

"Yes, Lake Powell will fill up first."

"When? Tell me *when*?" Dominy was now shouting.

"In a hundred to two hundred years," Brower said quietly.

"That's crap! The figures you work with aren't reliable."

"They come from reliable people."

"Nonsense."

"Oh."

The Colorado, Brower reminded us, used to be known as Old Red. This was because the river was full of red mud. It would never have been possible for Dominy to dip his cup in it in order to get water to go with his bourbon unless he wished to drink mud as well. On arriving at a campsite, rivermen used to fill their boats with water, so that the mud would settle to the bottom of the boats and they would have water for drinking and cooking. Except after flash floods, the Colorado in the Grand Canyon is now green and almost clear, because Lake Powell is catching the silt, and Glen Canyon Dam—fifteen miles upstream from the beginning of the Grand Canyon—is releasing clean water. "Emotionally, people are able to look only two generations back and two generations forward," Brower said. "We need to see farther than that. It is absolutely inevitable, for example, that Lake Powell and Lake Mead will someday be completely filled with silt."

"Nonsense, nonsense, complete nonsense. First of all, we will build silt-detention dams in the tributaries—in the Paria, in the Little Colorado. And, if necessary, we will build more."

"Someday the reservoirs have to fill up, Floyd."

"I wouldn't admit that. I wouldn't admit one inch!"

"Someday."

"*Some*day! Yes, in geologic time, maybe. Lake Powell *will* fill up with silt. I don't know how many thousands of years from now. By then, people will have figured out alternative sources of water and power. That's what I say when you start talking about the geologic ages."

Brower then began to deliver a brief lecture on the phenomenon of aggradation—the term for the final insult that follows when a reservoir is full of silt. Aggradation is what happens to the silt that keeps on coming down the river. The silt piles up and, in a kind of reverse ooze, reaches back upstream many miles, following an inclined plane that rises about eighteen inches per mile—a figure reckoned from the site of the now mud-packed and obsolete dam.

Brower was scarcely halfway through sketching that picture when Dominy ended his contributions with a monosyllabic remark, walked away, put on his pajamas, delivered to the unlistening moon his attack on the space program, and, forgetting Brower and all the silt of years to come, fell asleep. He sleeps on his back, his feet apart, under the mesas.

5 A.M. The sky is light. The air temperature is eighty degrees. Brower sleeps on his side, his knees drawn up.

7 A.M. Eighty-eight degrees. We will soon be on the river. Dominy is brushing his teeth in the green Colorado. Sam Beach, a big, bearded man from White Plains, New York, just walked up to Dominy and said, "I see God has given us good water here this morning."

"Thank you," Dominy said.

And Brower said to Beach, "I imagine that's the first time you ever heard Him speak."

And Beach said, "God giveth, and God taketh away."

Georgie White Clark

Conquering Glen Canyon

This account from the autobiography of river runner Georgie White Clark recalls her memories of floating through Glen Canyon. Preceding chapters present her Chicago girlhood, a hike across the country to California, her marriage and its failure, and her eventual lifelong fascination with and devotion to the Colorado River, which sparked after a slide presentation on the canyonlands.

After I developed the three-boat concept and then the big boat, I began to expand my trips considerably. Now instead of just running the Grand Canyon I would link the trip together with the Upper Colorado and its tributaries. Starting at Green River, Wyoming, I would run the Green through Labyrinth and Stillwater Canyons, through Catarac and Glen and finally through the Grand Canyon to Lake Mead, almost eleven hundred miles.

This extended trip sampled a wide variety of scenery and river conditions and took almost thirty days to complete. The upper portion was pretty much high desert. Labyrinth and Stillwater Canyons contained many colorful plateaus and mesas. In Catarac Canyon the walls became sheer and the river became a wild beast dropping 415 feet in fifty miles to produce a series of what were probably the most exciting rapids in the United States. Glen Canyon was one of the most fantastic areas on the river with tremendous red limestone cliffs, Indian petroglyphs, ruins and unusual formations. There probably isn't an area anywhere in the world like Glen Canyon before they built the dam. Sometimes I would make the entire eleven hundred mile run as

---

From *Thirty Years of River Running* by Georgie Clark (San Francisco: Chronicle Books, 1977).

one continuous trip. Other times I would break it up going from Green River, Utah to Hite, from Hite to Marble Canyon, or from Lee's Ferry to Lake Mead.

As a variation of this I would also come down the Escalante or San Juan Rivers to the Colorado River. The Escalante River was fun in high water, but in low water we literally had to push the rafts across the sandbars to the Colorado River. The first trip through, Harry and I hit the flood waters of the Escalante just right and managed to float all the way through without difficulty. The next year, Randall Henderson, publisher of Desert Magazine, and his wife decided to go with me. I had fortunately warned them that we might have to walk some of the way, but I wasn't prepared for what we found. The water ran only a few inches deep, and Harry and I had to push both rafts the entire seventy miles to the Colorado River. I never ran the Escalante River again, but in later years, I often pulled about five miles up the canyon as I came down Glen just to let the people with me see the tapestry-like beauty of the canyon.

The San Juan River was something else. It ran through spectacular red sandstone country with towering spires and some of the most fantastic formations to be seen anywhere. Especially intriguing were the Goosenecks of the San Juan where the river has cut a series of unusual loops that wind snake-like through the desert. People often came on this trip with me just to experience the rugged, almost inaccessible back country, as well as the river itself.

I would pick up my passengers in Marble Canyon, Arizona, pile in the car and a pickup truck and head off on a narrow dirt road across the incredibly beautiful Monument Valley. I always went first in the pickup because I knew that when I came to a difficult spot, the first vehicle would probably get through, but the second would usually become stuck in the sand. When this happened, everybody would pile out. I would unload the shovels and the boards that I always carried and begin to dig the sand out from around the stuck wheel. Finally when I had it clear, I would shove the boards underneath and together we'd push and drive the car out of the sand. This became a vital part of the trip and somehow people were always disappointed when it didn't happen.

The San Juan was an unusual river. During the low water period, many sandbars would appear, making boating difficult. In low water too, the river would break into a number of channels, and finding the right channel could be a problem. I learned early how to deal with this. I would simply run the motor slowly and wait. Invariably someone would say, "What are you doing, Georgie?"

"I'm letting the motor pick the channel."

They wouldn't believe me, but I found that when I ran the motor slowly enough, the boat would automatically find the channel with the most current. After learning this method on the San Juan River, I later used it quite successfully on Lake Mead to pick my way through the driftwood.

In the very early days Harry and I hiked a great deal in Glen Canyon. Glen, at that time, was probably the hottest spot on the river. The sun on that red sandstone turned the side canyons into radiating ovens.

That didn't bother us much, however; I can take heat well and after hiking the canyons as long as we had, we didn't really seem to feel it. By this time, I needed little food and water. I used to take along just a few small cans of tomatoes to eat and found this quite satisfactory. I hiked better and was more alert. I also found that water bothered my stomach while hiking so I seldom drank anything in the canyon.

In Glen, the canyon walls were extremely steep. To protect themselves from enemies, the ancient ones, or Anasazi, as the present day Indians call them, always built their mud buildings under an overhang high up on the canyon walls. To reach them, they had made tiny foot and hand holds called Moki steps which went hundreds of feet straight up the walls. When I saw these I just shook my head. They were so tiny. Did these Indians have smaller feet than the white man? Did they have an unusual sense of balance? Had they perfected some method of climbing I hadn't heard about? I really couldn't figure it out.

By using extreme caution I could climb into most places over these steps. My problem was, however, that I wanted to take people into the side canyons since I felt it would add considerable interest to the river trip. But the Moki steps as they existed were too small. Very few people were even going to try them.

"We're going to have to enlarge those steps," I told Harry. "They'll just never work that way."

He protested at first, then finally agreed I was right. We took a hammer and began to enlarge the backs and edges of several steps. That didn't work. The sandstone was so brittle that often we'd destroy a whole step. I soon realized that I'd have to go about it the Indian way. So we then took hard smooth rocks and rubbed them back and forth on those steps for hours on end, until we had them just right. In those days I spent so many hours enlarging Moki steps that I often found myself making steps in my dreams.

Actually, it took awhile to get the knack of it. The Moki step itself has a peculiar back slant. I realized that the Indians made them this way to give a better foothold. So we rubbed until we got the backslant just like the Indian steps only several times larger, of course. When we got through they were big enough to provide good foot and hand holds all the way up the cliff.

One of the first places Harry and I opened was Moki Canyon. The canyon itself contained a tremendous collection of ruins. The buildings reminded me of pictures of mud and adobe houses in early Jerusalem built with flat roofs. They literally stair-stepped up the slope in very tight clusters. With little effort I could recognize granaries and a few other buildings. Even after a couple of thousand years some buildings remained in remarkable shape. Others consisted of just a broken wall or two.

I knew that people would really enjoy that canyon. When we finished enlarging the steps, the first groups I took in consisted of Boy Scouts and their leaders. Although I couldn't get a lot of people to go with me in those days, I frequently got a number of Scout troops from the Los Angeles area who wanted to explore the Glen Canyon area.

Since I was a woman, the mothers seemed to feel safer letting their sons go out in the wilderness of Glen Canyon with me. Later I often thought that if only those mothers could have seen their children climbing those high canyon walls they would have quickly changed their minds. I found that the scouts absolutely loved Moki Canyon. If I had let them alone they probably could have spent several days exploring that one canyon alone.

Heights didn't bother me, and I thought nothing of climbing hundreds of feet unprotected up those small Moki steps. Neither did the Scouts. They seemed to have no fear at all. So I guess it was natural that after a couple of years I began to treat these climbs in a matter-of-fact manner. A few years later, however, when I first took the Sierra Club groups into Moki Canyon and started up into those ruins, they let me know in no uncertain terms how unsafe they felt that climb was.

They had been used to utilizing ropes on climbs like this. But because of the great heights of those walls, they couldn't belay their ropes in Moki Canyon.

"You're going to get someone killed up there, Georgie," they told me. "Some day one of your people is just going to peel off that cliff."

I felt at that time they were just being too cautious. Later, however, when I started taking a different type of person into the canyons their message came home rather dramatically.

One spring day in 1956, I started into the Moki Canyon ruins with a group of eight people. Everyone went up without difficulty and we spent several delightful hours poking through the ruins and looking at some petroglyphs. Then we started down. I had one passenger called Jack who apparently hadn't paid any attention to the height when he was climbing the wall. Neither had he thought much about it while scrambling in the ruins. When we started down however, he let out a wild scream. "How did I get up here? I'll never get down!"

"Oh, yes, you will," I told him. "Just turn around. Don't look. Go down like you came up."

But he could hardly move. He was trembling all over and his knees were shaking visibly. I sat down and studied the problem for a while. I find that in a situation like this it doesn't pay to act in haste. In most cases if you consider the possibilities quietly you can often come up with a pretty good solution.

Finally, I got below Jack and with a lot of pleading, managed to work his feet into those first steps. That's how we went down. I would talk to him for awhile, then I would take hold of his foot and slowly work it down to the next step. Then I would quietly talk to him again.

That descent took almost two hours, but I got him down safely. It was then I realized that some people were going to have a lot of trouble with those heights and I would have to quit taking everyone up there. After that, I only took a select few up Moki Canyon to see the ruins. It's a shame too, because that was one of the most interesting sights in the Glen Canyon area.

Harry and I spent many days enlarging the Moki steps onto Rainbow Bridge. The bridge was a moderate seven-mile hike from the river, but very few people took this trip. Today Rainbow Bridge is a national monument and accessible over an easy one-mile trail from Lake Powell. As a result, thousands now visit it every spring and fall. The bridge itself is a fantastic sight. It's the greatest known natural bridge with a perfectly formed arch 309 feet above the stream bed and 278 feet wide. When I first hiked to the bridge, the access down was over tremendously tiny Moki steps and I could hardly put my toes in them. Harry and I spent hours there rubbing them with a large rock. When we finished, they were big enough to easily accommodate anyone who wanted to climb down. I even hammered in a piton and tied a rope to it so people would have something to hang onto.

In those days, I took hundreds of Scouts and others onto the bridge. Today, however, since it's in a national monument, the general public is no longer allowed to climb on the bridge itself and the Park Service has since removed the pitons.

The Scouts I used to take on the river loved this trip. There were a whole series of pools along the entire seven-mile route. I would hike them to the bridge and three miles beyond. Then I would let them swim their way down through the pools to the river. This was a total of twenty miles and qualified them for their twenty-mile hike. As far as most of them were concerned, this trip to Rainbow Bridge was the easiest twenty miles they had ever hiked.

One of my other favorites on the Glen was Smith Canyon, right on the river. The Indians here used the walls almost like a gigantic art gallery. The cliffs contained over 1000 petroglyphs. A few of the petroglyphs were very simple drawings. Others were very complex panels. Some interpreters read elaborate legends into the placement of the figures and designs. I'm afraid I never tried to interpret what I saw but I enjoyed the variety. There were sheep in many forms, great serpents, spirals, open hands and flute players. Sometimes the flute player would be standing with a hump on his back, other times sitting and in a few cases, lying down. In addition, in Smith Canyon, I found pictures of hunters attacking sheep and Indians harvesting corn. Some people have told me that sheep represent hunting magic or a hunting adventure; serpents, meandering bends of a river; the hand, an oath of allegiance. I have never heard a satisfactory explanation for the flute player. Some say that it is a man seeking a wife; others say a legendary figure among the Indians. I never studied the petroglyphs from a scientific standpoint, but they were an enjoyable part of the river and the people I took with me always liked to see them.

Harry and I hiked to and enjoyed other areas during those years: Hidden Passage, Music Temple, Lake Canyon, Slick Rock and more. I think it's fair to say that there was a beauty and a uniqueness in those canyons that will never be duplicated anywhere else in the world. Today, all of that is under the water of Lake Powell. This, I think, is one of the crimes of modern bureaucracy. Most experts outside the government will tell you that dams have just about outlived their usefulness. They don't produce enough power to justify the tremendous expense, and the dams of the Southwest aren't really useful for diverting water for other purposes. The only reason they seem to exist is to keep the vast bureaucracy of the Bureau of Reclamation going and to provide a few outside jobs.

Like many other things, however, the pressure to build Glen Canyon Dam, and indeed, other dams on the Colorado River, was enormous. I opposed the dam vigorously and always urged anyone who came in contact with me to write his senators and congressmen in protest.

In many ways, I blame early environmental groups (the Sierra Club) for this fiasco. At the time the dam was in the planning stage, they didn't seem really very interested in the river. I think they used Glen Canyon Dam as a trade-off to keep a dam out of Dinosaur National Monument, Utah. Of course, this is only an opinion, but I do know that they expressed very little opposition and always urged me to temper my opposition. To me, this dam is a travesty for which we shall all pay forever.

Those early days on the Glen were, without a doubt, extremely pleasant ones. The Scouts that went with me on many trips loved being out in the canyon and they also loved the horseplay that went with it. I have to admit that during those years, so did I. I was always thinking up jokes to play on them. I made this into a sort of ritual at Hidden Passage. Hidden Passage is simply a passage between two canyons. Along the lower part were a number of pools where we could swim, then to get across to the other canyon, it was necessary to crawl on our elbows and toes along a ledge just slightly narrower than our bodies. Beyond that, we reached the top, the passage became steeper and narrower. The higher we climbed, the narrower it became. From below, it was impossible to see above until we popped out of the passage on top. On every trip, I would go first and take several dozen fresh eggs with me. Then as the boys came up, I would crack an egg on their heads. After several reached the top, they took great delight in cracking eggs on the heads of those below. It was like an initiation and the boys who had been there before always kept quiet so it would be a surprise to the others. They would laugh and shout and once everyone was up, they would kid each other about who looked the funniest. It was one of the highlights of the trip.

The fun and kidding that went on between myself and the Scouts seemed to prevail with the scoutmasters and other adults too. On these trips I always let the adults act as boatmen, but they were rather inexperienced and pretty rough on boats. As a result, they frequently sheered the pins in the outboard motors, by becoming tangled in the driftwood or hung on the rocks. We had a standing rule that if any boat sheered a pin, the other boats would come along and literally drown them with buckets of water. By this time, I had had so much experience and knew the area so well that I seldom had any trouble. While this wasn't a sore point between myself and the adults, it rather bruised their egos that a woman was better at it than a man.

On one particular trip as we approached Lee's Ferry, one of the scout leaders on my boat kept saying, "Georgie, how far to Lee's Ferry?"

"Why?" I asked.

"No reason; I just wondered." Then about half an hour later he'd ask again.

"Boy," I thought, "he's really anxious to get out of here this trip." Then suddenly I sheered a pin. I hadn't hit anything that I could see. I was in the middle of the channel away from all rocks and driftwood. I couldn't figure out what happened, when I turned to look at the scout leader he was grinning at me.

"Boy, am I glad that happened. I thought that pin would never let go."

Then he explained that all of them were getting so disgusted at sheering pins while I never did, that they decided to gang up on me. They had filed the pin in my motor almost in two. They were positive that I wouldn't go more than a couple of miles before it sheered all the way through. As it turned out however, I almost made it to Lee's Ferry. And the closer we got to Lee's Ferry, the scoutmaster told me, the more he began to sweat. "I knew we were out of food. And if that pin broke at the last minute and we couldn't put in there, we'd be swept right on down the canyon."

He was right, of course. In those days we could go two or three weeks in the Grand Canyon without seeing another person, and once committed below Lee's Ferry, we couldn't come back. We'd have had to go all the way to Phantom Ranch before we could get additional supplies. It would have been a rather uncomfortable predicament. He was so glad to have that pin break that he pitched in to help me change it before the others caught up to throw water on us. We changed the pin in the record time of ten minutes and still beat them into Lee's Ferry. I'll never forget the look of relief on his face when that pin broke. While I thought he was just anxious to go home, he was just getting nervous about the possibility of being swept on down the canyon on an unscheduled trip.

I always found Glen Canyon to be one of my favorite trips. My main interest in running rivers of course, was to experience the rapids. There weren't many on Glen, but the scenery more than made up for this. Glen Canyon itself was completely isolated and miles and miles from the nearest civilization. During the 1950s there probably weren't more than four or five people in hundreds of square miles of desert. Sometimes I found it rather difficult to bring that point home to others. Everyone wanted to judge the Grand or Glen and other areas on the Colorado by their own standards. I've never really understood this. No matter how much experience or knowledge you have they still don't want to believe you. Sometimes even my own boatmen have to learn the facts the hard way.

On one particular trip in Glen, I had taken a German girl named Heidi who had gone on a number of kayak trips in Europe and expected the American experience to be similar to the European. In Europe, apparently, at night, the kayakers change their clothes and go to the villages to dance. The nearest village was at least two hundred miles away across some of the roughest, most rugged country in the United States. I thought I had made this clear in the very beginning.

After a day or two on one of these river trips, everybody begins to become pretty informal in his dress. I, for instance, wore one leopard-skin bathing suit the entire trip. Another girl wore ragged cut-offs. Most of the women let their hair go entirely and none wore lipstick. After all, it's hard to look your best when you're in the water all day and camping on a sandbar at night. We looked exactly like what we were: river rats out for a several-week trip on the river. About the third night I looked up and there stood Heidi dressed to the teeth. She was a fairly small dark girl and that night she looked terrific. Her hair was combed smooth, she had put on bright red lipstick and an electric blue dress. If I hadn't known better I would have sworn she was about to go out for a night on the town in Las Vegas. I must say, against the rugged river background, she looked really out of place.

"What's the occasion?" I asked her.

"Why I'm going to the village just like we did in Germany."

"Where did you get a crazy idea like that?" I asked her. "Even if you were to hike 125 miles across that desert country, you probably wouldn't find one other person let alone a whole village."

"It's right out there," she insisted. "It's got to be."

"This country just hasn't been settled as long as Europe," I said. "It's still pretty much frontier out here. Why, most of the roads aren't even paved yet. It's just different in the American West."

She shook her head, turned around and walked back towards the boat. When I saw her half an hour later she was again dressed like a typical river runner. Actually I'm not sure that I convinced her. She seemed determined to believe there was a village out there somewhere with a nightlife. I, for some unknown reason, was trying to keep her from finding it.

During those years on Glen and Upper Colorado, life was never dull. Something unusual happened on nearly every trip. Not all of these experiences were exciting, of course, but some were unusual enough that they really stood out in my memory. On one occasion a movie company hired me to help make a movie called "Six Girls Against the Colorado." All of the girls were under eighteen so they asked me to play chaperone as well as run the boats. When they showed up at Hite, they looked like a traveling circus. They had brought six gorgeous Hollywood girls, an entire camera crew, and a number of other people to handle the miscellaneous functions. The first thing the director did after they unloaded, was to pop down in his chair on the beach and order martinis. I remember watching him drink that martini and thinking, "Boy, this is going to be some trip."

We started out in Glen Canyon where they took a lot of general background scenes. Then they took the girls and a camera crew to Rainbow Bridge. Finally they began to photograph the dangerous scenes. The script called for the girls to overcome all sorts of hazardous experiences on the rugged Colorado. It was then I learned the real truth about motion pictures. Everything is fake. First they set girls up to take a fall from a high cliff. They took a long shot of one of the high cliffs. That set the scene. Iris McCollough, a tall, dark, buxom girl, handled many of the dangerous scenes. They had trouble with Iris, however, because she had been a model for several years and always had difficulty remembering not to strike a static pose.

Next, they had Iris walk along the top of the cliff. Actually it was just a little spot outside camp. Next she fell and grabbed the top of the cliff. Next scene, the camera zoomed in to show her hanging hundreds of feet above the river. I almost died laughing over that one. They actually made that girl hang from the top of a little rock with her feet barely a foot above the ground.

All she had to do was let go and drop easily to safety. They did a good job of creating an illusion, though, for in the finished movie it looked quite dangerous. It went on like this for the next few days while they filmed rattlesnakes, scorpions, girls falling into the water and a number of other hazards. All of it was fake.

After that we came downriver to Lee's Ferry to run the boat sequences and the upsets. Just below Lee's Ferry there is a small riffle with a few waves that can be made to look like a large rapid. Actually it doesn't amount to much and generally I go through this riffle without paying attention. This trip, however, it was different. I was supposed to go through in a single boat and upset. Then I was supposed to show the girls in dangerous rough water. So I shot through the rapids, caught a wave just right and upset. I thought that would be that. But it turned out that they wanted to use different types of upsets throughout the picture. So I ran that same rapid over and over and over again. I never was so sick of anything in my life. I'd simply run through, do whatever they asked, put the raft on a truck, take it back to Lee's Ferry and start all over again. It got to be pretty boring after the tenth time.

They did a marvelous job of editing, though, and when the movie came out, they had interspersed bits of that rapid throughout the picture. It really looked like the girls were in trouble every inch of the way down the river. Not very authentic, but effective as far as the picture was concerned.

That was the only full length commercial film I ever helped make, but I did get in on several short films. First I was hired to help make the Disney short called "Grand Canyon." The crew for that twenty-one-day trip consisted of a director, a cameraman, a Park Service ranger, his wife, myself and a boatman. To make pictures of the rapids, without excess motion, they installed some sort of a gyroscopic tripod on the front of my raft. With this they took some excellent pictures of the river. When it came time to photograph the logs and trees floating down the Colorado, they just couldn't seem to take the shots they wanted. Finally the photographer picked out a few small pieces of wood from the bank, threw these in the current and took his pictures. I understand they looked like the real thing on the screen. They also got some marvelous shots of mules crossing the bridge near Phantom Ranch, the burros, the lightning over the canyon. These were synchronized later with the music of the Grand Canyon Suite.

When we came to camp, I cooked for myself and my boatman. The ranger, however, waited on that director hand and foot. He cooked, gathered wood, and even held the director over the bow of the boat while he took pictures. I didn't particularly enjoy this trip because I don't like people who expect special privileges like this. But I will admit, that finished picture turned out to be a work of art.

Fox and Paramount also made documentaries on the Colorado River, but these were an entirely different story. Both companies sent two men down the river with me to make their pictures. The cameras used on the river were large, shoulder-mounted 35 mm types. I felt extremely sorry for the cameramen who had to lug those big cameras over the rocks or carry them considerable distances to gets the shots they needed.

The Paramount crew got excellent pictures. I was, however, disappointed in Fox. On Lava I made a special effort to make sure they got shots of the boats going through the hole. Instead of concentrating on the rapid, the cameraman got a perspective shot showing the boat and the top of the canyon. It showed the contrast, all right, but not good detail of the rapids. In general though the Fox photographer did a good job in the 95,000 cubic-feet-a-second water we had on that trip. Since his footage was supposed to show the entire canyon trip, the Fox photographer also wanted camp scenes such as people putting out their sleeping bags, fixing dinner and similar shots. Every time I'd find a good one, I'd point it out and say, "Why not take that?"

Usually he was relaxing and chatting, so he'd say. "Tomorrow, Georgie. There is plenty of time." The last night came and he still didn't have any camp shots. Finally, in desperation, he just lined a few people up against a wall and shot the camp pictures. Later, in Chicago, I spotted a theatre running the Fox film so I got a number of river people together and we went to see it.

"Be quiet," I said, "and listen to what people say about this film."

They were saying, "Those people must be idiots . . . they're crazy . . . why would anyone do that?"

The picture, despite these comments, went over well and wound up being shown around the world. In my opinion, it did an overall excellent job of representing white water adventure as it really was.

As long as I'm talking about films, I might as well stop here and discuss two that I didn't make, but about which I have some strong opinions. The first is the Major John Wesley Powell expedition down the Colorado River called "Ten Who Dared." I believe strongly in making films of historic events. But in my opinion that film used history as a vehicle to tell a very warped version of the story. First, the company made the film in the studio, not on the river. That, to me, is unforgivable fraud. The only positive aspect was that they used the right kind of boats. But instead of showing the struggle the party had against nature and the river, they concentrated on the feuding that went on. In my opinion Powell told a terrific story, but the film really didn't depict the feat of running the river. It just showed the men fighting with each other.

A lot of people have asked me how I feel about the movie "Deliverance." I actually consider that film on a par with "Six Girls Against the Colorado." It was a fair story, but it wasn't authentic. All that was really seen of rapids there was a very small bit of film used over and over again. If a film is turned upside down, it looks like a different river. In "Deliverance," they made a small number of shots go an awfully long way. I really can't find fault with that technique of course, but when I see rapids, I like to see real ones. I guess I just can't get used to the methods used by Hollywood movie makers. The few movies I did help make were enjoyable and they taught me to look at movie making in an entirely different light.

One of the most unusual experiences I ever had on the Glen was my uranium prospecting trip. During the middle 1950s, the United States needed large quantities of uranium and there were indications that the Four Corners area of Utah, New Mexico, Colorado and Arizona contained huge deposits. As a result, prospectors from all over the country rushed to the area in a stampede that could well be compared to the California gold rush of 1849. Armed with Geiger counters, prospectors set out across the vast desert in search of uranium and instant wealth. As with most prospecting ventures, a few found uranium at the end of the rainbow, but most just got a lot of exercise for their effort.

At the height of this uranium craze in January 1955, I received a letter asking if I would be available to take a group of prospectors on a month-long trip in Glen Canyon. The fee sounded good. My brother had been mining for years so I was familiar with prospecting and rather enjoyed it. I agreed to the idea and on April 15 I met a group of fifteen prospectors at Hite, Utah.

They had brought a huge mound of equipment with them, including Geiger counters, scintillation counters and other electronic gadgets. I took one look at all that stuff and wondered how I was going to get it in the big boat. I managed to stuff every last piece in somehow, and three hours later we shoved off.

My prospectors were all men in their thirties and forties and I learned as we went along that they all had a good knowledge of mining and geology. Their leader, a man called John, explained that they wanted me to stop wherever they asked. I could hike with them but I was not to take pictures of anyone or anything on this trip including the scenery. I agreed, and every morning we would start down the river, go a few miles, then stop at some designated spot where everyone would get out and explore.

Before coming on this trip, the group had signed up with a number of backers who had paid to have them go down the river for them and stake a claim. There was a lot of fraud at that time and some companies simply took the money and forgot to stake the claim. Not this one; they would search with their equipment until they found a pretty good vein of uranium, then they would give me a bucket of paint and I would paint the rocks around the area. After that, they would fill out the claim forms and have me sign as a witness. Later, they were filed to make it legal. Every one of those claims actually contained uranium. Today three-quarters of the claims are under water.

Every night, the men would sit around the campfire and tell tall tales of riches. I don't think I ever heard a figure under a million dollars the entire time we were together.

One day there was a lot of excitement about the next canyon downriver. When we pulled in, they divided into three groups and set off in different directions. I went along with the first party. No sooner had we scrambled into a side canyon than the scintillator went wild. I've never seen so much scrambling around. Finally, they drove stakes, marked the spot, made some notes, took a few rock samples and started back to the boat. When we got there we discovered that the two other parties had had almost the same experience. Everybody swore me to secrecy. I told them I didn't care how rich they got. All I wanted was to run the river in peace.

Three weeks later we pulled into Marble Canyon. The leader thanked me and they drove away in several cars that had been left for them. I never did know whether anything ever came of their big strike up in that canyon, but I had enjoyed the company and the experience. I had, once again, spent an entire month on the river and had the time of my life, so it was well worth it to me.

The coming of Glen Canyon Dam, of course, overshadowed everything on the Glen and Catarac Canyons from the late 1950s on. The Bureau of Reclamation first began to prepare the site in 1957 and on every trip I took through the canyon after that, I could see the progress. The site itself was quite isolated and the initial preparation took years. River running wasn't really affected too much until the 1960s when they began to divert the river around the dam base. From then on I could still come down most of the way. But just above the dam, I had to take the rafts out and truck them to Lee's Ferry.

Then in 1964 they completed the dam, an all-concrete affair which rises 710 feet from bed rock, and began to fill Lake Powell. We stopped going through Glen at that time, but since I knew it would take several years to fill the lower lake, we kept running Catarac Canyon for another two years. There probably isn't any water anywhere in the world quite like Catarac Canyon. For a day and a half, we ran through an area known as the big drop. The canyon walls were extremely steep here and unlike the Grand below, the water simply rushed on through the canyon without stopping. There was no back-water. When I reached the entrance to Catarac Canyon, I would have my people try swimming in life preservers. The chance of getting tossed out somewhere along the way was pretty good, and I wanted them to know something about the water. If they wanted to slow down, for instance, they brought their feet up; if they wanted to take off, they put them down. There were a few tricks I thought they needed to know and this seemed like a good place to practice.

Catarac was always different in different kinds of water, but it was especially fierce in high water. During the 1957 trip, for instance, there was a tremendous flow of water in Catarac, approximately 115,000 cubic feet per second. That's probably the biggest water I have ever seen there. The waves were just huge, some at least fifty feet high, and those thirty-foot pontoons of the big boat just stood on end. That river contained enormous holes which we fell into with a sickening thud. I couldn't believe it.

Sometimes the water became so bad on Catarac that people just panicked. On one trip, we ran well until we came to Satan's Gut, which is an extremely vicious rapid. The three-boat started out wrong and just literally bounced through the rapid. Below, it ran smack into a rock and set out in midstream. At this point one of the passengers became so terrified, he grabbed that rock and hung on for dear life. The first boat bounced off and went on with him still hanging there. There he was, clinging to a rock two feet above the raging water. The second boat managed to come in against the rock in spite of the fast water, but he wouldn't jump. Finally we put a rope on another fellow who jumped over and pried his hands off the rock and almost carried him hollering back to the boat. We then took him over to the big boat and gave him something to drink. When he left, he wanted to take his life preserver home because, as he told me, it had saved his life. It's always strange to me when people go into shock like that and I'm always amazed at the funny ideas they come up with. That life preserver had nothing to do with saving his life, but we couldn't tell him that.

I ran 1964 and 1965 without trouble. The water was now rising fast, but I thought that I'd be able to get in the Catarac Canyon run at least one more year. So in 1966 I started down from Green River, Utah, once again. We came through Labyrinth and Stillwater Canyons, and with me holding my breath, entered Catarac. For the first three hours, we shot through those rapids like we always had. Then suddenly we hit the backed-up water. The next rapid was almost under water, and the next, the big drop was completely gone. I pulled in and just stared at it. I had to admit I was extremely sad, but I decided to put off telling the rest of the party until next morning. They had been so hoping they would get in one last good run. But they were on to me. One girl who had been there before came over and said, "We're here at the big drop, aren't we Georgie? It's all over, isn't it?"

I nodded, and as the girl turned away to tell the others, the tears streamed down her cheeks. An era had come to an end.

Today, we don't run the upper canyon anymore. Some river runners run the Catarac and San Juan, but it's a float trip. I am, of course, still running the Grand Canyon. But the dams have really destroyed the entire Colorado adventure as I used to know it, and have changed the entire complexion of river running everywhere, forever.

Philip L. Fradkin

Canyon Country: The Ultimate Ditch

This lament of the ecological effects of dams on the Colorado is framed by the story of a father-son trip on the river. A River No More *also includes chapters concerning the agricultural and mining industries in the watershed and the politics of water in the West.*

The preparation for a trip down the Colorado River seems interminable. First, there is the decision of what to take. We will be on a river whose water temperature varies between 45 and 50 degrees at the start, yet passes through a broiling desert. It can rain and be chilly, or the sun will shine and the temperature climb to 120 degrees. A hat and long pants are needed so one will not become parboiled, yet no one wants to be overdressed when there is a chance to go swimming or work on a tan. The brochure makes it clear: Bring as little as possible. Space is at a premium in the small wooden dories.

Having made our choices, my twelve-year-old son, Alex, and I drive from the San Francisco Bay area to the Grand Canyon Dories' boathouse in Hurricane, Utah. There we are instructed to repack our clothes into watertight bags and park the car. It is clear that our lives will be run by others for the next eighteen days. We are driven by van to a motel near Lee's Ferry, where we spend the night. The other twenty-four passengers, many of whom have come much further, gather at the motel that evening along with the seven boatmen and two women cooks. We are given a short lesson in how to pack the Navy-surplus bags. This first group experience shows we are a diverse

---

lot. Early to bed was a pattern that was to repeat itself on the river. Alex is excited and it takes him a while to get to sleep, as it does me. The air conditioner is faulty and there are crickets in the room.

In the morning Martin Litton arrives, piloting his own small plane from the scores of places he has just been. The peripatetic Litton shepherds the launching of his dories not only on the Colorado, but also the Green, Snake, Salmon, and Owyhee rivers. He has just come from the south rim of the Grand Canyon, where he had flown to check the accuracy of the park rangers' lecture to tourists on the river. Not very accurate, he reports. A former director of the Sierra Club and one of the first two hundred persons to run the river, Litton is afflicted by the same disease most persons contract who spend some time on the Colorado—an almost zealous possessiveness, a sense of proprietorship. I have noticed this not only about the river, but desert areas in general.

With the complicated logistics of getting seven boats launched and thirty-five people into them with all they will need for two and a half weeks ahead of us that morning, we go tearing off in the van for Lee's Ferry. Litton gives us a running commentary about how the Bureau of Reclamation has misnamed Marble Canyon, the money he is losing on the trips, the names of different rock formations, a short discourse on the Mountain Meadow Massacre, why Navajos are selling necklaces with Japanese-made glass beads at the bridge, and so on. There is a brief stop at the paved launching ramp at Lee's Ferry, where Litton chats with the park ranger who is going over his checklist. Then the group splits, nine to hike into the canyon with Litton and the remainder electing to float down the river to Badger Creek Rapids.

I choose to go with Litton, since I have ridden that stretch of river on a previous trip and want to soak up some additional folklore. He doesn't tell any of the passengers, but by getting some of them to hike in, Litton saves user days from his annual allotment that can be applied to other trips. The way down is over the lip of Kaibab limestone, the topmost layer of which will eventually tower over us as we float deeper into the Grand Canyon. The day warms up as Litton regales us with further tales. Grand Canyon rattlesnakes are chicken, he assures one passenger. True enough, we see a number of rattlers on the trip but suffer only one scorpion bite.

The river is a cool blessing, and once we reach it we swim. Lunch is eaten and then Litton departs, hiking back up the canyon to fly off somewhere else that day. We rejoin those who have come by boat and gaze down at our first rapid. It is the practice of the boatmen to scout difficult rapids. But Badger Creek is only in the moderate class and I get the feeling the pause is mainly for the benefit of the passengers to become used to the idea of dropping off sharp inclines in small boats into roiling whitewater. I assure Alex it is a piece of cake, that we will just slide down that smooth V-shaped tongue and be carried through the standing waves in a few moments. I am not sure he buys that.

Our boat, rowed by Greg Williams, is next to last to push off from the bank. From the start, I am a bit apprehensive. I learn later Williams has been down the river before, but never rowing a wooden dory which is more touchy than the rubber rafts most people use. As we are pulled by the current toward the tongue, Williams stands a number of times to make sure the boat is positioned correctly. Too many times. He is unsure. We enter the rapid too far to the right, the boat dips into a large hole, teeters on its left side, and Williams is thrown out. Alex and I are sitting in the stern, facing backward. The violent angle makes me look back. I spot Williams in the water by the left gunwale. With my left hand I hold Alex down. His principal interest is to get out. With my right I lean down to give Williams a lift back into the boat, which has righted itself, minus one oar. It is over in an instant, shorter than I had promised Alex. We recover the oar, bail out, and make for the shore where we will camp that night.

"A piece of cake, huh?" is Alex's later comment.

There is a tendency to think of the Colorado River through the Grand Canyon as one continuous set of booming rapids. It is not. It is a series of long, slightly angled pools and short, steep rapids. The river descends about 2,200 feet within the canyon, and rapids account for only 10 percent of this drop. In the first 150 miles of the river there are 93 rapids averaging a distance of 1.6 miles between each other. Altogether there are about 160 rapids on the total river run, with many being barely noticeable but still technically qualifying for the designation. Badger Creek Rapid, through which we had just run, drops 14 feet in a horizontal distance of 860 feet, a not uncommon rate. Speeds of the river's current through the flat sections are about 4 mph, with the water at a few steep drops approaching 30 mph. A trip down the river is essentially a long, lazy float interspersed with very brief, sometimes violent descents. Like books about sailing cruises that tend to emphasize storms at the expense of the more prevalent calms, accounts of the river journey tend to overly dramatize the whitewater.

The justifiably famed rapids of this stretch of the Colorado River are formed in one of four ways. Most of them are the result of storms dumping large amounts of water in short periods of time higher up in the canyon-country tributaries to the river. The resulting flash floods deposit gravel, small rocks, and large boulders into the bed of the master stream. An underwater barrier is flung across the river and its flow is constricted by the debris collected at the mouth of the tributary. A pool is formed above the new rapid caused by the resulting rise in the riverbed, and turbulent water rushes through the constriction.

Crystal is the classic example of this type of rapid. Fourteen inches of rain fell over the drainage of Crystal Creek on December 4 and 5, 1966, and the resulting floods carried away Indian ruins that had stood since the twelfth century. Thousands of tons of gravel and rock, with large boulders mixed in, hurtled down at speeds of up to 50 mph. The mass of material pushed the Colorado River toward the opposite shore, and overnight the second most dreaded rapid on the river had been formed. A U.S. Geological Survey crew that had made the first detailed survey of the rapids and river depth the year before had noted nothing significant at Crystal Creek. This was to be one of the two rapids we were required to walk around while the boatmen ran them alone.

The granddaddy of them all, Lava Falls, is just that, a falls, the second form of rapids. It is formed by an outcrop of hard basaltic rock, the result of a number of lava flows that had plugged the river only to be worn down over a period of time by the persistent force of water. Other rapids are formed by huge slabs of rock that peel off from the canyon walls periodically, or by gravel bars extending partway into the channel.

It is not the waves formed by these obstructions that are feared so much as the holes found on the downstream side. These holes are the black spaces of the river. The average depth of the river is about 40 feet, but one measurement of 110 feet has been obtained. The boatmen's terminology for such phenomena is descriptive of the havoc they can wreak. They are known variably as souse holes, suck holes, stoppers, reversals, or keepers. With water pouring over a boulder or ledge, a void is formed below, while the towering wave just beyond it keeps trying to rush back into the hole. Some boats have been literally kept in such holes. Others are held, then spat out. While the water in the curling wave vainly seeks to fill the hole, other water dives deep to travel at high speeds along the river's bottom to emerge as a large boil, or upwelling, as far as one-quarter mile downstream. These boils form powerful eddies below the rapid. Here river currents may be going in opposite directions with only a thin shear line separating them. Boats are pulled one way, then another in these unpredictable currents. I found the holes and boils the most powerful forces in the river.

Glen Canyon Dam is changing the nature of the rapids, along with riverside beaches, vegetation, and wildlife in the Grand Canyon. It is, in effect, a new river with different forms of life dependent upon it. Before the dam was built no thought was given to what it would do to the downstream river and only a cursory examination was made of the effects of the reservoir on the Lake Powell area. These decisions came before the era of voluminous environmental-impact statements, which now attempt to predict such effects, and possible alternatives, with relative precision. What was not taken into account was the fact that the great flood flows of the past would exist no more, the average amount of silt passing Phantom Ranch was going to drop from 500,000 tons a day to 80,000 and the cold, clear water released from Glen Canyon was no longer going to fluctuate from near freezing to 80 degrees.

The rapids are in the process of changing because the flood flows no longer flush boulders downriver. Some researchers think this will make the rapids generally easier to run, since the remaining boulders and rocks will now tend to rearrange themselves within the rapid, resulting in a more even cross section and filling in some holes. There are exceptions to this thesis, and one is the possibility that rocks may pile up at the toe of a rapid, thus creating a shallow area. With less rock being swept away, the common theory among boatmen is that the gradual accumulation of such obstacles will make the river more difficult to run. Another set of researchers has also come to this conclusion, stating the "rapids may become impassable to river traffic" in time.

To date, the change in beaches used extensively for camping in the summer months has been more dramatic than any alteration in the regimen of the rapids. Boatmen who have been on the river for a number of years can point to beaches where the volume of sand has decreased markedly. With most of the silt now being trapped behind Glen Canyon, this essential beach-building material no longer replenishes downstream areas. What has happened already in the fifteen-mile stretch between Glen Canyon Dam and Lee's Ferry is, in the words of one technical report, that beaches have "been degraded and stabilized with an armor bed of self-sorted riprap ranging from small cobbles to large boulders." Behind their new armored coating, some beaches have disappeared while a few are still being eroded. The report continues, "The lessons to be learned here should be applicable shortly to the river below Lee's Ferry." A comparison between aerial photographs taken in 1965 and 1973 shows the beach degradation process to be slow, perhaps taking a few decades to work its way downstream. But with less silt, it is sure.

The most noticeable change has been in the riverside vegetation. Prior to the completion of Glen Canyon there were three vegetation zones parallel to the river. Adjacent to the water was the ephemeral zone subjected to periodic flooding. This zone consisted mostly of such plants as seep willows, desert broom, and the true willows that would desperately try to put down roots before the next flood. Above the high-water line of these floods was the second zone, typified by such species as Apache plume, redbud, hackberry, mesquite, and acacia. On the dry talus slopes above, in a typical desert environment grew brittle brush, various cacti, creosote bush, and Mormon tea. With the dam came the establishment of a new riparian community at the lowest level. Here the ubiquitous tamarisk took hold, along with arrowweed, coyote willow, and other herbaceous plants. The new zone replaced the old ephemeral zone in many areas, and the plant life in the ephemeral zone then changed to such dominant species as red brome, tansy mustard, and fescue. Two exotic species, Russian thistle and camelthorn, found their way into the ephemeral zone.

With the increase in plant life along the river, the diversity and density of animal life have grown accordingly. During periods of blooming the lowest zone, dominated by tamarisk, contains nearly three times the number of insects as the next higher zone. Lizards have found an abundant source of food, and one species, the whiptail, feeds on small crustaceans when the daily "tide" goes out. More mice are found in this zone, and such birds as the yellow warbler and blue grosbeak have taken up residence along the river. With the change in water temperature and turbidity, the fish life has been altered. The humpback chub, an endangered species, has all but disappeared, while an excellent trout fishery has developed in the cold, clear water just below the dam.

With all these changes, it is hard to say the river and its immediate surroundings could be considered to be in their natural state any longer. But unless you whisper this repeatedly to yourself while floating down the river, it is difficult to realize that the Colorado within the Grand Canyon has become the ultimate ditch in the efficient transport of water from Lake Powell to Lake Mead.

There is a special river routine, and we get our first lesson in it from Bego, the wiry, bearded trip leader who once spent a hundred days in the canyon during the winter. Bego, whose single Indian name has replaced a more prosaic Anglo one, is a veteran of the technical rock-climbing scene at Yosemite National Park who drove out to the Grand Canyon one day and became ensnared by its geological charms. He is now one of those wandering young people—like ski patrolmen and climbing guides—who manage to eke out a living off the natural assets of the West. Bego is also quite possessive about his domain. He doesn't realize it but there is a strong tie between river boatmen and the Bureau of Reclamation employees back at the dam. They are the only people to make a living directly off the river.

A conch shell blown by Bego with a great deal of lung power summons us to meals and the first group meeting on the river. He tells us to put on life jackets when the boatmen do, and never to sit on them or the air pocket inside will burst. We are shown the proper position to assume in the water when we are thrown out of the boat. High-siding, whereby one leans into the waves to help keep the boat on an even keel, is explained—a bit too late for Alex and me to be of any help to Greg. Urinate in the wet sand, and the yellow rubber glove on the stick will show if the portable toilet is occupied or not. "Don't forget to dump the snow"—(lime)—"on the mountain," Bego reminds us. All human wastes and garbage are carried out on the one rubber raft accompanying the six dories. The raft is nicknamed T.O.B., for "turds on board." Life is rather basic in the canyon, and dealing with those basics begins to bring the diverse group together.

Bego has a nice habit. Each evening he will read us those sections of Powell's book we will be experiencing the next day. Tonight:

> Riding down a short distance, a beautiful view is presented. The river turns sharply to the east and seems inclosed by a wall set with a million brilliant gems. What can it mean? Every eye is engaged, every one wonders. On coming nearer we find fountains bursting from the rock overhead, and the spray in the sunshine forms the gems which bedeck the wall. The rocks below the fountain are covered with mosses and ferns and many beautiful flowering plants. We name it Vasey's Paradise, in honor of the botanist who traveled with us last year.

Around the corner from Vasey's Paradise is Redwall Cavern, which Powell estimated would seat 50,000 persons. Next day we pull up just as another group in large rubber rafts, referred to disparagingly as "baloney boats" by us proud dory riders, departs from this major river attraction. The river is rather crowded at times.

Edward Abbey

Down the River with Henry Thoreau

The float trip which is the subject of Abbey's Down the River *commenced on November 4, 1980, at Mineral Bottom on the Green River. This selection begins on November 10 at Stillwater Canyon on the Green and follows his progress through Cataract Canyon on the Colorado down to Lake Powell where he arrived November 14.*

November 8, 1980.—Who won the election? What election? Mere vapors on the gelid air, like the breath from my lungs. I rebuild the fire on the embers of last night's fire. I construct the coffee, adding fresh grounds to yesterday's. One by one, five human forms reassemble themselves about me, repeating themselves, with minor variations, for another golden day. The two vegetarians in our group—Rennie and Lorna—prepare their breakfast oatmeal, a viscous gray slime. I dump two pounds of Buck-sliced bacon into the expedition's wok, to the horror of the vegetarians, and stir it roughly about with a fork. Stir-cooking. The four carnivores look on with hungry eyes. The vegetarians smile in pity. "Pig meat," says Lorna, "for the four fat pork faces." "Eat your pussy food," says Dusty Teale, "and be quiet."

The melody of morning. Black-throated desert sparrows chatter in the willows: *chirr . . . chirr . . . chit chit chit.* The sun comes up, a glaring cymbal, over yonder canyon rim. Quickly the temperature rises five, ten, twenty degrees, at the rate of a degree a minute, from freezing to fifty-two. Or so it feels. We peel off parkas, sweaters, shirts, thermal underwear. Ravens croak, a rock falls, the river flows.

The fluvial life. The alluvial shore. "A river is superior to a lake," writes Henry in his *Journal,* "in its liberating influence. It has motion and indefinite length. . . . With its rapid current it is a slightly fluttering wing. River towns are winged towns."

Down the river. Lorna rows the dory, I row the raft. We are edified by water music from our string trio, a rich enchanting tune out of Peru called "Urubamba." The song goes on and on and never long enough. The Indians must have composed it for a journey down the Amazon.

Fresh slides appear on the mud banks; a beaver plops into the water ahead of us, disappears. The beavers are making a comeback on the Green. Time for D. Julien, Jim Bridger, Joe Meek, Jed Smith, and Jim Beckwourth to reappear. Eternal recurrence, announced Nietzsche. Time for the mountain men to return. The American West has not given us, so far, sufficient men to match our mountains. Or not since the death of Crazy Horse, Sitting Bull, Dull Knife, Red Cloud, Chief Joseph, Little Wolf, Red Shirt, Gall, Geronimo, Cochise, Tenaya (to name but a few), and their comrades. With their defeat died a bold, brave, heroic way of life, one as fine as anything recorded history has to show us. Speaking for myself, I'd sooner have been a liver-eating, savage horseman, riding with Red Cloud, than a slave-owning sophist sipping tempered wine in Periclean Athens. For example. Even Attila the Hun, known locally as the Scourge of God, brought more fresh air and freedom into Europe than the crowd who gave us the syllogism and geometry, Aristotle and his *Categories,* Plato and his *Laws.*

Instead of mountain men we are cursed with a plague of diggers, drillers, borers, grubbers; of asphalt-spreaders, dam-builders, overgrazers, clear-cutters, and strip-miners whose object seems to be to make our mountains match our men—making molehills out of mountains for a race of rodents—for the rat race.

Oh well . . . revenge is on the way. We see it in those high thin clouds far on the northern sky. We feel it in those rumbles of discontent deep in the cupboards of the earth: tectonic crockery trembling on the continental shelves. We hear it down the slipface of the dunes, a blue wing moaning out of nowhere. We smell it on the air: the smell of danger. Death before dishonor? That's right. What else? Liberty or death? Naturally.

When no one else would do it, it was Thoreau, Henry Thoreau the intolerable bore, the mean skulker, the "quaint stump figure of a man," as William Dean Howells saw him, who rang the Concord firebell to summon the villagers to a speech by Emerson attacking slavery. And when John Brown stood on trial for his life, when all America, even the most ardent abolitionists, was denouncing him, it was himself—Henry—who delivered a public address first in Concord, then in Boston, not only defending but praising, even eulogizing, the "madman" of Harpers Ferry.

We go on. Sheer rock—the White Rim—rises from the river's left shore. We pause at noon to fill our water jugs from a series of potholes half filled with last week's rainwater. We drink, and sitting in the sunlight on the pale sandstone, make our lunch—slabs of dark bread, quite authentic, from a bohemian bakery in Moab; a serious hard-core hippie peanut butter, heavy as wet concrete, from some beatnik food coop in Durango, Colorado (where Teale and Corson live); raspberry jam; and wild honey, thick as axle grease, for esophageal lubrication.

"What is your favorite dish?" another guest asked Thoreau as they sat down to a sumptuous Emersonian dinner.

"The nearest," Henry replied.

"At Harvard they teach all branches of learning," said Ralph Waldo.

"But none of the roots," said Henry.

Refusing to pay a dollar for his Harvard diploma, he said, "Let every sheep keep its own skin." When objections were raised to his habit of exaggeration, Henry said, "You must speak loud to those who are hard of hearing." Asked to write for the *Ladies' Companion*, he declined on the grounds that he "could not write anything companionable." He defines a pearl as "the hardened tear of a diseased clam, murdered in its old age." On the art of writing he said to a correspondent, "You must work very long to write short sentences." And added that "the one great rule of composition . . . is to speak the truth." Describing the flavor of a certain wild apple, he wrote that it was "sour enough to set a squirrel's teeth on edge, or make a jay scream."

And so on. The man seemingly composed wisecracks and epigrams in his sleep. Even on his deathbed. "Henry, have you made your peace with God?" asked a relative. "I am not aware that we had ever quarreled, Aunt," said Henry. To another visitor, attempting to arouse in him a decent Christian concern with the next world, Henry said, "One world at a time."

One could make a book of Henry's sayings. And call it *Essais. Areopagitica. Walden.*

Many of his friends, neighbors, relatives, and relative friends must have sighed in relief when Henry finally croaked his last, mumbling "moose . . . Indians . . ." and was safely buried under Concord sod. Peace, they thought, at long last. But, to paraphrase the corpse, they had *somewhat hastily* concluded that he was dead.

His passing did not go unnoticed outside of Concord. Thoreau had achieved regional notoriety by 1862. But at the time when the giants of New England literature were thought to be Emerson, Hawthorne, Alcott, Channing, Irving, Longfellow, Dr. Lowell, and Dr. Holmes, Thoreau was but a minor writer. Not even a major minor writer.

Today we see it differently. In the ultimate democracy of time, Henry has outlived his contemporaries. Hawthorne and Emerson are still read, at least in university English departments, and it may be that in a few elementary schools up in Maine and Minnesota children are being compelled to read Longfellow's *Hiawatha* (I doubt it; doubt that they can, even under compulsion), but as for the others they are forgotten by everyone but specialists in American literature. Thoreau, however, becomes more significant with each passing decade. The deeper our United States sinks into industrialism, urbanism, militarism—with the rest of the world doing its best to emulate America—the more poignant, strong, and appealing becomes Thoreau's demand for the right of every man, every woman, every child, every dog, every tree, every snail darter, every lousewort, every living thing, to live its own life in its own way at its own pace in its own square mile of home. Or in its own stretch of river.

Looking at my water-soaked, beer-stained, grease-spotted cheap paperback copy of *Walden*, I see that mine was from the thirty-third printing. And this is only one of at least a dozen current American editions of the book. *Walden* has been published abroad in every country where English can be read, as in India—God knows they need it there—or can be translated, as in Russia, where they need it even more. The Kremlin's commissars of literature have classified Thoreau as a nineteenth-century social reformer, proving once again that censors can read but seldom understand.

The village crank becomes a world figure. As his own Johnny Appleseed, he sows the seeds of liberty around the planet, even on what looks like the most unpromising soil. Out of Concord, apples of discord. Truth threatens power, now and always.

We walk up a small side canyon toward an area called Soda Springs Basin; the canyon branches and branches again, forming more canyons. The floor of each is flood-leveled sand, the walls perpendicular sandstone. Each canyon resembles a winding corridor in a labyrinth. We listen for the breathing of the Minotaur but find only cottonwoods glowing green and gold against the red rock, rabbitbrush with its mustard-yellow bloom, mule-ear sunflowers facing the sunlight, their coarse petals the color of butter, and the skull and curled horns of a desert bighorn ram, half buried in the auburn sand.

The canyons go on and on, twisting for miles into the plateau beyond. We turn back without reaching Soda Springs. On our return Dusty Teale takes up the bighorn trophy, carries it back to the dory and mounts it on the bow, giving his boat dignity, class, an unearned but warlike glamour.

We camp today at Anderson Bottom, across the river from Unknown Bottom. We find pictographs and petroglyphs here, pictures of deer, bighorns, warriors, and spectral figures representing—who knows—gods, spirits, demons. They do not trouble us. We cook our dinner and sing our songs and go to sleep.

November 9, 1980.—Early in the morning I hear coyotes singing again, calling up the sun. There's something about the coyotes that reminds me of Henry. What is it? After a moment the answer comes.

Down near Tucson, Arizona, where I sometimes live—a grim and grimy little-big town, swarming with nervous policemen, dope dealers, resolute rapists, and geriatric bank robbers, but let this pass for the moment—the suburban parts of the city are infested with pet dogs. Every home owner in these precincts believes that he needs whatever burglar protection he can get; and he is correct. Most evenings at twilight the wild coyotes come stealing in from the desert to penetrate the suburbs, raid garbage cans, catch and eat a few cats, dogs, and other domesticated beasts. When this occurs the dogs raise a grim clamor, roaring like maniacs, and launch themselves in hot but tentative pursuit of the coyotes. The coyotes retreat into the brush and cactus, where they stop, facing the town, to wait and sit and laugh at the dogs. They yip, yap, yelp, howl, and holler, teasing the dogs, taunting them, enticing them with the old-time call of the wild. And the dogs stand and tremble, shaking with indecision, furious, hating themselves, tempted to join the coyotes, run off with them into the hills, but—afraid. Afraid to give up the comfort, security, and safety of their housebound existence. Afraid of the unknown and dangerous.

Thoreau was our suburban coyote. Town dwellers have always found him exasperating.

"I have traveled a good deal in Concord; and everywhere, in shops and offices and fields, the inhabitants have appeared to me to be doing penance in a thousand remarkable ways. . . . By a seeming fate, commonly called necessity, they are employed, as it says in an old book, laying up treasures which moth and rust will corrupt and thieves break through and steal. It is a fool's life, as they will find when they get to the end of it, if not before. . . . I sometimes wonder that we can be so frivolous. . . . As if you could kill time without injuring eternity."

Oh come now, Henry, stop yapping at us. Go make love to a pine tree (all Nature being your bride). Lay off. Leave us alone. But he will not stop.

"The mass of men lead lives of quiet desperation. What is called resignation is confirmed desperation. . . . A stereotyped but unconscious despair is concealed even under what are called the games and amusements of mankind. There is no play in them."

But is it *true* that the mass of men lead lives of quiet desperation? And if so, did Henry escape such desperation himself? And who, if anyone, can answer these questions?

As many have noted, the mass of men—and women—lead lives today of *un*quiet desperation. A frantic busyness ("business") pervades our society wherever we look—in city and country, among young and old and middle-aged, married and unmarried, all races, classes, sexes, in work and play, in religion, the arts, the sciences, and perhaps most conspicuously in the self-conscious cult of meditation, retreat, withdrawal. The symptoms of universal unease and dis-ease are apparent on every side. We hear the demand by conventional economists for increased "productivity," for example. Productivity of what? for whose benefit? to what end? by what means and at what cost? Those questions are not considered. We are belabored by the insistence on the part of our politicians, businessmen and military leaders, and the claque of scriveners who serve them, that "growth" and "power" are intrinsic goods, of which we can never have enough, or even too much. As if gigantism were an end in itself. As if a commendable rat were a rat twelve hands high at the shoulders—and still growing. As if we could never have peace on this planet until one state dominates all others.

The secondary symptoms show up in the lives of individuals, the banalities of everyday soap opera: crime, divorce, runaway children, loneliness, alcoholism, mental breakdown. We live in a society where suicide (in its many forms) appears to more and more as a sensible solution; as a viable alternative; as a workable option.

Yes, there are many who seem to be happy in their lives and work. But strange lives, queer work. Space technicians, for example, busily refining a new type of inertial guidance system for an intercontinental ballistic missile bearing hydrogen bombs. Laboratory biologists testing the ability of mice, dogs, and chimpanzees to cultivate cancer on a diet of cigarettes and Holsum bread, to propel a treadmill under electric stimuli, to survive zero gravity in a centrifuge. And the indefatigable R. Buckminster Fuller hurtling around the globe by supersonic jet with six wristwatches strapped to each forearm, each watch set to a different time zone. "The world is big," says Fuller, "but it is comprehensible."

And also, to be fair, young dancers in a classroom; an old sculptor hacking in fury at a block of apple wood; a pinto bean farmer in Cortez, Colorado, surveying his fields with satisfaction on a rainy day in July (those rare farmers, whom Thoreau dismissed with such contempt, we now regard with envy); a solitary fly fisherman unzipping his fly on the banks of the Madison River; wet children playing on a shining, sun-dazzled beach.

Compared with ours, Thoreau's was an open quiet, agrarian society, relatively clean and uncluttered. The factory system was only getting under way in his time, though he took note of it when he remarked that "the shop girls have no privacy, even in their thoughts." In his day England, not America, was "the workhouse of the world." (America now in the process of being succeeded by Japan.) What would Henry think of New England, of the United States, of the Western world, in the year 1980? 1984? 2001? Would he not assert, confidently as before, that the mass of humans continue to lead lives of quiet desperation?

Quiet desperation. The bite of the phrase comes from the unexpected, incongruous juxtaposition of ordinarily antithetical words. The power of it comes from our sense of its illuminating force—"a light which makes the darkness visible." Henry's shocking pronouncement continues to resonate in our minds, with deeper vibrations, 130 years after he made it. He allows for exceptions, indicating the "mass of men," not all men, but as for the truth of his observation no Gallup Poll can tell us; each must look into his own heart and mind and then deny it if he can.

And what about Henry himself? When one of his friends, William Ellery Channing, declared morosely that no man could be happy "under present conditions," Thoreau replied without hesitation, "But I am." He spent nearly a year at his dying and near the end, too weak to write any more, he dictated the following, in answer to a letter form his friend Blake:

"You ask particularly after my health. I *suppose* that I have not many months to live; but of course I know nothing about it. I may add that I am enjoying existence as much as ever, and regret nothing."

When the town jailer, Sam Staples, the same who had locked Thoreau up for a night many years before, and had also become a friend, paid a visit to the dying man, he reported to Emerson: "Never spent an hour with more satisfaction. Never saw a man dying with so much pleasure and peace." A trifle lugubrious, but revealing. Henry's sister Sophia wrote, near his end, "It is not possible to be sad in his presence. No shadow attaches to anything connected with my precious brother. His whole life impresses me as a grand miracle. . . ."

A cheerful stoic all the way, Thoreau refused any drugs to ease the pain or let him sleep; he rejected opiates, according to Channing, "on the ground that he preferred to endure the worst sufferings with a clear mind rather than sink into a narcotic dream." As he would never admit to a vulgar sadness, so he would not allow himself to surrender to mere physical pain.

It must have seemed to Henry during his last year that his life as an author had been a failure. Only two of his books were published during his lifetime and neither received much recognition. His contemporaries, without exception—Emerson included—had consigned him to oblivion, and Henry could not have been unaware of the general opinion. But even in this he refused to acknowledge defeat. Noting the dismal sales of his books, he wrote in his *Journal:* "I believe that the result is more inspiring and better for me than if thousands had bought my wares. It affects my privacy less and leaves me freer."

Emerson declared that Thoreau was a coldly unemotional man, stoical but never cheerful; Emerson had so convinced himself of this that when, in editing some of Thoreau's letters for publication, he came across passages that indicated otherwise, he deleted them. But Ralph Waldo's son Edward, in his book *Henry Thoreau as Remembered by a Young Friend*, wrote that Henry loved to sing and dance, and was always popular with the children of Concord.

In her *Memories of Hawthorne,* Hawthorne's daughter Rose gives us this picture of Thoreau ice skating, with Emerson and Hawthorne, on the frozen Concord River: "Hawthorne," she writes, "moved like a self-impelled Greek statue, stately and grave" (the marble faun); Emerson "closed the line, evidently too weary to hold himself erect, pitching headforemost . . ."; while Thoreau, circling around them, "performed dithryambic dances and Bacchic leaps."

But what of the photographs of Henry referred to earlier, the daguerreotype in his thirty-ninth year by B. W. Maxham, made in 1856, and the ambrotype of E. S. Dunshee, made in 1861? Trying to get some sense of the man himself, in himself, which I do not get from his words alone, or from the accounts of Thoreau by others, I find myself looking again and again at these old pictures. Yes, the eyes are unusually large, very sensitive and thoughtful, as is the expression of the whole face. The nose is too long, the chin too small, neither an ornament; the face deeply lined, the brow high, the hair and beard luxuriant. A passable face, if not a handsome one. And it still seems to me that I read in his eyes, in his look, an elemental melancholy. A resigned sadness. But the man was ailing with tuberculosis when the former picture was made, within a year of his death when the second was made. These facts should explain the thoughtful look, justify a certain weariness. In neither picture can we see what might be considered a trace of self-pity—the *vulgar* sadness. And in neither can we perceive the faintest hint of any kind of desperation. Henry may have been lonely; he was never a desperate man.

What does it matter? For us it is Henry's words and ideas that count, or more exactly, the symbiotic and synergistic mutually reinforcing logic of word and idea, and his successful efforts to embody both in symbolic acts. If it were true that he never had a happy moment (I doubt this) in his entire life, he surely had an intense empathy with the sensations of happiness:

". . . I have penetrated to those meadows on the morning of many a first spring day, jumping from hummock to hummock, from willow root to willow root, when the wild river valley and the woods were bathed in so pure and bright a light as would have waked the dead, if they had been slumbering in their graves, as some suppose. There needs no stronger proof of immortality."

The paragraph is from the springtime of Henry's life. *Walden* is a young man's book, most of it written before his thirtieth year. But the infatuation with the sun and sunlight carries on into the premature autumn of his years as well; he never gave them up, never surrendered. Near the end of his life he wrote:

"We walked [jumping has become walking, but the spirit remains the same] in so pure and bright a light, gilding the withered grass and leaves, so softly and serenely bright, I thought I had never bathed in such a golden flood, without a ripple or a murmur to it. The west side of every wood and rising ground gleamed like the boundary of Elysium, and the sun on our backs seemed like a gentle herdsman driving us home at evening."

And concluding: "So we saunter toward the Holy Land, till one day the sun shall shine more brightly than ever he has done, shall perchance shine into our minds and hearts, and light up our whole lives with a great awakening light, as warm and serene and golden as on a bankside in autumn."

November 10, 1980.—Onward, into Stillwater Canyon. We have left Labyrinth behind, though how Major Powell distinguished the two is hard to determine. The current is slow, but no slower than before, the canyons as serpentine as ever. In the few straight stretches of water we gain a view of Candlestick Tower, now behind us, and off to the southwest, ahead, the great sandstone monadnock three hundred feet high known as Cleopatra's Chair, "bathed," as Henry would say, "in a golden flood of sunlight."

We row around an anvil-shaped butte called Turk's Head. Hard to see any reason for the name. Is there any reason, out here, for any name? These huge walls and giant towers and vast mazy avenues of stone resist attempts at verbal reduction. The historical view, the geological view, the esthetical view, the rock climber's view, give us only aspects of a massive *presence* that remains fundamentally unknowable. The world is big and it is incomprehensible.

A hot, still morning in Stillwater Canyon. We row and rest and glide, at two miles per hour, between riparian jungles of rusty willow, coppery tamarisk, brown cane, and gold-leaf cottonwoods. On the shaded side the crickets sing their dirgelike monotone. They know, if we don't, that winter is coming.

But today is very warm for mid-November. An Indian-summer day. Looking at the rich brown river, jungle on both banks, I think how splendid it would be, and apposite, to see the rugose snout of an alligator come sliding through the water toward us. We need alligators here. Crocodiles, also. A few brontosauri, pteranodons, and rocs with twenty-five-foot wingspan would not be amiss. How tragic that we humans arrived too late, to the best of our conscious recollection, to have witnessed the fun and frolic of the giant thunder lizards in their time of glory. Why was that great chapter ripped too soon from the Book of Life? I would give ten years off the beginning of my life to see, only once, *Tyrannosaurus rex* come rearing up from the elms of Central Park, a Morgan police horse screaming in its jaws. We can never have enough of nature.

We explore a couple of unnamed side canyons on the right, searching for a natural stone arch I found ten years ago, on a previous river journey. Hallucination Arch, we named it then, a lovely span of two-tone rosy sandstone—not shown on any map—somewhere high in the northern fringes of the Maze. We do not find it this time. We pass without investigating a third unknown canyon; that must have been the right one.

We camp for two nights at the mouth of Jasper Canyon, spend the day between the nights exploring Jasper's higher ramifications, toward the heart of the Maze. If the Maze has a heart. We go on the following day, down the river, and come sailing out one fine afternoon into the confluence of the two great desert streams. The Green meets the Colorado. They do not immediately merge, however, but flow along side by side like traffic lanes on a freeway, the greenish Colorado, the brownish Green, with a thin line of flotsam serving as median.

Henry never was a joiner either.

"Know all men by these presents that I, Henry Thoreau, do not wish to be considered a member of any incorporated body which I have not joined."

A crusty character, Thoreau. An unpeeled man. A man with the bark on him.

We camp today at Spanish Bottom, near the first rapids of Cataract Canyon. Sitting around our fire at sundown, four of us gnawing on spareribs, the other two picking at their pussy food—tofu and spinach leaves and stewed kelp (it looks like the testicles of a sick octopus)—we hear the roar of tons of silty water plunging among the limestone molars of Brown Betty Rapid: teeth set on edge. The thunderous vibrations rise and fall, come and go, with the shifting evening winds.

We spend the next day wandering about the top of the Maze, under the shadows of Lizard Rock, Standing Rock, the Chimney, looking down into five-hundred-foot-deep canyons, into the stems, branches, and limbs of an arboreal system of part-time drainages. It took a liberal allowance of time, indeed, for the rare storms of the canyon country to carve out of solid rock these intricate canyons, each with its unscalable walls, boxlike heads, stomach-turning dropoffs. A man could spend the better part of a life exploring this one area, getting to know, so far as possible, its broad outline and its intimate details. You could make your summer camp on Pete's Mesa, your winter camp down in Ernie's Country, and use Candlestick Spire all year round for a personalized private sundial. And die, when you're ready, with the secret center of the Maze clutched to your bosom. Or, more likely, never found.

Henry spent his life—or earned his life—exploring little more than the area surrounding his hometown of Concord. His jaunts beyond his own territory do not amount to much. He traveled once to Minnesota, seeking health, but that was a failure. He never came west, although, as he says, he preferred walking in a westerly direction. He never saw our Rocky Mountains, or the Grand Canyon, or the Maze. He never reached the Amazon, Alaska, Antarctica, the Upper Nile, or the Mountains of the Moon. He journeyed once to Staten Island but was not impressed.

Instead, he made a world out of Walden Pond, Concord, and their environs. He walked, he explored, every day and many nights, he learned to know his world as few ever know any world. Once, as he walked in the woods with a friend (Thoreau had many friends, we come to realize, if not one in his lifetime with whom he could truly, deeply share his life; it is we, his readers, over a century later, who must be and are his true companions), the friend expressed his long-felt wish to find an Indian arrowhead. At once Henry stopped, bent down, and picked one up.

November 14, 1980.—Today will be out last day on the river. We plan to run the rapids of Cataract Canyon this morning, camp on Lake Powell this afternoon, go on to Hite Marina and back to civilization, such as it is, tomorrow.

I rise early, as usual, and before breakfast go for a walk into the fields of Spanish Bottom. I see two sharp-shinned hawks roosting in a cottonwood. A tree of trembling leaves, pale gold and acid green. The hawks rise at my approach, circle, return to the tree as I go on. Out in the field, one hundred yards away, I see an erect neck, a rodentian head, a pair of muley ears displayed in sharp silhouette against the redrock cliffs. I stop, we stare at each other—the transient human, the ephemeral desert mule deer. Then I notice other deer scattered beyond the first: one, two, three, four, five—nine all told. Two with antlers.

My first thought is *meat.* Unworthy thought—but there they are, waiting, half of them standing broadside to me, their dear beating hearts on level with the top of the sand sage, saltbush, rice grass. Two of them within a hundred yards—easy range for a thirty-thirty. Meat means survival. Survival, by Christ, with honor. With *honor!* When the cities lie at the monster's feet, we shall come here, my friends, my very few friends and I, my sons and my daughter, and we will survive. We shall live.

My second thought is more fitting, for the moment. Leave them in peace. Let them be. Efface yourself, for a change, and let the wild things be.

What would Henry say? Henry said, "There is a period in the history of the individual, as of the race, when the hunters are the 'best men,' as the Algonquins called them. We cannot but pity the boy who has never fired a gun; he is no more humane, while his education has been sadly neglected." But then he goes on to say: "No humane being, past the thoughtless age of boyhood, will wantonly murder any creature which holds its life by the same tenure that he does. The hare in its extremity cries like a child. I warn you, mothers, that my sympathies do not make the ususal *philanthropic* distinctions." Is that his last word on the subject? Hardly. Henry had many words for every subject, and no last word for any. He also writes, "But I see that if I were to live in a wilderness, I should become . . . a fisher and hunter in earnest."

So let them be for now. I turn back to camp, making one step. The deer take alarm, finally, and move off at a walk. I watch. Their fear becomes contagious. One begins to run, they all run, bounding away toward the talus slopes of the canyon wall. I watch them leap upward into the rocks, expending energy with optimum ease, going farther and rising higher until they disappear, one by one, somewhere among the boulders and junipers at the foot of the vertical wall.

Back to camp and breakfast. We load the boats, secure the hatches, lash down all baggage, strap on life jackets, face the river and the sun, the growing roar of the rapids. First Brown Betty, then Ben Hur and Capsize Rapids, then the Big Drop and Satan's Gut. Delightful names, and fitting. We feel the familiar rush of adrenaline as it courses through our blood. We've been here before, however, and know that we'll get through. Most likely. The odds are good. Our brave boatman and boatwoman, Dusty and Lorna, ply the oars and steer our fragile craft into the glassy tongue of the first rapid. The brawling waters roar below, rainbows of broken sunlight dance in the spray. We descend.

Henry thou should be with us now.

I look for his name in the water, his face in the airy foam. He must be here. Wherever there are deer and hawks, wherever there is liberty and danger, wherever there is wilderness, wherever there is a living river, Henry Thoreau will find his eternal home.

Bill Beer

Rapids, Icewater and Fire

This excerpt is the second chapter of Bill Beer's We Swam the Grand Canyon, *which recounts Beer and his friend Jim Daggett's twenty-six-day adventure swimming 280 miles of the Colorado River from Lees Ferry to Pierce Ferry on Lake Mead.*

We said goodbye to a solemn-looking Dave who was to take John's car back to L.A. and then waded into deep water and swam out to the main current. We were carried along surprisingly swiftly while Dave and the fishermen rapidly dwindled to small figures, Dave waving sadly and the fishermen indifferent.

The water again seemed pleasant, the canyon quiet, and John and I could talk easily to each other even when we were separated by a hundred yards or so. We didn't have much to say; we were already overwhelmed by what was happening and were each lost in our own thoughts. The small, jumbled cliffs near Lees Ferry quickly gathered themselves into steep walls which then steadily grew higher. We imagined ourselves climbing out of the canyon and looked to see how many places it seemed possible. Before too long there didn't seem to be many.

Then the quiet ended; ahead of us the river was making a noise. We pointed nervously downstream to each other, even though we knew we hadn't gone far enough to get to the first rapid. We quickly reached the noise; the river gathered speed, there were a few ripples and waves and then it was calm again. Not a rapid, just a little riffle, but the noise was new to us.

We had gone only a couple of more miles before the vagaries of the currents separated us by a quarter of a mile or so, and swim as hard as we might, it seemed the river wouldn't let us get back together. Neither of us wanted to be that much alone, so John swam over to the narrow bank and climbed out to wait for me. After I joined him we spent a few minutes aiming John's 35mm camera at the cliffs and taking a few snapshots. When we got back into the water, we both remarked on how cold it was—much colder than it had seemed at first.

The cold water began to get downright uncomfortable as we drifted down a long corridor of cliffs. And when we rounded a slight bend and saw another long passageway with Navajo Bridge hanging high above, it became obligatory to stop again and take some movies. On our second return the water felt icy.

Drifting toward the bridge we were fascinated by its lacy arch so high above us—the last work of man we expected to see for days. Dave was supposed to be up there waiting to see us, but the bridge was so high we could barely detect whether there were any people on it, much less recognize one of them. To them we must have looked like small pieces of driftwood, if they even saw us.

Just as we passed under the bridge the canyon was rocked by an explosion that sounded like a 120mm cannon going off. Then another, and another. People were dropping small boulders off the bridge! Falling from nearly 500 feet, the boulders exploded when they hit the water. We waved frantically, but only when we were safely past the bridge did we finally see one of the little figures up in the sky seem to wave back. Must have been Dave.

The water was really beginning to seem cold now. My rubber shirt had leaked and all I could think of was getting out of that water and getting warm. The Lees Ferry hydrographer notwithstanding, the actual temperature of the water that day was 51 degrees F. This is but 19 degrees above freezing and humans don't last long in water that cold.

Not only were we freezing, but we were being blinded by a wind that blasted sand and water into our eyes so that we had no recourse but to drift downstream backward. John complained bitterly that no one had mentioned the wind in the books he had read and I had to admit the same. We agreed that if it were to blow like this all the time we just might quit and go home . . . if we could.

We turned another bend and passed out of sight of the bridge and the wind blew even harder. There was nothing to do now but get out of the water and find shelter. We searched for a campsite but saw only piles of big boulders below the cliffs—not even enough room to lay out a sleeping bag. I was so cold now that I felt I would turn to stone if we didn't find a campsite soon.

Around another bend we saw a small side canyon which made a break in the cliffs on the right. Where it joined the river we saw a pile of sand and scattered boulders that had been pushed out of the side canyon during flash floods. We swam, kicking our fins with all our strength to get to the bank before being swept past. Pushing the bulky boxes through the water and not being able to use our arms to swim made it slow going, but at the last moment the current weakened and we landed on the powdery beach just at the mouth of the little side canyon.

The wind still blew furiously as we looked for a place to build a fire and camp out of the wind. The best we could find was a little pocket among some boulders where the wind became a whirlwind blowing sand round and round with only slightly less fury than the blasts outside. When the fire got going ashes and sparks were added to the whirling sand.

When John opened up his boxes to get out his warm dry clothes, he found that water had gotten in, and while the wind and sand and ashes blew furiously outside, the Colorado River lapped calmly around his clothes and food, defying him to be comfortable. He was stunned—too miserable to rage, he could only mutter.

He rigged a clothesline and hung his clothes up, philosophically remarking that "dry and gritty is better than wet and muddy." Fortunately, most of his other things—double wrapped in plastic—were saved from the water, though he did lose some cookies and candy.

The real disaster was that the movie camera was soaked and the film loaded in it ruined! With its enormous load of silt, the river water left everything it touched gritty. And even though I stripped the camera down as much as I could—even to cleaning the shutter mechanism—it still sounded suspiciously wheezy when it ran. Another casualty was our river map. I had wrapped the first sheet in plastic and tied it to the top of one of my boxes. The plastic leaked and of course our map was a sodden mass of pulp.

It, too, was gingerly dried and though barely legible we could see that we were camped at a place called Six Mile Wash. If the river could do all that damage in only six miles, what would the next 274 miles be like? Not a comforting thought.

Finally, well after dark, we set about making dinner—no simple matter with the air full of dirt and ashes. We dined on an unpretentious canned stew flavored with cinders, sand and ashes, and washed down with strong coffee made with muddy river water. Even though we kept our pans covered between bites, whenever we lifted the lid to sneak out a forkful the wind added to the fine brown and black layer already over our meat and potatoes. It was dangerous to linger too long over a bite; in seconds the morsel would be coated. That night we found why we had brought diving masks. Wearing them around our windy campfire we could at least keep the sand and ashes out of our eyes.

Dropping off to sleep later I wondered what the rapids would be like. Would we be able to get through? Or would we be hurt—a leg broken, or a concussion? And what if we got pinned to a rock by the current? How to get free? Obviously this wasn't the first time these thoughts had surfaced, to the contrary, we had talked them to death. But now the problem was at hand.

The next morning the wind still blew, and as the sun reached over the canyon walls and forced us awake I looked over to see John with matted eyebrows, muddy face, scraggly beard, unkempt hair, face blotched with yesterday's zinc oxide ointment, all covered with a fine layer of light-colored sand and ashes. He peeked out of his sleeping bag like a dirty old caterpillar called too soon out of the cocoon. I told him he couldn't have sold life insurance to a condemned man. He in turn warned me that the first cop we saw would arrest me for vagrancy.

We were clumsy getting breakfast, having to wait for a short lull between gusts to open a box, retrieve an item and quickly close the flap before the wind blew in another cupful of sand and ashes. We fumed and muttered and the wind added sand to the flour and sand to the water and sand to the butter and sand to the syrup and our hotcakes tasted like mud pies. John still had some water in his boxes which now was mud. After breakfast we went to the river to wash dishes but in the minute it took us to walk back our dishes were dirty again. Then, as if sorry for what it had done, the wind died.

Despite the late hour, John felt an urgent need to clean all the mud out of his boxes, so he emptied them and spread all his gear out to scrape it off and let it begin to dry.

From down the canyon came a sound we had already learned. It was approaching fast. A few hundred yards away the brush bent under the approach of a tan cloud; little dust devils danced and twisted their spiral columns of sand here and there in advance of the cloud.

"Oh no!" shouted John. We both dove for his gear, scrambling and clutching, trying to stuff it willy nilly into the boxes. But too late. We were surrounded by blowing sand and there was nothing for poor John to do but sigh pitifully, turn his back to the wind and cover his eyes and nose. I did likewise. When we finally packed, it was not without a fair measure of sand in along with everything else.

We hurried into our river clothes and hustled the heavy boxes one at a time to the water's edge. Our side canyon had made a little riffle here, but the riffle was almost obliterated by the seamless texture of choppy little waves the wind made on the surface of the river. The water looked extra cold and we recalled that when we had washed dishes in it our hands had hurt from the cold. The sun was high, and though we had no watch we knew it was getting late. Even so, after looking at that forbidding water, each of us found some very necessary last minute adjustments.

John had been experimenting with a coiled lanyard and some sort of clever quick-release knot so that he could let his boxes out on a long line if he needed to. The coil was miserably snarled and needed careful attention. As soon as he finished, I realized that I had again put our mutilated map on the outside of my box; obviously that hadn't worked before, so I needed to memorize the next few miles and put it inside.

John had been waiting while I secured the map, then he saw that he ought to do a better job of sealing the waterproof flap to his boxes. After watching him take such great care, I worried that I ought to do likewise and so resealed each of mine.

Then it was the rubber shirts that needed adjustment, one after the other, then our inflatable Mae West lifejackets, and then we felt the socks we wore under our fins to prevent chafe were too full of sand so these had to be rinsed out in the muddy water. Each of these steps demanded careful discussion and experimentation.

This little one-act play in ankle-deep water must have taken about an hour, but ultimately there was nothing more we could do but get into the cold water.

It was an agony we were to feel many times a day in the weeks ahead. Wading off the silt bank into gradually deepening water, pushing our boxes ahead of us, we resisted the increasing current as long as we could, putting off the moment when we had to surrender and get swept off our feet to begin swimming toward midstream. The moment we stopped swimming we could feel our bodies try to fight off the cold. The water, of course, was relentless. Water is so much more efficient than air at conducting heat, and at little more than half the body temperature it can swiftly carry away much of whatever warmth the body is able to produce.

Our cheap little swimming outfits, rubber shirts, sweatshirts and woolen underwear helped slow down this numbing loss of heat, but only inadequately. Our bodies, to survive, had to keep our central temperature up. Faced with rapid heat loss, the body retreats, first abandoning the skin and its underlying tissues by closing off blood circulation. In arctic temperatures this can result in loss of fingers and toes to frostbite. In our cold water, frostbite was not the problem; hypothermia, or lowering of temperature of the whole body, was. The next part of our bodies to be abandoned to the cold would be our muscles and with their loss our chances of survival would diminish seriously.

We were very conscious of this from almost the first day. We could not keep warm in the river; we could not be comfortable. But to endure for the long periods we would have to stay in the water, we had to keep active. This sounds easier than it was.

On first getting into the water we felt pain everywhere on the surface of our bodies from the shock of the cold water. Soon after, especially if we stopped swimming, came a tingling, the first stage of numbness, and our reaction was to fight it, to shiver, to flex our arms, legs and feet, to swim—even to shake our heads. Soon the numbness passed, replaced by a weariness that made us think we were getting used to the cold. If we could stay in the sunlight and keep our heads dry we could forget for a while the cold creeping into our muscles from our necks down. But before long we would begin to feel stiff and resisted movement of any kind. It became easier to make no effort at all. Finally it became painful to move, we hurt all over. We became aware that something more than discomfort was happening; bones felt like icicles and wouldn't bend at the joints. We could no longer actually feel our feet, and when we struggled to limber up it hurt quite a lot. Even when we ignored the pain and forced ourselves, we could hardly move.

This was the time to get warm—the last chance. Otherwise, next would come a drowsiness from which there would be no escape; the temperature in our central organs would begin to drop and our lives would be threatened.

The noise woke me up. I was almost unaware of the last half mile, but when I heard the rumble ahead over the wind, I knew I had to act. John heard it at the same time and we both forced our nearly helpless legs to push us toward shore. We could barely see 50 yards through the blowing sand ahead but we could feel the current speeding up. At first we seemed to make no progress out of the center of the river, we were being carried against our will toward the noise. Then gradually, as before, we made more progress and the current lessened—the effort took about all the strength we had left. When we finally touched the bank we fell exhausted into the warm sand, lying there in the noise, grateful for the little bit of sun shining on us. Grateful, too, for the black rubber shirts which, if they didn't conserve our own warmth too well, certainly absorbed the sun's heat quickly.

Semi-restored, we got up and made our way down through the pile of huge boulders disgorged from the little canyon that had split the massive cliffs. We slipped and stumbled as our paralyzed muscles refused to perform their duty. We were at Badger Creek and soon saw the source of the noise, Badger Creek Rapid. We had landed at its very head—just barely before we would have been swept down it. We found a spot alongside the midway point, sat on a boulder and soaked up more sun while we studied our first rapid.

It's not a big rapid, though to us at the time it seemed big enough. On the brink there were rocks sticking up all over the place and now and then the water swirled, revealing other rocks just under the surface. Out in the middle of the river there seemed to be a clear channel, but we saw that from where we had landed we could not swim out that far before the river carried us down the vicious edge of the rapid. The only way to get enough room to swim to midstream would be to haul our boxes well up river before launching ourselves. That didn't sound like much fun.

Another possibility was to turn our boxes loose to go through the rapid by themselves while we swam vigorously through what seemed to be the safest channel. But supposing a box or boxes were lost or pinned under a rock by the current?

We could portage, that is, carry our boxes around the rapid, but that would be more work than carrying them up river and, of course, would not be in the spirit of the whole enterprise.

We concluded that we would be best off if we tried to swim, stumble and drift along the boulder-strewn edge of the rapid. The current there seemed slower and the volume of water did not seem as if it would overpower us. Short of being pinned against a boulder or dragged over one, we should make it okay.

We guessed that it was nearly noon; anyway, we were hungry, so before returning to the icy water we dined on dried fruit and candy—quick energy but not too filling. Already we were wishing we had brought more food. Living off our rations for a few days in Los Angeles had been a good idea, but we had failed to account for the extra calories we were burning out here. And then the movie camera and film took up so much room.

Badger Creek was a fight. We writhed and squirmed and fended off rocks while our contrary boxes pulled at us or jammed in between rocks and fought our efforts to pull at them. John let out his quick-release line and at once his boxes swept around one side of a boulder while he was forced around the other side. The line naturally caught up on the rock and there was John, trapped. He couldn't pull the boxes around his way, so he had to go hand over hand up the thin nylon line against the pressure of the current to work his way around the rock. John's boxes held fast under the steady pressure of the flowing water, but as soon as he got halfway around the boulder they shot downstream, jerking John off the boulder and dragging him underwater. He came up a few yards downstream, sputtering and cursing, but in the clear.

This was not the way to swim a rapid. Even at the slower rate along the edge, the current was much stronger than we were and there were just too many boulders. It was dangerous.

As we drifted below Badger Creek, we speculated that our theory of running rapids was still valid, though untested. Swimming alone we could easily avoid rocks we thought—especially if we could see them. But the problem still remained of what to do with the boxes. Without them we had all the freedom of movement we needed, but they were too bulky to shift quickly around in the water or to swim fast with. Cutting the boxes loose was simply unacceptable. We had tried to keep track of particular pieces of driftwood or logs as they went through Badger Creek Rapid and had seen how easy it was to lose sight of them. And to lose our food, clothing, matches, etc. might be really dangerous. There is not much chance of living off the land in these canyons, which were starting to get very deep.

The plateau into which the Colorado has cut its canyon rises to the west from Lees Ferry; only nine miles downstream the rim was already a thousand feet above the river, only 40 feet of that was the drop in the river bed itself. Trying to leave, to give up the attempt, was getting to look very difficult indeed. Better to stay on the river.

We were cold again, but this time we weren't going to be lulled into drifting almost to the brink of the rapid. Soap Creek Rapid made so much noise we heard it from two miles upstream. There was a booming and crashing tone to the roar which had not been there at Badger Creek. It was quite alarming. We could see the side canyon, Soap Creek Canyon, coming in from the right almost from the time we first heard its rapid, so well upstream we began to edge to the right side of the river. But soon it began to appear that we weren't going to make it: the bend in the river and the delta of Soap Creek were creating a current angle we couldn't overpower. Reversing course, we headed for the left bank, only a narrow band of boulders below the cliff, which we reached well above the beginning of the rapid. It appeared to us that at higher stages of water there would be no bank here at all, only sheer cliffs dropping straight into the river.

When we had clambered down alongside the rapid, feeling like ants on a gravel pile, it was obvious that the Badger Creek technique was out of the question. The river raged at our very feet with no appreciable slowing at its edge. It was a lot bigger rapid than Badger Creek: steeper, longer, wilder, with bigger waves and more noise. There was little likelihood we could get to the other bank without being swept over the rapid. Our only choice seemed to be to swim straight through the safest part of the rapid.

After inspecting the maelstrom from several sites, guessing at the location of a number of unseen but suspected boulders in the rapid, we concluded that a little left of center was the best course.

The place had a nasty reputation, having caused one of the early drownings—that of Frank M. Brown during an attempt to survey the Grand Canyon for a proposed railroad through it. Several of those early expeditions had dumped their boats in Soap Creek, so most had chosen to laboriously portage around. In 1929 a party of young men on a strictly-for-fun trip became its first conquerors.

Now John Daggett was about to become the first person to swim through Soap Creek Rapid. We hoped.

In addition to the camera and tripod, I had brought my fins and life jacket from upstream. From where I stood, well below the brink of the rapid, it would not be hard to scramble downstream and launch myself into the river below the rapid if John needed help.

What did John think about as he was stumbling back upstream to get ready to swim the rapid? Mostly, he said, that he didn't want to get back into that cold water. Regardless of what other dangers the river might offer, as far as John was concerned the most immediate was its temperature. He had no fear of death. Since the loss of his wife and two little girls less than a year previously, it was something that really didn't matter much. He was somewhat afraid of being seriously injured—especially with no help available except old Bill sitting down there on his rock.

He put on his fins and life jacket rather quickly and, with a deep breath, shoved off into the river.

He found himself lying face down between his two boxes, which were loosely joined by their straps, with one arm draped over each. He could hoist his head a foot or so off the water to better see where he was going and he had his legs free for kicking.

Down on my rock I was busy practicing with the camera, following chunks of driftwood as they slid down the long smooth tongue of the rapid and were lost in the boiling waves and confusion below. It was hard to follow them—about the best I could do was to hope to pan the camera with the flow of the water so that when the chunk of driftwood did surface it was still in the frame.

Then I saw John at the top of the rapid waving. I checked that the camera was wound and aimed it at him. Through the viewfinder, like looking through the wrong end of a telescope, I saw only a wall of water with a tiny figure perched on top. The little figure swooped down the smooth wall and was immediately lost in the angry, noisy water. I could feel the camera grinding the film as I tried to follow the path through the water I thought John would travel. But where was he?

Suddenly he popped to the top of a wave, very close, almost filling the viewfinder. I could see his expression. Pain? No, more like intent. Then he dropped down behind a wave. Just as he came out on the other side of it, another wave reached over and smacked him on the side of the head and he disappeared again. Then almost as fast as he had disappeared, he reappeared. He was only a spit away from me and I could have jumped in next to him. The camera stopped and I had to rewind it.

I was diverted for only a moment, but when my attention turned back to John he was 50 yards downstream and waving to me that everything was all right. I could see him shouting something, but couldn't hear over the noise of the rapid. I kept the camera pointing at him, filming until he faded away into the gloom that now filled the canyon.

Drifting in the shadows below Soap Creek Rapid, John was relaxed and elated. He had had a whale of a good time going through that rapid, but now that the excitement had passed, he realized that he had been very tense during the ride. He wondered why; there wasn't anything to it—he had seen and swum in much more dangerous waters in Pacific breakers. He thought of me and wished he could have told me what fun it was. He realized that though I would be a bit worried, I'd have no trouble. So he turned his thoughts to finding a good place to camp and getting a warm fire going.

Back at Soap Creek I was all alone. And believe me, there's no place lonelier. John was out of sight around a bend and what I had to do I had to do all by myself—nobody to even watch. I gathered up the camera, tripod, fins and lifejacket and went back upstream to my boxes. I wasn't as frightened now—after all, John had gotten through all right—all I had to do was jump in and swim the rapid and get downstream to where John had started camp. I packed the camera, sealed the box and got in the water.

It was late afternoon and the water was really cold! I kicked hard to get out in the middle and got there sooner than needed. So there was nothing to do for a few moments except drift toward the noise of the unseen rapid. I hung suspended in the smooth water not moving. Little pieces of driftwood hovered a few inches away barely cracking the glassy surface. Nothing moved. And yet everything was moving rapidly toward the brink. I could hear the noise and beyond the brink I could see plumes of the waves leaping up here and there. But of the rapid itself I could see nothing.

Then in a moment I was on the brink. With no time to think I dropped swiftly down the fast, smooth, undulating slide into the waves and fury. I was immediately pulled under, or maybe through the first wave. I came up and the spray smashed into my face so that I couldn't see a thing. I went under again, came up, got twisted around and was bounced up and down like a ping pong ball on a water fountain. The waves were so powerful I could hardly keep my feet under me. I was hanging onto my boxes with all my strength while the river pulled at me from all directions. It even tried to pull the swim fins off my feet. I was a little alarmed at my helplessness.

Almost instantly I was in control again in the choppy tail of the rapid that streamed down the river for a quarter of a mile. Now I could see what was happening to me.

It had been a wild ride but a lot of fun. I lost a lot of fear of rapids there and then—in fact, I looked forward to the next one. This was a great sport! It reminded me of the first thrill of skiing or riding a breaking wave. The only thing wrong was that it was so cold.

In all the violence, water had leaked in again under my rubber shirt and my sweatshirt was drawing in cold water like a wick, making me ever colder. And I was lonely. The canyon wasn't awesome and beautiful anymore—just gloomy. I wanted to rejoin John and sit by a warm fire and gloat about swimming our first big rapid. I began to search the darkening shore for smoke or flame or John. Perhaps he was up around the next bend.

As I came around slowly I searched every inch of shore. A small rapid chattered away and I ran it without hesitation. Of course I got my face and head wet again and was colder still. Now it was my teeth that chattered. There was another bend around to the left, and as I came around I was facing a straight calm stretch of water almost two miles long. Here and there were piles of boulders that had fallen from the vertical cliffs and I knew that in one of them John was right now setting up camp. I drifted along colder and stiffer by the minute, occasionally yelling so I wouldn't drift by without his noticing. He might be busy behind a rock where I had no chance of seeing him. The wind was still blowing hard and he would naturally seek a very protected site. With the long run it had in this straight corridor, the wind whipped up bits of spray and sand and blew this mixture into my eyes making it hard to see.

Then I heard another rapid. It had a deep sound—probably not a small rapid. Of course John would camp above it. As I approached the rapid I looked for the side canyon which had formed it. Everything was shadowy and I couldn't see it, so not knowing which bank the side canyon delta and John would be on, I stayed in the middle of the river. As I got closer I saw that there wasn't any side canyon! The cliffs were unbroken above and below the rapid on both sides. This turned out to be Sheer Wall Rapid, so named because it had been formed by chunks of cliffs falling off on both sides. I could land and scout it but had better hurry up.

To hell with it! I was so helpless with cold that I didn't even want to get out of the water to look over a rapid. If I got out, I wouldn't have been able to get back in again. All I wanted to do was get to a fire. After all, John must have run the thing. Or at least he had if I hadn't already passed him. So down I went.

I was too cold to really appreciate it at the time, but it was fun. It had a ten-foot drop and some nice big bouncy waves. Just beyond the rapid there was another big bend, and as I glided around I saw another straight stretch of more than a mile. And still no John.

Where was he? Didn't he know I was freezing? Wind rushing up the canyon smacked me in the face and I swore. I was not only cold, now I was getting angry. John wasn't showing any sense getting so far ahead; he should have waited in shallow water or on a mud bank. But maybe he wasn't ahead? Maybe I had passed him near one of the rapids where I was too blinded or too busy to look? Now I didn't know whether to go on to catch up or stop to wait. What if I did stop and he never showed up? Then he would be as baffled as I, not knowing whether I had passed him or stopped short. His best guess would have to be that I had gotten in trouble and was still upstream of him. Then of course he'd have to try the nearly impossible—go up the Colorado. In that event, if I'd already passed him, he would be struggling futilely.

We each had a pistol for signaling in an emergency, but with all the cliffs and echoes such signals would probably be only confusing.

I was really cold by now, desperately so. I had to stop soon simply to survive. I had already traveled four miles downstream from Soap Creek and had been in the water for what seemed like half a day, though it was more like an hour. It was virtually dark, so I resolved to go around the next bend and, if I couldn't see John, to stop anyway and set up my own camp. I was rather glad now we had packed for self sufficiency.

Just at the head of that next bend was another small rapid. I stayed in the center of the river, playing it safe. Then miraculously, there was John over on the left bank just above the rapid waving frantically.

Too late.

I tried to swim over to him. I wanted so much to get out of the water immediately. But the river as always had too much strength. I was dragged over the little rapid, not in the nice deep water but along the shallow edge, bouncing and swearing and barking my shins and thumping my ankles until I finally made a landing just below the rapid. Then I had a long, muddy 75 yards to carry my heavy boxes, one at a time. By the time I made camp I was the wettest, coldest, maddest, tiredest, stiffest, sorest man in Arizona.

I barely had strength to plop down in the lee of the boulders in the little sandy spot John had picked for camp and start giving him hell. But I couldn't get too angry, after all, we were back together again with good reason to celebrate the afternoon, and John did have a satisfactory explanation for going so far. He had been particularly anxious to find a spot out of the wind after last night, and had even gotten out of the water once or twice at likely spots, but none had satisfied him so he had gone on. As a matter of fact, he had arrived at our camp just a few minutes before I came around the bend and hadn't even started the fire.

I never knew what a blessing to mankind fire was till at last we got our bit of flame going. I didn't care if I never moved away from the fire—I was so exhausted that I had no appetite and only wanted to crawl in a warm sleeping bag and sleep. It had been a day of doubts and fears, triumphs, tribulations and exhilarations that neither of us would forget for the rest of our lives. For the moment, contemplation had to take a back seat while we enjoyed the miraculous restorative powers of the hot chicken soup John served up.

Ellen Meloy

Gravity in a Fluid Medium

This essay appears in Raven's Exile, *a poetic and philosophic record of Ellen Meloy and her husband's experiences on and off the Green River and their observations of Desolation Canyon's geological, botanic, and zoological features.*

> For years we lived anyhow with one another in the naked desert, under the indifferent heaven. By day the hot sun fermented us; and we were dizzied by the beating wind. At night we were stained by dew, and shamed into pettiness by the innumerable silences of stars.
>
> —T. E. Lawrence, *The Seven Pillars of Wisdom*

The Mongols, who live on a high grassland plateau on the divide of the great rivers of east Asia and Siberia, take their home to be a mound at the center of the world. The Zuni and other Pueblos square things off, and a square requires edges, over which the world, at least for the Zuni, ends. The Yurok Indians, fishermen of northern California, believe they live under a dome of sky on a disk surrounded by ocean, a relatively small island crossed by the Y of the confluence of Klamath and Trinity Rivers. Physically and cosmologically the Yurok orient themselves by the Klamath River, which reduces directions to two: upstream and downstream. Since the river turns and twists, never running straight, upstream and downstream can indicate all points of the compass. Symmetry comes from the river, not cardinal points.

Yurok geography best describes Desolation Canyon. The overturned cauldron circumscribes the Tavaputs Plateau, a heart-shaped table of wrinkled peaks cleaved by the sinuous river as a hot wire cuts through ice. Beyond the plateau, off the disk, we—like the Yurok—are vaguely aware that other humans exist. The sun may set upstream or downstream, depending on the night's camp. Deep inside its stone carapace, the river runs a graceful labyrinth, and surely the weight of its will, if not its silty burden, could shift the tectonic plate beneath it.

From a flying carpet Desolation is revealed in slow motion: Long before the river comes into sight, there is a sense of its cool, muddy refuge from parched, rough-hewn badlands and terraces the color of bleached bones, slumped in the loose collapse of oyster middens. Deep in the cleft the river writes itself—an infinity of facets molded into one meandering tale. It shifts, sifts, sorts, and reshapes its load. It appears to move slowly, if at all, yet it runs at considerable velocity over a sandy bed that offers little resistance. Around sweeping bends it flows not as a flat, uniform sheet but in a helical, corkscrew roll that picks up sediment on the outside of a curve and deposits it as a point bar on the inside. A grain of sand can move an inch, two miles, seventy miles, or, lodged in a bank, nowhere in a hundred years, until its next hop. Channels, braids, sandbars, beaches, and islands form, but they may migrate or change shape from one water level to the next. Deeper inside the Tavaputs Plateau the current quickens, the bends tighten into a series of pools, constrictions, and rapids, the configuration of a steep-gradient, canyon-bound river. The water's rasp over sand, its whisper through smooth stones shaped like moons and turtles' backs, its roar over boulders fallen from rims or flushed into the mainstream from side canyons, these sounds tell you how the river reads the earth's surface, which rock resists, which succumbs.

Lateral canyons tilt green fans of greasewood, rabbit brush, and sage toward a necklace of cottonwoods, cobbles, and sand, then river's edge. The monsoon rains that departed with August left flash flood scars at Tabyago, Wire Fence, Snap Canyon, and other washes, "flood" being a loose term for a slurry of rock, sand, mud, and other solids unleashed by violent cloudbursts. With experience one can read which washes have flashed merely by the color of the river. Spates from Big Canyon erode red sand across the white sand of Moonwater Rapid's beach, turning the river a rich terra-cotta. Rains in the Price River watershed northwest of Desolation release a sludge of Mancos Shale, spilling viscous, blue-gray, cheap diner gravy into the mainstream. We have seen a black river, as well, when rainfall after a fire in the high country flushed ash and charcoal into the river at Coal Creek and Rattlesnake Canyon. This week, beneath a chain of glorious, sunny days, the river color is smoked green glass, dazzling silver where it throws back the sun.

In the upper canyon wildlife biologists lean over a holding crate, open the latches, and release ten sleek river otters that, they hope, will reclaim Desolation—nearly otterless during the past century—for the species. At Stampede Flat rogue watermelon plants grow on the beach, sprouted from seeds spit into the water by boaters then germinated as the river dropped. In Desolation's middle earth mule deer keep pace with hereditary improvements in mountain lions, a pace slower than the sand grain's hop. Bighorn sheep nap in crevices of rock three hundred feet above the river, stand up, bash heads, then lie down to rest again. At Rabbit Valley, beneath a boulder where black widow spiders live, fleets of tiny progeny storm out of egg cases. The season's closing parenthesis, a migrating snowy egret, works a riffle at the mouth of Saleratus Canyon, wiggling its yellow feet underwater, tricking fish into thinking its toes are food. Off the disk ravens tweak the dome to see that we pay attention. At Flat Canyon, above a grove of ghost trees, the vernal equinox sun rose in the east, upstream in Yurok terms. Morning brought a night heron, rarer and shorter in neck than a great blue heron, and an ache in the back of my skull. We float through Desolation on the last trip of the year. Ranger season has come to an end, and when I think of this I wish I were on the Lethe, river of forgetfulness and oblivion.

Flying carpet parked, start at river's edge below Flat Canyon Rapid and walk away from the water through a thatch of knee-high cottonwood seedlings. Pass through a second terrace of older, taller saplings and on to the third terrace, trying not to trip over the ranger, who scribbles his paperwork and repairs an oar sleeve, or the camp stove, wafting a pungent aroma of strong black coffee into the cool morning air. This third gallery of cottonwoods is twenty or more years old, gangly trees about seven inches in diameter at bases scarred by the spring floods that engorged the canyon during the big waters of 1983 and 1984. The trees lean slightly toward the canyon wall, bent upstream by gales. Their lustrous, shimmering leaves throw back the sun in a dazzling dance of green light. Seldom is the air so still that there is no motion of cottonwood leaves. This tree is restless, like the river. To understand the cottonwood is to understand the river.

On the fourth, highest terrace lie the ghosts: an enormous grove of aged cottonwoods strewn over the floodplain like elephant bones. The recumbent boles, some of them five feet across, feel smooth under one's fingertips, shed of their rough plates of deeply furrowed bark, pale and polished silver-gray, intricately grooved by the jaws of beetles. Blackened wood scars the hollow of each fallen tree. The deadfall has opened this end of Flat Canyon's debris fan to the sky save for a half-dozen living monarchs, spared the fire and wing that toppled their ranks. Although some of Desolation's cottonwoods spread their canopies outward in the fashion of live oaks and others swoop thick, gnarled branches to the ground in a Laocoön of branches and exposed roots, the fire survivors, the oldest cottonwoods at Flat Canyon, rise a hundred feet straight up, clear of branches until the last sixty feet.

Narrowleaf cottonwoods grow here but most of Desolation's riparian cottonwoods are *Populous fremontii*, a member of the willow family and one of the Colorado Plateau's most common broadleaf deciduous trees. Fremont cottonwoods thrive in saturated soils, store great quantities of water, and grow at phenomenal rates. Wind knocks them over; drought turns their soft, rainlike rustle to a dry rattle; lightning incinerates them; drops in the water table starve them. Compared to other trees, they don't live long, a hundred or so years, but their prodigious seed crop, borne on silky, cottonlike tufts of trichomes, showers the canyon in white blizzards. Beaver use saplings for homes and food; eagles, ospreys, and harriers perch in leafless snags where the view is unobstructed. Hopi carvers seek cottonwood roots from driftwood on rivers and streams and from these roots they chisel kachina dolls, saving in the doll the tree's heart, turning the soft wood into figures like a toothy-jawed So'yoko, or Black Ogre, or a Mastof Kachina, whose cheeks the carvers paint black with sprays of white dots, the Pleiades on one cheek, the Big Dipper on the other.

Cottonwoods tie their lives to the river with tight, spare threads. All life hinges on an exhalation. Timing is everything. A cottonwood runs its sex life on a swelling river. By the time the spring floods recede, it has ripened and dispersed its future—fragile, tiny seeds a millimeter across, blown through the air with the help of a canyon breeze and its own airy tuft, seeds born with only three weeks, more or less, to live.

Floods bathe the river's edge in fresh silt, leaving a moist alluvial substrate ideal for cottonwoods. Here the seeds germinate and grow quickly, sending young roots into subsurface waters before summer's heat dries the topsoil. Far from the main channel, the ghost grove may be the progeny of a hundred-year flood that stretched wide across the canyon bottom. Looking down from high on the canyon rim, you can see the scars of these old floods. You can also trace the water table along the canyon floor by following the live cottonwood galleries that grow in sweeping stands as if on a subterranean river.

Without Desolation's grand cottonwoods, one's brain would fry for lack of shade and comfort, soil would wash away, creatures whose lives depend on them—flycatchers, warblers, and other birds, as well as the insects they eat—would lose food and cover, the wind its symphony. In the arid West cottonwoods mean wet. In Desolation they rise along the riverbanks like upright veins, a main stem and capillaries, the river itself transformed by solar extravaganza. They grace nearly every camp, soothing each night's dreams or edging sleep with their restless leaves. Downriver their glory wanes. They grow sparingly in Gray Canyon; tamarisk reign in Labyrinth and Stillwater Canyons. Cataract and the Grand Canyon gouge a byzantine storm of rock where few trees can find purchase, and Glen Canyon's cottonwoods disappeared long ago beneath Lake Powell. In this light Desolation's cottonwoods grow like treasures.

Flat Canyon abounds with ghosts. Sometimes they force themselves upon you—the river voices that catch your ear, or the scent of your own history, mapped in hundreds of days on the river, in bone marrow and thrum of blood. Often the ghosts merely hint a past, a faint remnant of an extraordinary event. On either side of the dry wash that cuts through Flat Canyon, seventy yards away from the cutbanks, another phantom forest: hundreds of logs, straight-trunked, branchless trees scattered over the canyon bottom. The fallen trees measure eight to ten inches across, toothpicks compared to the monsters in the burned grove, and they are conifers. Deep grooves whirl around the trunks, an etching of lines riding up from base to tip like contour lines on a topographical map. The ridges of wood between the grooves break off easily, dry and brittle, gray on the outside and rose where light has not bleached them.

Desolation's firs live above the river in altitudes of greater moisture and in crevices so high and steep only winged creatures have touched them. Usually one must climb the canyon walls to reach a Douglas fir, but in some places a few trees sneak below their range. The firs strewn across Flat Canyon did not sneak down; they came from higher country on a flood, an entire forest passing in a heartbeat, rafting atop a wall of water and debris that spread across Flat Canyon. Imagine sitting on a sandstone ledge, rattling turkey bones and sorting through tangled dreams about a raucous obsidian bird with sun on its feathers like boiled rainbows when suddenly 600 cfs of water roars out of the high country in a roiling swath. Here lies another ghost grove, another story, another mystery. By the time we return to the river next year, after a winter's absence, Desolation will have laid in many more.

For thousands of days my life has been ruled by a river, by its flow and the distance it takes us each day, by its speed and volume, its ever-changing light. This morning the river is noisy—the kicking tailwaves of Flat Canyon Rapid—and it is red, not from sediment but from the reflection of salmon-red sandstone walls illuminated by the sun. Raft loaded, we shove off the gravel bar and pinball across the rocky shallows into the current. We float a lean river this time of year, about 1,200 cfs, a volume no longer augmented by the rainy season. Now that Flaming Gorge Dam has become a card-carrying tree hugger, the flow regime upriver from Desolation simulates the stable fall and winter flows of a damless river—about 1,100 to 1,800 cfs. Through November the Bureau of Reclamation will warm the river reach directly below the dam by releasing water drawn from high in the reservoir. Releases from greater depths, standard practice since the sixties, proved too frigid even for the artificial trout fishery below the dam. The flows will remain stable as winter's ice forms along the river. Until spring break-up, Reclamation uses this period of deep winter to store water in the reservoir.

Low water demands caution. The raft floor barely skims over shallow bars like Deviated Septum Riffle, named when an oar blade struck bottom and propelled the shaft like a spear into my nose, painful lesson about the consequences of rowing too deeply. After twenty days a month with oars in the fists, the river's muscle shows itself in our arms and backs and in calluses so thick, winter's respite won't be long enough to soften them. Our hands will be ready to take the oars next spring without blistering. Sun, papery dry air, and swims have mapped themselves on our hides. Tenderness lives in the lines at the corners of my husband's eyes. When I stand against the sandstone, he says, there is no difference between me and the red-gold canyon. I have turned the color of Desolation.

For the week, summer has returned in all respects but one: the strength of the light. While temperatures reach the low eighties, the robust brilliance of the hot season, the desert light that swallows everything, has thinned. A new season sits atop the Tavaputs Plateau, glimpsed when the canyon rims open to high country dressed in a quilt of gold aspens, yellow-brown oaks, bright red maples, and shapely green firs. Inside the river gorge fall slips beneath the warm air, beginning in the cool blackness of cottonwood shadows and sandstone overhangs. The box elders and cottonwoods, which now display only a branch or two of yellow among their emerald leaves, will soon turn. On the banks tamarisk fronds change from smoky green to pale gold. Rabbit brush still blooms yellow torches tipped with a delirium of white moths. On a lower, autumn arc the sun angles into the canyon so sharply its dazzling glare splinters the river's surface into blinding fragments. Above rapids Mark cannot see the runs through the glare and he guides the raft by memory. At this low volume the rapids' tongues narrow, the rocks are meaner, and some passages require threading-the-needle maneuvers and a folding in of oars to avoid smashing them in a maze of exposed boulders.

At the edge of a rincon above Fretwater Falls, we pass the scant remains of an old cottonwood incinerated by lightning a month before. Although most trees survive direct hits, passing the current to the ground, this strike exploded the tree and instantaneously scorched a nearby juniper from green to brown. Ground zero: an island of black carbon, gray ash, and scattered tree bits. When we stopped to investigate the burn, the seared soil still bore enough heat to warm the soles of our river sandals. A cloudburst had followed the strike quickly, dousing the flames before the fire leapt into the dry grasses of the rincon.

Lightning has been called "a river of electricity rushing through a canyon of air." For a split second it dipped into the canyon of stone. Surely the earliest river inhabitants loved and feared Desolation's monsoon lightning. In the desert varnish of a cliff face downriver, they etched a row of hump-backed figures chasing a zigzag line, a motif repeated on the chests of looming anthropomorphs elsewhere in the canyon, whose job it may have been to tease out the lightning from the clouds that brought rain to the corn.

The change in season or the decrease in human traffic, possibly both, bring the big mammals down from the high country. Black bears move frequently along the cutbanks and beaches, leaving tracks distinguished by a faintly pigeon-toed register. Their feet etch the soft mud with delicate whorls of skin punctuated by claw marks. Compared with Montana's *Tyrannosaurus rex*–sized grizzlies, Desolation's ursae are small, young, oxymoronic: desert bears. They are swimmers. We connect river-bound tracks on one bank with a receding trail on the opposite shore, downriver a bit, accounting for the current. Mule deer and coyote travel the river corridor, too, but the elk won't slip off the high peaks until the first heavy snow atop the Tavaputs Plateau. Amid this calligraphy of tracks we do not find the tracks we long to see.

Major Powell's 1869 crew noted river otters along the Green, and they killed them, which is what most river folk did. (In a journal entry written in upper Desolation, Jack Summer droned his meat mantra: "Passed 2 rapids today; killed 2 otter and 4 wild geese; made 34 miles and camped on the east side.") As early as 1899 trapping had decimated otter and beaver populations so severely, the state of Utah controlled further harvest. Where the pressures of the fur trade left off, water pollution and habitat loss took over, and the otter's resilience remained weak despite a century of protection. Between 1978 and 1988 a study revealed only fifty-eight otters in the entire state, twenty-three of them in the Green and Colorado Rivers, country less assaulted by mining, agriculture, and suburbs than the intermontane valleys in northern and central Utah. On the canyon rivers the otter's future looks promising. Using stock from stable otter populations in Nevada and Alaska, state wildlife biologists released nine otters below Flaming Gorge Dam in 1989 and more at downstream points over the following years.

Historically, Green River otters were *Lutra canadensis* subspecies *sonora* or *pacifica*: the taxonomic distinction of *sonora* is still under debate. They are weasels, or mustalids, and this is what they need: food (catfish, carp, frogs, crayfish); foraging areas such as meanders, oxbows, pools, backwaters, and logjams; long reaches of riparian cover for dens and escape; and space for the dispersal of juveniles. They do not need chemical pollutants, to which they are very sensitive. The less human intrusion the better, but let there be lots of beavers. Rather than build their own dens, otters use old dens dug into riverbanks by beavers and muskrats. With their underwater limb caches and other river work, beavers also create habitat for otter food. In Desolation an otter can find these life requirements; here it can eat carp, catfish, and suckers, fish doomed by their slowness to be pinned against the bottom and captured. Swift, agile swimmers like chubs rarely show up in otter diets.

People love otters. Those sparkly eyes, pudgy cheeks, thick Wilford Brimley whiskers, the shiny button nose. That adorable way they hug those frogs against their chests, bite the little frog heads off, crunch those little frog bones. The rubber torpedo swim, the nimble body-toboggan down a slide, the affectionate snuffling chuckles to mates and siblings, the instinct for play and amusement, all this warms the endearment nerve. That is, unless you want their fur, in which case you break the law, try to ignore that little nose, and think this: just another aquatic weasel.

Ten otters were slipped into the waters of upper Desolation this month, released by Utah Division of Wildlife Resources biologists working their otter reintroduction program downstream from Flaming Gorge. Out from their crate nine otters headed downstream. The tenth swam upstream. Who can herd an otter? The plan—not the otter's, obviously—was to release this set for downriver territory. Ultimately the otters will work out the river among themselves. They will pair, breed, and bring back to the canyon one of its natives. Desolation's first ten otters came from Alaskan stock. Not long after they arrived Mark saw one limping about with cactus spines in its paw. On this trip we examine banks for tracks and otter rolls, scenting areas where the creatures emerge from the river and roll on the ground, pushing aside debris and vegetation to make a bowl-shaped depression. We look for noses and whiskers among the bankside willows or sleek backs slipping through the current, signs that the otters are alive, making themselves at home undeterred by prickly desert life.

Is the canyon safe for otters as the river rangers depart for the winter? Otters arrive, peregrine falcons nest, wild black bears visit our heads. Flaming Gorge Dam sports an environmental conscience. Squawfish hold steady, humpback chubs cling by a fin, but razorback suckers and bonytail chubs may slip into oblivion. All season long we removed the most blatant signs of human presence, everything from tires and barrels of illegally disposed agricultural pesticides to boxer shorts and gum wrappers.

Political Desolation, however, is far less manageable. The canyon remains in limbo as a BLM Wilderness Study Area, protected until Congress makes it an official wilderness or drops it from the roster. Opinions differ radically on how large it and adjacent study areas should be, with proposals ranging from zero acres to over a half million. Few other issues polarize westerners like the wilderness issue, little else like the debate over preserving or developing public lands thrusts blood pressures off the charts. As we leave for the season, the Utah wilderness stalemate enters its second decade.

Although livestock munch and oil and gas wells perforate Desolation's peripheries, remote, rugged gorges like this one allow neither easy nor cheap access to range and energy resources. The upper canyon's oil shale deposits lie dormant until markets and technology make extraction more attractive. So far methods for processing oil shale—separating the goop from the shales—range from fracturing the rock with underground nuclear explosions to mining, crushing, and heating, a method that requires three and a half barrels of water for each barrel of oil in country already pushing its water resources beyond their limits.

For now Desolation Canyon remains the domain of river runners and hikers who see the river not as an enemy or tool or "resource" but as a refuge and playground. Regulations control their numbers but not their styles.

A. Henry Savage Landor, an early-twentieth-century explorer, climbed Himalayan peaks without mountaineering gear because he considered paraphernalia "cheating." Powell and his men careened through the Green-Colorado canyons in pseudo–walnut shells. Ken Sleight nudged his passengers into river literacy using little more than army surplus boats, good boots, and a fearsome curiosity. He fed them wienies and beans from a can. The next wave engaged with every fiber but dumped the wienies for freeze-dried apples and cheap Chianti. We listened to haute curmudgeon Edward Abbey, who advised desert pilgrims to "walk, better yet crawl, on hands and knees, over the sandstone and through the thornbush and cactus. When traces of blood begin to mark your trail you'll see something, maybe. Probably not."

A small but visible number of today's open-air hobbyists are a puzzlement. Progeny of an irrevocable marriage between technology and the acquisitive nerve, they bring into this wilderness volleyball sets, solar blenders, battery-powered blow dryers, sauna tents, and cellular telephones that work poorly, if at all, inside the canyon. They use words like *ensorcelled* and pack in enough fluorescent underwear, power animals, and companions to ensure that the canyon's Cenozoic silence won't make them edgy. In chats with river runners I have lauded my oars. "There is nothing quite like a fine set of oars," I will sigh with dorky nostalgia, evoking no response from a commercial boatman packing her raft with a portable hot tub, which she will assemble in camp, heat with a propane tank, and fill with grateful customers. Who can blame them for choosing a relaxing soak over the dementia of sunstroke or a death march through a gauntlet of desolate rock and angry spiders? Not even the wildest places remain immune from the constructs of contemporary travel styles, the careful arrangement of experience, and often the environment, on the traveler's behalf.

Desolation's ultimate fate, however, depends, as it always has, on one measure: water. Water is the canyon's bounty. Water, present or absent, insinuates itself in every fin, bone, and leaf, on every surface and in each crevice. By geographical quirk, perhaps, the Green River through this remote corridor is one of the longest sections of unnailed snake. The free-flowing Yampa River feeds it vital fluids. A cynic would say we should thank neither geography nor the Yampa for the Green's semiwild nature. Instead, we should thank California. The Colorado River watershed brings life to twenty-one million people in seven states and two countries. The majority of consumers lives in southern California and in Arizona's Sun Belt cities. By compacts negotiated early in the Dam Century, the Green River Basin must deliver California's share. Ironically, a sandstone canyon like this, left in its natural state, makes a decent pipeline.

The sun's ferocity lingers only a few hours each day, leaving cool air in its wake and raising heretofore unseen (since April) visitors: goose bumps. After months in loincloths, we wear teddy-bear-pelt jackets on the raft late in the day. At each bend I crane my neck around to memorize cliff against sky, ribs and spines of rock, the shape and sweep of water. My mind must hold these images over the winter. I feel strong enough to row upriver, to go back and start over, but we never do.

The linguistic world of Navajo is split into long things and round things. The shapes and textures of the physical world affect verb stems. In Navajo you need one verb stem for a round thing, a different verb stem for a long thing, other verb stems altogether for a granular thing or something that is bundled up. A single word might also consider the object's direction—is it above you, are you lowering it, or does it fall on its own accord? So often Desolation's riches, real or sensory, flow over me like the riches of this intricate native language. I will never understand them, sort them, make the finest distinctions and nuances, store them in my mind to be brought out properly during winter's exile. It would take several more lifetimes to become literate here; my passage will only carry knowledge like a strong taste on the tongue.

Late in the afternoon we row the raft to shore and tie the bow line to a tamarisk. In a series of muscular hurls followed by squishy, rubber-bag plops, a toad jumps across the sand and disappears under the raft's upturned snout. More often these toads are active at twilight and end up in the raft's shady, damp shelter by morning. We will shove the bow off the beach with an explosion of popcorn *Bufos* around our ankles. On the open beach they are not entirely vulnerable. Several species excrete a nasty fluid that can gag if not temporarily paralyze a coyote that tries to mouth their delectably pudgy bodies. The toads' high-pitched trills—summer's night chorus—have waned along with their sex frenzies. Soon the loner under the bow will enter a prolonged winter retreat.

We leave the raft and hike a tributary mouth where on an earlier trip Mark had placed markers for an aerial survey. He made each marker from two broad strips of plastic crossed in giant X's and anchored to the ground with rebar and rocks. The markers lay at considerable distance from one another—it had taken us several hours of walking to place them—so that four X's set corners and a fifth located the center of a rough rectangle. Seen from the airplane the rectangle helped the photographer frame the shot. The aerial survey was completed; we were to pack the plastic and rebar out of the canyon.

Two mice, male and female, scurry out from under one of the markers—no nest yet, merely *coitus interruptus* as we rudely peeled back their ceiling. Near the marker we also find a round, dimpled object: a golf ball. Desolation's sportsters are using the canyon as a driving range; no wonder they need hot tubs. I assume the limp stance of disbelief, eyes glazed over and staring into space. "Mark, honey," I babble. "We're nerds."

"Rangers are supposed to be nerds." He rolls up the plastic strips and stashes them in his pack.

"No one asks if you play golf or otherwise questions your cool when his raft is wrapped midstream around a boulder, shredding neoprene and spilling coolers, and he needs your help, your ropes, and your come-along to pry it loose."

River runners must assume their own risks in Desolation. If the ranger happens by, he is always willing to help, and people in trouble appreciate Mark's strength. This season, thank the river gods, we haven't assisted a single rescue; everyone has traveled the canyon safely. The last person to die in Desolation was a seventeen-year-old who oversniffed the glue he robbed from an outfitter's raft repair kit, a terrible and bizarre tragedy that overshadows the fact that several thousand people make it through the canyon with nothing worse than a bad sunburn.

We cannot decide about the golf ball. Should we pack it out or leave it for the phantom Fremont Indian scavengers who would then give anything to get their hands on a couple of drivers? "In solitude one finds only what he carries there with him," someone once said. We toss the ball into the sack with the survey markers and haul it back to the raft. The river will always provoke an asceticism in us; it's simply our nature. What the river means is nearly inexplicable, and each person harbors his or her own inexplicable meanings. One can only hope that, as diverse as this canyon's recreationists may be, they will defend Desolation when the time comes to speak up for wild places.

We pull into camp early. The days shorten; the light fades before we can finish our gypsy chores. In the soft dusk, two beavers swim to shore and feed along the bank. Their wet fur dries quickly, spiking outward, doubling their body size. The turbid Green loads their pelts with sand, and sandy pelts have less market value. This pair would make hats and coats so heavy, your neck would crack and shoulders implode, knuckles would drag the ground. The beavers never leave one another's side, they snuffle and cuddle like two electrocuted bowling balls. Beaver swim in one another's "arms," rub noses, and munch the same twig, rolling it like an ear of corn. Their affection incites ear nuzzling and fat-puppy noises among all beings within a mile radius.

As we slip into our bags atop the ground cloth, Mark wonders if we should have set up the tent. The odds for rain appear to be fifty-fifty. Half the sky is clear, with a slice of waxing moon and stars; half is obscured by a bank of clouds. Simultaneously the tiny moon glows, a shooting star streaks across the blackness, and a jagged stroke of lightning flashes above the rims. One hell of a raven tweak on the big dome.

Ann Zwinger

Badger Creek and Running Rapids

Down Canyon *is a meticulous record of naturalist Zwinger's observations on the length of the Grand Canyon during all four seasons. This excerpt is set in the summer months.*

Summer is irrevocably connected in my mind with running rapids. Every river trip must negotiate around sixty of them between Lees Ferry and Diamond Creek. I do not particularly enjoy running rapids in 45°F water and 20°F air. Ideally rapids should be not a matter of survival on the cusp but a welcome wetting down on a hundred-degree day. Rapids should be a glorious orgy of splash and spray, splinters of shattered sunlight, brilliant turquoise shadows, screens of white lacy foam edged with rainbows, an entrance into a glittering, sparkling world, tilted off the horizontal and incandescent with light.

The rapids begin at Badger Creek. Once upon a time, at Mile 7.8, slabs peeled off the deep beige of the weathered Coconino Sandstone cliff like a paint scraper skins off paint, leaving an ivory scar pointing to one of the joys of summer and the unwary river passenger's first baptism, Badger Creek Rapid. Ellsworth Kolb's description of a rapid says it all. A youngster from Pennsylvania, he came west and discovered the Grand Canyon, decided to make a profession of running and photographing the Colorado River, and persuaded his younger brother, Emery, to join him. The brothers left Green

---

River, Wyoming, on September 8, 1911, and reached Needles, California, on January 18 the following year, having made the first moving pictures of the Colorado River in the Grand Canyon.

It may be small comfort to the first-time passenger that Badger, named because Jacob Hamblin shot a badger there, has confounded as well as terrified many passengers. Claude Birdseye, the U.S. Geological Survey engineer who led the 1923 expedition, wrote on seeing Badger that "the water looked forbiddingly rough," and their first boat knocked a hole in its bottom from striking one of Badger's boulders. On a trip in 1934 with outfitter Bus Hatch, Clyde Eddy, who didn't like rapids much at all, was "so frightened he got down in the bottom [of the boat] just like a wet hound." But in 1937 Buzz Holmstrom figured out how to run it beautifully, despite feeling "kind of blue this morning when I got up, but after breakfast felt much better. I kept looking at the rapid and thought I saw a way to run it." The classic run is still Holmstrom's, to "drop over the top on the right side of the main channel, which runs square into the rock below, and the suction below the rock sort of pulls the boat to the right so as to miss the rock. It worked fine."

When approaching Badger, one sees only a smooth, innocent line of river surface behind which an occasional gobbet of white water flies up and falls back, inexplicable handfuls of spray, flung as provocatively as the lacy garments ladies of the theater used to toss out from behind dressing room screens. The momentary calm in the pool above Badger, a quiet current running between 1 and 3 miles per hour, is deceptive, especially compared to the 4 to 6 mph the river generally runs in straight reaches. Not until the current accelerates and plunges the boat into the tongue is the roar and bombast of the rapid manifest.

In a configuration common throughout the canyon, the V-shaped tongue, a slick rolling chute, constricted and shaped by strong lateral waves, points to a path of no return. An unexpectedly crisp breeze smacks you in the face and then the rapid breaks loose—there is little to compare with that first frightening look into the maw of chaos and the river's careless and hypnotic power. Even at low-flow velocities, the speed of the current can increase more than ten times and may jump to as much as 20 mph in the rapid itself, creating turbulence that charges the water with so much air that it froths like beaten egg whites, a meringue gone wild.

The drop of fifteen feet at Badger takes place in a sixth of a mile, making it one of the steeper rapids in the canyon. Grand Canyon rapids have their own rating system from one to ten, and every good river guidebook also notes each rapid's difficulty at various levels of water. Larry Stevens's excellent river guide, *The Colorado River in Grand Canyon*, rates Badger's fifteen-foot drop as 8-7-6-5, the four numbers denoting difficulty at water levels of very low, low, medium, and high, warning that at lower water levels it becomes much more difficult.

From being a well-behaved, sensibly horizontal vehicle, the boat bounds and bucks and plunges into an incoherent mass of splashing, fuming chaos, where it's every wave for itself. The flow does not increase linearly but bunches in "hydraulic jumps," manifested in big haystack waves—standing waves that remain perpendicular to the current, spewing foam off their crests. Then the haystacks lessen to undulating rolling waves that finally peter out from the twin frictions of air and river bottom. The river returns to its usual swirling flow as if nothing had ever happened.

At the foot of the rapid the wrinkled ridge of an eddy line, interrupted by boils and small whirlpools, divides the upstream flow of the eddy from the downstream flow of the river. Where the bore of fast water from the rapid emerges and encounters the slower water along the edge of the river, a sheer line forms that sets the slower water spinning in the opposite direction: eddy flow is firmly upstream, and the only way to exit it is to row vigorously in that direction. Eddies usually form at the foot of rapids, but they may also form wherever the channel bends or obstacles interrupt or deflect the current. When a motor raft crosses an eddy line, the propeller's sound changes as different underwater currents give it different messages. Water within an eddy generally flows slowly, around a foot per second, not fast enough to hold sand and silt in suspension so they settle out and form sandbar beaches.

The boat rotates around into the eddy to wait for following boats. I look back at waves galloping upstream, peaking into great larruping pyramids of water, mantling menacing holes into which they break. Wind carries the roar away and without the rapid's fist-shaking fury, following boats seem to hover tranquilly, removed from the slam-and-spray reality, a slow-motion silent movie of a river ballet, graceful and lyrical.

To someone who has not run a rapid before and questions the need to do so at all, the lure of this charging volume of water pointing toward your very own vulnerable, frangible body is difficult to explain. For some it is the challenge to "beat the river." Those who row have the intellectual and physical challenge of coordinating head and hand and doing something difficult well, *very* well, even with grace and precision. For others rapids give an edge to living, a baptism that blesses with a reminder of mortality. Still others need the willingness to risk, to push the limits one more time, to cherish the sense of monumental natural power into which one must fit in order to survive. Once is enough for many, and forever not enough for some.

Rapids on the Colorado River account for a scant tenth of the river's length but for half its drop in elevation. Through its total fall of some nineteen hundred feet within the Grand Canyon, it drops an average eight feet per mile, about twenty-five times that of the Mississippi. Half that drop occurs in 160 rapids spaced an average 1.6 miles apart.

The influx of debris brought in by Badger Creek and washed slightly downstream of its mouth formed Badger Rapid, a process characteristic of all but a couple Grand Canyon rapids. Debris flows, shooting down steep side canyons, are responsible for 54 of the 57 major rapids in the Grand Canyon. The ability of small side canyons to contribute to the river anything from gravel fans and cobbles to tool-shed-sized boulders derives from the steepness of their gradients, which follow fault lines and fracture zones in the cliffs. The side canyons affect the river out of all proportion to their size through debris flows that combine high density with high velocity. The size of rock a flow can move is directly proportional to the square of the velocity of the water—that is, if the stream's velocity quadruples as debris flows have been known to do, the size of the rock it can carry multiplies a whopping sixteen-fold.

Badger initially formed in a relatively open channel. A debris flow cascaded down the side canyon and may have completely dammed the river or, more likely, shoved the river against the opposite bank. The river usually overtops or breaches an obstruction fairly quickly, leaving a narrow channel through which the river surges. Over time a rapid usually achieves some stability in the relationship of its width to that of the normal river channel, expressed as the "constriction ratio." The Colorado River has molded its rapids with remarkable constancy, to a surprisingly uniform ratio of 2:1, indicating that the regular channel has twice the width of the constrained channel in a rapid.

John Wesley Powell ran cumbersome, round-bottomed wooden boats with two rowers facing upstream, a man on the tiller, and the fourth man shouting instructions, hardly a comforting arrangement for oarsmen rowing as hard as they could into a disaster they could not see. Brown and Stanton used oarsmen in the same manner on the railroad survey. Both made laborious portages and suffered unnerving upsets.

The change in the way rapids were run and the kind of boats used came in late summer of 1896, when a trapper from California named George Flavell, inspired by an article Stanton wrote for *Scribner's* in 1890, decided to run the river from Green River, Wyoming, to Yuma, Arizona. Arriving in Green River with Rámon Montéz, a shadowy figure about whom little is known, in eight days Flavell built himself a flat-bottomed boat, fifteen and a half feet long, with a square stern, a narrow prow, and a double-thick planked bottom, which he christened *Panthon*. They started down the river on August

17, "First, for the adventure; second, to see what so few people have seen; third, to hunt and trap; fourth, to examine the perpendicular walls of rock for gold."

Flavell's technique was to face the bow, which he pointed downstream, and to stand up so he could see better, pushing through with his oars. By the time he and Montéz reached Lees Ferry in early October, Montéz, tired of sitting behind Flavell and getting soaked, announced he was leaving. Flavell's often-quoted and perhaps apocryphal reaction was, "You can come along with me or you can float down dead." At any rate, Montéz went. They portaged Soap Creek Rapid, which turned out to be "a little more exercise than we were used to," but otherwise ran every rapid in the Grand Canyon proper, without upsets or irrevocable damage, a remarkable accomplishment in a single boat.

That same winter of 1896–97 Nathaniel Galloway with another trapper from Utah ran the Colorado River from Green River, Wyoming, through the Grand Canyon to Needles, California, the common takeout for early river trips. With more than a dozen white-water trips under his oars before this run, Galloway also realized the futility of handling a large boat with a single oarsman or trying to build a boat strong enough to endure battering. He too designed a slender boat for speed and lightness, shallow and narrow with a definite rake at bow and stern, about the size of the modern dory, with watertight compartments bracketing an open cockpit. In rowing rapids, Galloway swiveled the boat to make the stern face forward into the white water as rowers do today, giving him not only better vision but also the ability to pull back from danger, since control in a rapid depends on going either faster or slower than the current.

Reportedly, Flavell met Galloway when he arrived at Needles in February 1897. Both had gone down the Green and Colorado Rivers ostensibly to trap furs. Galloway netted $600, which he did not consider worth his time, perhaps the last serious fur-trapping trip in the canyon. Flavell's name does not appear again on the river (he died four years later), but Galloway's does. In January 1898 he was working at Robert Stanton's placer mines in Glen Canyon. Stanton's gold-dredging operations were partially bank-rolled by industrialist Julius Stone. Stone, checking out his investment, met Galloway, judged him ingenious at fixing anything, "so dexterous that one would not be surprised to see him run a boat on a heavy dew." In 1909 they launched a trip together, only the sixth trip of the canyon's whole length, and Galloway became the first man to make two trips the whole length of the canyon—Powell's second trip ended at Kanab Creek.

At Soap Creek, where Mr. Hamblin's raccoon turned to soap when he tried to soak it overnight, and the only rapid that Flavell and Montéz did not run, the brothers Kolb looked long and hard at the rapid with the practical and jaundiced eyes of someone about to run it in a chilly October, in wooden boats without support. They knew that their predecessors, Stone and Galloway, in October two years earlier, had chosen to line Soap Creek Rapid, that is, to let the boat down by standing on the bank and jockeying it through the rapid, holding on to painter and stern lines. Nevertheless, the Kolbs ran Soap Creek, without mishap.

Hum Woolley chose to line Soap Creek in 1903 on the fifth trip of the river. Next to the trip of Bessie and Clyde Hyde, historian David Lavender finds Woolley's trip one of the most enigmatic. A certain Madame Schell, a widow living in Los Angeles, hired Woolley to do the legally required improvements to maintain mining claims she owned near the Grand Canyon. Rather than sensibly setting out overland, Woolley built a boat in Mrs. Schell's back yard, disassembled it, shipped it to Flagstaff, and reassembled it at Lees Ferry in August 1903. As helpers, he hired his two cousins, who obviously didn't know what they were getting into and spent most of the trip clinging to the decks in abject terror as they sluiced through rapids. On September 4 cousin Arthur Sanger wrote with desperate gratitude, "Thank God we are still alive, it is impossible to describe what we went through today."

Woolley made it through the canyon and got around to visiting Mrs. Schell's claims, then vanished into the nowhere whence he came, leaving the question of who on earth such a skilled boat designer and oarsman really was.

House Rock Rapid at Mile 17 takes its name from House Rock Valley. Father Escalante, approaching the river from the northwest on his reconnaissance of the Southwest in 1776, noted "the gorges and large rocks of the river basin which, seen from the western side, seem like a long chain of houses." Recently bighorn sheep have been brought into the valley, and one June morning, sixteen sheep, two lambs in a flock of females and young males, came down to water as the raft wallowed past.

House Rock is a ten-foot drop, caused by rocks brought down Rider Canyon. The river sweeps into a V, picks up speed, lathers into a white froth—except that "froth" is too dainty a word for the thick foaming maelstroms that churn off the left wall. Water in the huge hole in the middle of the rapid glints emerald green in the sunshine, icy teal blue in the shadows. In big rafts you can be as much as five feet above the water and the splash often depends upon the boatman's fancy. Not so in a dory. When you sit in a dory, the waves in House Rock are eye-level, in-your-face affrontive. Sitting high on the back hatch of a dory, I look down into a hole that transmogrifies into a huge obese wave and buries my present, my past, and my future being. I come up sputtering and drenched to the ribs. Water fills the dory up to the gunwales.

"Bail!" I never realized the urgency of that clarion call until I calculated the weight of the amount of water I heaved out in a calibrated five-gallon bailing bucket. A pint being a pound the world around, I figure I threw at least three hundred pounds over the side. Add roughly the same amount in the other bilge, and you're rowing a baby hippopotamus. On the plus side, the effort of bailing significantly warms up a body recently immersed in 46°F water.

Running rapids in a dory or a small oar-driven raft (both are sixteen to eighteen feet long) fosters a very intimate association with the river. In the 1920s the Norwegian Torkel Kaahus modified the Mississippi River "sweep scow," then used to barge up and down the Salmon River. He canted bow and stern upward, leaving less hull surface to interface with the water so it was easier to rotate, elongated the square stern into a point to cut through waves better, and used it on the McKenzie River in Oregon. Martin Litton and P. T. Reilly saw in the McKenzie boats the potential for Colorado River navigation and worked with boat builders to design and construct a boat sixteen feet long, with airtight compartments and oarlocks set at the widest part of the boat to get maximum leverage on the nine-foot oars, essentially today's dory.

At Mile 75, less than two miles above Hance Rapid, shale cliffs backing the beach radiate back the afternoon heat. Shade is virtually nonexistent on this June afternoon rapidly approaching the far edge of insufferable.

The guides huddle: to stay or not to stay, that is the question. The river runs just under 5,000 cfs and is falling, uncomfortably low to run Hance in the big thirty-seven-foot rafts of this trip. If we get there and cannot run, the campground at Hance has less shade than here and, according to the boatmen, is two hundred degrees hotter.

I believe them. If I don't believe them I don't believe anything. Experienced Grand Canyon boatmen and boatwomen are the best in the world, bar none. They deal with a fluctuating river whose fickle flow alters how rapids are fun from hour to hour. They know how each rapid runs at each flow, and what river mile they've reached at any given moment. They explain the complexity and use of "the unit" with such panache that even the most prudish of Victorian ladies would not take umbrage. They are born performers, shills for the preservation of the canyon, talented teachers intriguing even the geologically impaired with complex ideas and practical identifications. They are responsible for the lives of those in their boats, bonded by necessity to people they have never seen before and may not see again. Many are fabulous cooks—for ten, twenty, thirty, forty people. Every morning. Every night. From scratch.

They inflate and rig boats, lug massive amounts of gear, load and lash, unlash and unload, de-rig (one boatman compares manhandling a deflated raft to hauling a dead elephant), pack up, and drive back to Lees Ferry to do it all over again next week. They are a sister- and brotherhood who greet each other lavishly, loan each other a pound of coffee, share a six-pack, trade recipes, describe hair-raising rides through rapids with extravagant gestures, commiserate over each other's hangovers, flaunt senses of humor that ought to be bottled and sold. Inveterate gossips, they know where everyone else is and with whom, this happy few, this band of brothers (and sisters) whose Saint Crispin's Eve is just above Crystal or Lava Falls. As boatman-historian Scott Thybony writes, on dry land Colorado River boatmen wake up at night "listening for a sound that isn't there."

And they very patiently answer questions like, "Does the moon affect the tides in the Grand Canyon?"

After an hour of debate, looking at the river, looking at the sun, looking at the sand, the guides decide to stay here and run Hance on the rising water of morning. I dump my gear and go wandering.

Across a sandstone ledge mysteriously inscribed perfect circles the size of small manhole covers appear, outlined as precisely as if scribed by a compass. The crossbedded sandstone here at river's edge belongs to the uppermost member of the Hakatai Shale Formation, one of the four sedimentary formations of the Grand Canyon Supergroup. The Supergroup remains exposed until the Upper Granite Gorge some three miles downstream, outcropping elsewhere only as faulting wrenches it to the surface.

In the middle of a sandy path through the tamarisk, a tiny Grand Canyon rattlesnake has wound itself into a serene resting coil just four inches across. A resting coil is a flat spiral like a cinnamon roll, with the head at rest on the outer edge, very different from an aggressive striking coil, with the tail spread to serve as a stable base from which to launch a strike. Wavering dark gray lozenges pattern a back webbed with white, markings not yet clearly defined. The markings of an adult Grand Canyon rattlesnake are distinctive: discrete oval rings crosswise on a rosy pink ground, a background color that blends into the sandy soil eked out of reddish sandstones and shales. The little sleeper awakens and flicks out a threadlike forked tongue, two conjoined cylinders that diverge into a pair of distinct, delicate, and sensitive tips that sample the air and pick up odor particles. Slowly it unwinds itself to its full thirteen inches, its body not as big in diameter as my index finger. Its first retained rattle, only a button, gives a brave bumblebee buzz. The quiver probably developed to lure an enemy to focus on its tail rather than its head;

the rattle developed later, a heart-stopper that several nonvenomous snakes and burrowing owls are able to imitate with stunning effect.

Although rattlesnakes are usually thought of as inhabitants of dry, rocky places, the canyon rattler, *Crotalus viridis abyssus,* often occurs in riparian habitats within feet of water and dens in tamarisk thickets. Two rattlesnakes commonly prowl the canyon, speckled and Grand Canyon; the latter, endemic and more abundant, developed in the riverside "island habitat."

The population of both snakes appears to have increased since construction of the dam, as their food base of small rodents and lizards has burgeoned. Although night hunters, every one I've seen has been out during the day, albeit resting in the shade and not actively hunting. The rattler's success in the desert depends upon the two common adaptations to heat and desiccation: avoid or tolerate. Tracking prey by heat sensing, ground vibration, and smell enables them to be active at night, to avoid high temperatures, and to conserve body water. When prey is sparse they can fast for long periods, sustained by a low metabolic rate. Within the hour I meet a second rattler, two more than I usually see on a trip. It also snoozes, its broken diamond-shaped spots matching it to the webbed shadows of a silt-coated slab at river's edge. It unloops to a couple of feet in length and glides beneath a damp rock.

The next morning, Hance's ill-tempered grumble precedes it upstream. White streaks and a big burnt orange patch of Hakatai Shale color the left slope above the rapid at Mile 76.5. Some layers of the Hakatai (the Havasupai name for the Colorado River) contain brilliant purples and reds and startling patches of brilliant orange hornfels from the oxidation of iron-bearing minerals. When molten volcanic rock pushed into the shale, heat and pressure metamorphosed it to this vibrant color, which, where it outcrops, lights a canyon wall with hot coals. When polished by the rain it gleams like the elegant black and cinnabar red of Japanese lacquerware.

Hance was not always a rocky road to disaster. Once Red Canyon debouched into a narrow lake backed up behind a lava dam over a hundred miles downstream. Today the lake is long gone and debris flows now shoot down Red Canyon on the left and freight boulders of resistant diabase and Shinumo Quartzite directly into the water where their adamant hardness gives little away to the river. Hance has a thirty-foot drop in half a mile, the biggest drop in the Grand Canyon, and the black boulders make Hance look like the field where Cadmus sowed the dragon's teeth.

Across the river a wall of Hakatai displays the classic geology book illustration of a dike and a sill. Intrusions of molten rock create "dikes" when they wedge in along fractures and crosscut other rocks, and "sills" when they intrude along preexisting bedding planes. The dike traces a small diagonal fault up through the fine-grained sandstone layers of the Hakatai, then thins into a sill as it insinuates between the Hakatai and the overlying Shinumo Quartzite. Whereas the shale crumbles and the river handily carries it away, the lava intrusion has kept its integrity and stands in sharp relief.

High on the cliff ahead, tailings drizzle down the slope from John Hance's asbestos mine. When the great curtain with "ASBESTOS" emblazoned on it thudded down on the stage of a London music hall in the late nineteenth century, the asbestos likely came from Hance's mine—fire-resistant, asbestos theater curtains were much in demand in a time of open flame footlights. Asbestos is the common name for one of the serpentine group of minerals that occur in nature as green to yellow, silky smooth, more or less flexible fibers. Most asbestos fibers are short, slippery, difficult to spin and weave; only those a third of an inch or longer are suitable for weaving, and these are usually combined with a rough cotton for ease of handling. The fibers from Hance's mine were coveted for their three- to four-inch length. Ore ferried across the river was packed out by mule to the South Rim, shipped to San Diego, and thence carried around Cape Horn to London.

One in the long string of characters associated with the river, Captain "Honest John" Hance (his title presumably from the Civil War) first saw the canyon in 1883 while working at a ranch on the South Rim. In 1884 he improved an old Indian trail to the foot of the canyon. Although a prospector, he suspected that there might be more money in guiding tourists than in mining. As the "Münchhausen of the West," Hance enchanted guests with tall stories, vowing he once snowshoed across the top of the canyon when it was filled with clouds. Another time he claimed he couldn't save from starving the man whose new rubber-soled shoes kept him bouncing up and down in the canyon. As one euphoric guest wrote, after finding the Grand Canyon much grander and more sublime than Yosemite, Yellowstone, and Mont Blanc, "God bless our friend John Hance!"

The Hance Trail, until the Bright Angel Trail opened to the public in the 1920s, gave the only decent access to the river and boats some notable "firsts." The first woman to hike into the canyon, Emma Burbank Ayer (after whom Ayers Point is named), came down the Hance Trail in May 1885, a year after it was finished. C. Hart Merriam used this trail when he camped in the canyon, working out his theory of life zones. S. B. Jones, a park ranger, saw an eagle splashing in a pool at the top of the Red-wall and wrote that "this is the first definite record that we have of our National Bird in Grand Canyon." When the Birdseye Expedition was resupplied here in 1923, head boatman Emery Kolb took advantage of the supply train to bring his daughter Edith down. The river was so low that pack mules had to carry supplies to the foot of the rapid so boats could be run empty. When Emery let Edith ride on one of the unloaded boats, she became the first woman to run a major rapid in the Grand Canyon. Colonel Birdseye, horrified by the hair-raising run, disallowed any more women on *any* of the expedition's boats.

Flavell and Montéz were debating whether to run or to line Hance Rapid when three tourists came down the Hance Trail and said they wanted to see some action. Flavell's vanity got the best of him. In transit he broke and lost oars, tore out oarlocks, wedged in the boulders twice, and went down "sideways, endways, and every way," but he remained upright, thus being the first to run Hance.

The entrance of the rapid is forced far to the right. There is no neat tongue, no neat tail-wave train, no neat eddies, no neat run-out. There's no good cushion of water and not much margin for error, and the crack of a snapped oar signals that you're in the wrong place at the wrong time but it's too late now. George Bradley, with Powell in 1869, thought it "the worst rapid we have found today and the longest we have seen on the Colorado. The rocks are seen nearly all over it for half a mile or more—indeed the river runs through a vast pile of rocks." True. For Ellsworth Kolb it was the measure of a "nasty" rapid:

> While reading over our notes one evening we were amused to find that we had catalogued different rapids with an equal amount of fall as "good," "bad," or "nasty," the difference depending nearly altogether on the rocks in the rapids. The "good rapids" were nothing but a descent of "big water," with great waves . . . the "bad rapids" contained rocks, and twisting channels, but with half a chance of getting through. A nasty rapid was filled with rocks, many of them so concealed in the foam that it was often next to impossible to tell if rocks were there or not, and in which there was little chance of running through without smashing a boat. The Hance Rapid was such a one.

True again. Running Hance is like going down a river-sized pinball machine. The difference is that rocks don't go "ding" when they're hit but broadcast "blang" when a propeller contacts an underwater chunk of basalt, or emit a rich, ripping sound when a raft pontoon is sliced open by a can-opener edge, or crackle sharply when a dory's wooden hull confronts a boulder and loses. Some very good boatmen have gotten hung up in Hance and remember the occasion with no joy.

To look back up from the bottom is to wonder how anything larger than a toy duck can bob through. Most rapids can be and are run in less than a minute and a half. Hance takes almost three.

As in three lifetimes.

Colin Fletcher

Big Drop

Fletcher's "Big Drop" occurs in Cataract Canyon between October 3 and 5, 1989, and between miles 735 and 756 of a solo journey along more than 1,700 miles of the Colorado River from the Wind River Mountains of Wyoming to the Gulf of California. The entire trip, undertaken when Fletcher was sixty years old, took six months.

By mid-morning next day, even before I floated out from between Stillwater's sheltering walls, a south wind ruled the river. And as soon as I debouched onto the open water of the Confluence I felt thankful that, because it was only five miles from camp to Cataract's first rapid, I'd already battened down the raft into whitewater mode.

Out on the open water—much more open, suddenly, than I'd expected—the wind whipped upriver unimpeded. It brawled with swirling currents, whisked racing whitecaps. It sired sandstorms from sandbars and sent them billowing across the river. I found us being twirled like a toy. Even muscular oar work buffered the vagaries of wind and current only enough to keep us moving in more or less the right direction, and when I shipped the oars and took a few shots with my simple Olympus camera, we drifted almost aimlessly. Generally upriver, though. So back to battling with the oars.

Almost before I knew it, we were past the Confluence and heading down the Colorado. Down a river twice as big and powerful as the Green; maybe three times. A river still divided, right and left—in that piquant switch of name burdens—between murky Green and green Colorado. Before long,

---

From *River* by Colin Fletcher (New York: Alfred A. Knopf, Inc., 1997).

though, the murk triumphed, right bank clear across to left. It was excruciatingly difficult to believe that somewhere in that turbid expanse twirled even one molecule from my little source basin.

The river and I flowed on southward, toward the sea. But the river had notched up to a new stage of maturity. The Confluence had changed it—the way a dark experience can, overnight, render an apparently mature person mature in some deeper sense.

If anything, the wind had now intensified. Whitecapped waves. Surging gray currents. I battled the oars. To encourage myself I mouthed out loud, into the teeth of the gale, "Oh well, anything for a change, I guess."

Soon, on the right bank, a huge red-edged wooden sign:

DANGER
CATARACT CANYON
HAZARDOUS RAPIDS 2½ MI
PERMIT REQUIRED FROM
SUPERINTENDENT CANYONLANDS
NATIONAL PARK FOR BOATING
BELOW SPANISH BOTTOM

High overhead scudded small white clouds tinged with gray. Their shadows kept shrouding the battlefield in deeper gloom.

I swung us around, began to pull instead of push. Now I sat looking back upriver. But already it was difficult to locate the Confluence: it had blended with the general flow of the canyon walls, had become just another flat in the passing show. I kept pulling, hard. It occurred to me that you'd have difficulty finding a confluence of rivers of this magnitude—in the United States or anywhere else in the developed world—that had remained so free from human impact.

Yet there was no denying that the Confluence had been an anticlimax. I suppose I hadn't given any thought to how it would be when I passed through this place at which my river both ended and continued. This place where the Green died but the river lived on. I rather think I'd expected a mini-pageant, trumpets offstage. Instead, this battle.

The war dragged on all the way to Spanish Bottom. The only respite: when I looked ahead and saw high right, strung along the rim, a cluster of gay, toylike rock pinnacles that I knew spelled "Doll House" and "Land of Standing Rocks." Otherwise I fought wind and current and strove to adjust spirits and techniques to the bigger, more powerful river. A reasonable degree of success. But it was a relief to reach Spanish Bottom, just above the first Cataract rapid, and pull in for lunch.

After lunch I dozed, then sat debating. Should I scout Rapid 1 now, then run it? Or wait until morning, when the wind might have died? The way it was gusting now promised grim whitewater maneuvering. Still, running the first couple of rapids before I camped would be a confidence builder.

For a long time after lunch I sat and ruminated.

I was facing up-canyon and off to my right the wind scourged the river. Until it let up, forget the rapids. And cloud shadows kept plunging the scene into gray gloom. The far bank was a stark line of burnt trees: Dave Stimson, the Canyonlands river ranger, had said the fire was started by a backpacker burning toilet paper. No, if you came to this canyon from almost any other place it might, in its way, seem close to magnificent; but it was not Stillwater.

So, without question now, my peaceful ten-day cruise through Labyrinth and Stillwater was over. It had been an almost achingly perfect time. An idyllic interlude that had built slowly, so that it was all but over before I'd begun to recognize it. That was the way such things tended to happen: they crept up on you. And already the interlude was beginning to radiate a warm, nostalgic, Indian-summer glow.

A gust of wind caught the tethered raft. It bumped against the bank. A mini-avalanche of sand tumbled into the river.

Such a golden interlude could occur in any kind of journey. It might be a physical journey. Down a river, say. Or an individual traveling his life course. Or a civilization unfolding. (Europeans often saw the years just before World War I as such an interlude; Americans were now fingering the 1950s.) Or the journey might be that of a species evolving. Or of life evolving on a planet.

It seemed to me that you could—possibly without stumbling across the twilight zone that separates insight from crap—perceive a certain ancient pageant played out on the East African plateau as just such a halcyon interlude in the evolution of life on this planet. (Halcyon, I mean, if you viewed evolution as a whole: the times may not have looked that way at all to any single species, let alone any individual organism.) For a long and uninterrupted span beginning in the Permian age, just after the dinosaurs had folded their scales and silently crept away, the equatorial East African plateau—already uplifted a mile and more above sea level—was spared two kinds of disasters that often break the flow of evolution: ice-age glaciation and inundation by oceans. The mammals, a previously insignificant evolutionary twig that had just begun to prosper, were thereby given a chance to flourish, uninterrupted. They took it. They branched out; radiated to fill many niches. Eventually they built a rich and complex web across the savannah. Even today, when only tatters of that web remain, glimpses of it can be breathtaking. Human descendants flock from all over the world just to watch.

If we dollied the camera in toward the end of that stable and fruitful span we could view the savannah as the scene of another halcyon pageant of a lower order. (Or higher order; take your pick.) Near the end of that long post-dinosaur interlude—perhaps four million years ago—the mammalian branch sprouted hominids. (Again, of course, I mean "halcyon" from a collective, not individual, perspective: the life of an individual hominid who lived then was, when viewed from where we now think we stand, "nasty, brutish and short.") But if you accept that we began somewhere in the vicinity of Olduvai Gorge and also—though this demands a greater leap of faith—that we are indeed the current spearhead of mammalian evolution, even of planetary life, then it seems reasonable to regard that relatively recent little pageant on the East African plateau as a golden interval for both planetary life and its mammalian branch.

Out in the present, in midriver, I glimpsed a dark blob that might or might not have been a beaver's head. The wind had dropped a little but choppy waves still tended to obscure such matters.

Come to think of it, if we dollied the camera in on that ongoing East African pageant at a time that was virtually the present, and focused our lens down to the next life-system level—to individual organisms—and if we once again zeroed in on the only individual whose life journey I know and shall ever know in its entirety, we might glimpse scenes in what could be called, in hindsight, a halcyon interlude for that organism.

Co-managing a Kenya hotel with my wife turned out to be, as I've said, not my line. Its demands may have hastened the breakdown of our marriage. Anyway, we separated, and eventually divorced. I went into farming, first as pupil-assistant, eventually as a manager. Farming turned out to be the first occupation that really satisfied me for any length of time. Yet after five and a half years in Kenya, I left. (Without, strange as it may seem, having "discovered" the savannah's rich wildlife.)

In later years I had sometimes looked back through rose-tinted nostalgia mists and seen that spell of farming on the East African plateau as—in some ways, though certainly not all—a golden pause in the sun, before I moved on to face new challenges.

I left Kenya for a rainbow of reasons, spread across the human spectrum. But one purpose I recognized and voiced at the time was a wish to "get out and see something of the rest of the world." And when I left Kenya I launched myself into the currents of a much wider river. Even at the time, I think I understood, if not very clearly, the significance of what I was doing.

Four traveling years twirled me on a journey through Southern Rhodesia (now Zimbabwe), Britain, Canada and sundry waypoints—and deposited me in San Francisco, California. That journey changed my life, internally as well as externally. Toward the end of it, in Canada, a friend looked at me and said, "You may not know it, but you're going through a glorious metamorphosis." I had no idea what she was talking about.

In San Francisco I fell in love with the city and a damsel. Two years later, after an almost achingly perfect interlude, several routine quirks of fate left me standing for the first time beside the Colorado. Left me standing at the Mexican border with a pack on my back, facing Oregon. Facing an entirely new and intriguing challenge.

And now here I was, midway through another Colorado journey, at the end of another golden interlude, poised on the brink of Cataract Canyon, with Grand Canyon looming.

I felt myself shiver. Beyond my right shoulder, the sun had sunk behind the canyon wall. Cool gray shadow, reaching out across the Colorado, had enveloped raft and resting place. Had tranquilized the river, too. Gusts now churned it only rarely, and during the interludes between them the water's surface subsided. Subsided to an almost peaceful calm.

I glanced at my wristwatch: 3:53. I stood up.

For a split second I looked away from the rapidly approaching tongue, checked the watch: 5:11. Then my eyes flicked back to where they belonged—out beyond the left oar.

We were almost level, now, with those first small, wide-spaced rocks. Bisecting them perfectly. And gathering speed. At the foot of the tongue, right, I could now see, clear and unmistakable, that ugly boulder-hump with the horrendous hold behind it. We'd clear it all right, just as I'd planned when I scouted down the bank.

With the hump safely identified I push-pulled the oars, fiercely. We pivoted. Now I ferried bow-left, facing the new danger: a series of holes on the tongue's left edge—and below them, a whitecapped cauldron I couldn't yet identify but that I knew lurked in mid-rapid.

A gust of wind caught the raft. I corrected. No problem. Then we were racing past the series of holes, bow in just the right place, a foot or two clear, and I could see the white cauldron ahead. No need to correct. I spun us bow-first. And then the current had carried us past the cauldron and down the center of the rapid's tail—just as Ranger Dave Stimson had said it would and as my long scout down the right bank had seemed to confirm. Then we were out of the white water.

But not for long.

The second rapid was another down-the-tongue job. Or so Dave and my scouting had promised. Approaching the tongue I ferried, compensating for minor wind gusts, until we were headed dead-center into the drop-away; then, at the last moment, I spun us bow-first and pushed like crazy.

Instant bedlam. Walls of surging white water, tainted brown. But everything straightforward. Just a careening rush. Small oar pressures to hold the raft at right angles to each wave, nothing more. The waves were big, though. As big as any we'd taken. But the bulging blue bow rode up and over them, one after the other. At each wave, water showered us with glistening off-white cascades that were cold, very cold; but the little raft held true. No twinge of danger, only exhilaration. Then we were clear, floating level, and I was scanning the right bank for a sheltered campsite, above Rapid 3.

The freeze-dried Mountain Chili matured in its pot. The wine tasted good. The rare gusts of wind passed harmlessly overhead. A few yards below, the river slid into the first white water of Rapid 3.

I looked back toward Rapid 2. Yes, it had been important, getting those first two safely under my belt. With the wind gusting like that I wouldn't have fancied tackling anything too demanding, but Rapid 1 had been neither technically difficult nor bum-tingle scary. Just about right. Just enough of a challenge. (It was also called Brown Betty Rapid, after the cook boat of the ill-fated Brown-Stanton expedition that exactly a century earlier had surveyed a possible river route for a railroad through both Cataract and Grand Canyons; but *Brown Betty* was in fact lost about four miles downstream.)

Afterward, Rapid 2 had been fun. And the big waves had renewed my confidence in the raft.

Another sip of wine.

The river had in a sense reassumed its old identity as an overgrown trout stream. Only in one sense, though. In the rapids, things hadn't felt all that much bigger than in the Green; but there was no doubt, really, about the river's new maturity, its new power. I'd have to treat it with even greater respect. Would have to pay attention.

I tilt-slithered a helping of chili from pot into metal cup.

"Paying attention" meant doing what Les Bechdel had recommended in his *River Rescue* book: thinking carefully about "What if?" Above all, "What if I flip?" I knew the rules: getting back to the raft was normally the safest thing, whether it was upside down or not; failing that, get yourself ashore—and hope you can recapture the raft. But I ought to have a contingency plan in case I was separated from the raft. During dinner I decided that starting next morning I'd always travel with a waterproof matchsafe in one shorts pocket and a tiny Swiss Army knife, secured by a cord, in the other, along with a tightly rolled aluminum foil space blanket in a ziplock bag. Also some iodine tablets: I could purify river water in the space blanket. Should have done all this long ago. But better late than never.

I finished dinner, sat watching day dim toward night. Against pale sky, bats swooped and swerved to snare their insect breakfasts. The bats materialized almost every twilight, but until now I hadn't really noticed their extraordinarily abrupt maneuvers. Very different from the swallows' smooth, curvaceous sweeps. Sonar-directed, so the dying light made no difference. But my day-use eyes could hardly follow their dark little side-slipping shapes: they kept flicking into and out of existence. *Twinkle, twinkle, little bat / How I wonder what you're at.*

I looked upriver. Darkness had curtained off Rapid 2. And Rapid 3, just below camp, swamped its sound. But I was conscious, now, that those first two rapids had refreshed my memory about many things, piffling through ponderous.

The one-minute-after-the-hour nonsense, for example. Not until we were actually in the tongue of Rapid 1 had I remembered to check that my watch didn't read 5:01. By then it would have been too late, anyway. At a guess, this foolishness had its roots in my school days. The train that carried us all away at the end of each term, back out into the wide world and to our various homes, was scheduled to leave the local station at 9:01 a.m. So we sometimes used "the 9:01" to signify any ending or departure. For years the metaphor had lain fallow in my mind. But in the last couple of decades, with timepieces gone digital, it had been borne on my consciousness that when I glanced at any watch or clock it seemed to read, on an overwhelmingly unreasonable number of occasions, one minute past the hour. Bedside digital clock-radios, in particular, projected almost echoically vivid messages: their brilliant LED numerals beaconed out of the darkness into the dream-clouded canyons of your mind. Anyway, my clocks and watches had for years now seemed to say, with inordinate frequency, "1:01" or "4:01" or some rhyming cousin. As you know, I'm not superstitious. But I'd come to regard "XX:01" as a potential omen. I'd even offered comic wagers that when I died that's what the clock would read. So back up in Lodore Canyon I'd naturally avoided starting a run down any rapid when my watch proclaimed those ominous figures. Before Cataract's Rapid 1 I'd forgotten to check. Now, though, with memory refreshed, I'd resume sensible precautions. Knowing that the whole thing was a can of paper worms made, of course, no difference at all. (Not long ago, when I explained this drivel to a friend, she exclaimed, "Oh, but I feel the same—except that with me it's been *repeating* numbers. You know, '3:33' or '11:11.'")

The rapids had jolted my memory about serious things, too. Adrenaline tides, for example.

Back in Lodore and Desolation I'd learned that the scary times were the scouts. As you walked down the bank—ears drumming with the rapid's roar, eyes dazzled by glistening foam—or stood on a rock and pondered and repondered route choices, the adrenaline began to flow. As you walked back up to the raft, wondering if your choice was really the right one, flow surged to rush. And when you stood hesitating before you unhitched the bow line, rush built to flood. That was prime farting time.

But once you cast off and got your hands on the oars and began to peer ahead for markers, peace descended. Now, everything narrowed to specifics. To nitty-gritties. Picking up the marker: that small but distinctive camel-humped boulder right of the tongue. Picking it up early enough to let you ferry onto the precise line that would bring your bow past it very, very close indeed: brushing it would be good, but banging might trigger disaster. Feeling bow brush rock. By then, though, your mind was leapfrogging thirty feet downstream to the narrow gut between those monstrous twin rocks—the racing ribbon of water you had to hit dead center, bow-first, raft aligned arrow-straight. All this time your mind was so pinned to the present, so engrossed in doing what it had to do, that there was no time, no room for anything you could clearly call fear. Not even when you found yourself plunging down into the maw of the gut and it was steeper and faster and narrower than you'd expected, or when you hit the first tail wave a touch off kilter and had to correct frantically to line up for the second. You were too centered, too busy, to feel fear. And when you came clear at last into flat water you were smiling, grinning, laughing.

I'd learned all this before I got to Green River, Utah. There, I'd discussed the adrenaline pattern with Karen, the Holiday boatman. "That's right," she said. "I think we all go through the same routine. Terrific. No wonder they call us 'adrenaline junkies.' Seems you never get over it, either. Dee Holiday says that after thirty years at the game he still reacts much the same."

Now my adrenaline seemed destined to flow freely. In the next 10 miles we'd run more than twenty rapids, culminating in Lower Big Drop, alias Holy Shit. (Cataract once had fifty-two rapids, spread over 18½ miles, but Powell Reservoir—a.k.a. Lake Powell—had engulfed its lower half.)

Out on the river, night had taken over. Suddenly weary, I washed up, slid down into my sleeping bag. Far to the south, lightning flashed. I bantered around with what had become one of my standard wilderness gags: it had to be lightning, because if it was the start of World War III those occasional winking lights of commercial jets wouldn't still be creeping across the night sky.

The wind was blowing directly from the storm toward me but the lightning looked a long way off. I did put the big blue tarp ready, though, beside my bed.

That night it rained and I dreamed.

When the rain hit I came half awake and pulled the tarp over me and lifted it clear of the sleeping bag by draping it over half-empty dry bags and tucking its edges under them. But all night, every time I felt the wind blow, I came one-third awake and worried about the perfunctoriness of the tucking, and periodically did something about it. In between the caretaking, I dreamed. Dreamed dreams that were as idiotic as most dreams but more menacing and more unremitting. Or so it seemed. Anyway, I suffered one of my rare disturbed nights and woke still halfway weary.

Yet the morning went well.

The wind had died. Most of the rapids turned out to be simple. The rest, no more than interesting. And I felt pleased with the way I ran all but one.

After a long and careful scout of Rapid 5 I knew that the key to avoiding the bad-news obstacles that riddled its foot lay in entering close to but just left of a big submerged rock. Too far left, and I might hit a hole, just below. From above, though, the submerged-rock marker might be difficult to see.

It was. I picked it up late. Very late. Even after a spurt of frenzied ferrying I still passed it too far left and barely had time to straighten up before we hit the hole. We hit it hard, just right of center. The raft spun. I tried to counter. In that swirling white foam, though, the oars flailed. Sudden helplessness; then we were out of the hole—unscathed but spun around. For a moment, the bow faced directly upriver. But now, in less foamy water, the oars worked, and within seconds I'd pivoted us back with the bow pointing downstream again, facing danger, facing the bad news ahead. We rode the rest perfectly. But I remembered that moment when we faced upriver.

It was the only time all morning that I felt I did not have the raft under control.

Above Rapid 10 I landed river left to scout. Dave Stimson had warned of one hole that demanded respect—and this was apparently the rapid that sank the Brown-Stanton party's cook boat. Only later did I learn from Robert Brewster Stanton's book *Down the Colorado* that *Brown Betty* was actually lost during an attempt to line her down the rapid.

Stanton's book sheds light on the problems that pioneers faced:

> When we were going through Cataract [starting June 1], the River was rising, though it had not gotten to its full high water stage, and that year, 1889, the rise did not reach its average height, so that most of the rapids were full of rocks above the water, and their sharp edges played havoc with our thin cedar boats. It was not any individual rapid, but the eighteen and a half miles of continuous, boiling, tumbling waters among the rocks that wore them out, and so severely tried our powers of endurance.

In my noncedar raft (its design forged from a century of post-Stanton river-running), pampered by a river guide (ditto) and by Dave Stimson's advice, I ran Rapid 10 without difficulty. And its two successors.

Next on the agenda, Mile-Long Rapid.

Mile-Long consists of five closely spaced rapids, numbers 13 through 17, that at high water tend to merge. I landed river right, spent over an hour scouting the first four rapids. As I walked back up to the raft I kept running the sequences over in my mind: a succession of current-and-obstacle details that not only had to be precisely recalled in the right order but would also demand split-second translation of images viewed from the bank into images seen from directly upriver.

Above all, there was Rapid 15, with its endearing name of Capsize: a complicated series of moves, including one in which I'd have to pivot at precisely the right moment and pull across a line of white water. I'd pull rather than push in order to achieve enough momentum to carry us across the barrier line. This technique of pulling hard, stern-first, out of the main current into safer water on one flank—usually through side waves—is today known as "Powelling," apparently because it resembles John Wesley's method of barreling down all rapids.

Back at the raft, adrenaline or no, I felt tired. Could the disturbed night be taking its toll? I brewed my standard caffeine response and then, with juices seeping back, sat in the moored raft and for several minutes applied what I call "an Emmett": a relaxation technique known as Selective Awareness—by self-hypnosis out of Transcendental Meditation—perfected by an M.D. I know, Emmett Miller. Before long I felt relaxed, centered, ready.

The whole sequence went like clockwork. Particularly Capsize Rapid. Halfway down, pulling hard, I looked over my shoulder at precisely the right moment and immediately saw my rounded-rock marker on the barrier line of white water. I Powelled through dead on target. The relatively slack water beyond gave me even more time than I'd expected to pivot the bow so that it faced new bankside dangers. Adjust onto planned line. Ferry on down, under absolute control. Let bow brush, exactly as intended, a triangular-rock marker. Then, as I straightened out to run a final tongue down into the clear—even before we entered the tongue, because I knew we would hit it dead center—I laughed and shouted out loud, "Perfect!"

The elation still swirled as I threaded us through the rest of Mile-Long with the confidence of a pro who'd been at it for years.

Now, confidence can slither undetected into overconfidence. And hubris spells danger.

Just before either Rapid 18 or 19—I'm not sure which, because I hadn't bothered to check the guide—the full flow of the river, confined and swift but without white water, swung across at an angle from the right wall to left. In mid-swing it divided on each side of a huge boulder and dropped away in two smooth tongues. I could see the far tongue, left of the boulder, clear down to the place it leveled off into flat water. Without much thought, I chose the shorter route, right of the boulder, and floated languidly toward it—broadside on, bow left, ready to make minor adjustments to avoid any obstacles in the short stretch of it that lay out of my sight. I was almost at the drop-off when I saw, over the raft's right tube, that this tongue did not, like the other, glide serenely down into the flat water. It poured over into a horrendous hole that spanned the tongue's entire width.

No time to pivot, then pull left. So I pushed, frantically, on both oars. The imminent glassy lip of the drop-off and the seething maw below, now all too visible, goaded me on. Inch by inch we began to ease left, toward the big boulder—away from the lip, from the hole. Very slowly, we gained momentum. For a moment I thought we were going to be swept up onto the boulder and jam solid. But then we'd lifted onto the bulge of water above the boulder's sloping base. We hung there, almost motionless. Then we were sliding down into the safety of the far tongue.

Minutes later I pulled ashore above Rapid 20. The adrenaline was ebbing, fast. Suddenly I felt drained.

Dave Stimson had drawn my attention to Rapid 20 but had remained vague. When I asked for specifics, he smiled and said, "The guide rates it '1,' but . . . Well, you'll see." (The river guide rated each rapid on a scale of 1 to 10. Capsize was a 6; Lower Big Drop, 10.) By now I'd learned to appreciate the way Dave metered his advice: enough information to post warnings and plant signposts, not enough to tarnish expectation; plenty of latitude for me to deal with details. For Rapid 20, he'd left me wondering.

My first impression: a confusion of black boulders and white water. No hint of a route. Second impression: ditto.

By now it was nearly three o'clock. Lunch long overdue. I lunched, siestaed. Afterward, though, even wearier. No doubt now: the disturbed night had caught up with me.

I did walk slowly down and scout the rapid. Close up, it looked horrific. Mostly, a confusion of whitewater obstacles. At its foot, a curving drop-off that blocked all except a narrow channel, left. This channel guarded by a large boulder and its god-awful hole.

I dragged myself back up to the raft. I'd meant to camp that night just above Lower Big Drop. But by now I'd grasped that it was stupid and dangerous to run a "bad" rapid when you were operating anything short of peak performance. Besides, by morning light the run might look easier. So I camped where I'd pulled in.

Afternoon eased into evening. After dinner I leaned back against my drybag backrest. The food had injected enough energy for a reassessment.

All along, I'd known that Cataract posed a test. A test that would last little more than a day but would scan my fitness for the month-long run of Grand

Canyon. And ahead, now, lay Cataract's cusp. In the next two miles the river dropped 72 vertical feet—and climaxed in the cusp's cusp: Lower Big Drop. Yet for the moment I felt more nervous about this next rapid.

Briefly, I scouted the lining possibilities. But my heart wasn't in it. I had to *run* this one. If I balked, how could I pretend to be ready for Lower Big Drop, let alone Crystal and Lava Falls in Grand Canyon? (By now, I guess, I'd fully embraced, almost without further thought, the idea that I'd try to run all the river's rapids.)

Dusk deepened. Downriver, the canyon's irregular and crumbly red walls were sinking toward gray. "The attraction of Cataract," Dave Stimson had said, "is the rapids, not the rock."

I closed my eyes. Well, all right, I'd scout Rapid 20 again in the morning. And probably run it.

Close below me, the rapid roared something like defiance. I listened more intently. No, it didn't really roar: this one didn't intimidate with size. It snarled: its threat lay in confusion. But if you failed to sort out the confusion—to dampen the "noise" in its communication sense—and found yourself down at the foot, heading inexorably for that line of holes . . .

I comforted myself with two warring quotes. First, somebody's insight that "life is not a gift but an open-ended loan, liable to be called without notice at fate's whim." Then Nietzsche's edict: "That which doesn't kill you makes you stronger." You had to stomach the Nietzschean machismo and allow the underlying truth. Had to allow that facing physical danger can help raise you up from a condition in which you look out on a bleak world and ask plaintively, "Is this all there is?" Can help lift you back on track and leave you gushing "Oh, what a wonderful life!" Can help you, that is, to achieve just the kind of alchemy that long journeys are—whether you know it or not—often designed to engender.

I reopened my eyes. Downriver, the canyon walls had faded to ghost spaces. Overhead, a star-spangled wedge of night sky.

Now, I'm reasonably accustomed to facing physical dangers. Dangers keen enough to threaten life. And I've always accepted them. But sitting there at the head of Rapid 20 I found myself accepting in a new way. I was aware that the next mile, the next 200 miles, would strain my sketchy rafting capabilities to their limit. Aware that if things went wrong, down at the foot of Rapid 20, for example, and I flipped, out here on my own, with heavy water below, then I might not make it. And I found myself accepting that possibility in a new way. Looking back, I was no longer sure that in the past I'd done so. Not sure I'd faced the reality head-on, eyes open. But this time I felt I did accept. Did so with a certain stoicism. Stoicism of a new kind. I seemed to say to myself, "I've had a good life. And if this is it . . . well, all right."

Night displaced dusk. Down to my right, the rapid snarled on.

Mind you, I wasn't sure I trusted myself. My conversion probably went no more than intellect-deep. If things went wrong I'd fight like hell against extinction. After all, that was how we organisms are constructed. How we have to be constructed.

Next morning, after a good night's sleep, back to the nitty-gritty.

By morning light the run at first looked no easier. But a lengthy scout disclosed a possible way through. When I pushed out into the current, post-Emmett, semi-confidence ruled.

Halfway down the rapid. Ferrying bow right. Still on the chosen line. And the water ahead looking rather less fierce than I'd feared . . . Then we were not on line but being pulled right. Being drawn toward the line of holes across the foot of the rapid. Pull hard, both oars. Pull like mad. At first, no change. Then—painfully slowly—inching back toward the line that meant safety. Moments later we eased in behind and below the big boulder and its god-awful hole. Now ferry in close to the left bank, then spin the bow downriver. Done. We went through the narrow channel dead center, comfortably clear of the line of holes, and slowed into quiet water.

Rapids 21 and 22—Upper and Middle Big Drop, both rated 7—were big water but fairly straightforward. (Though Middle Big Drop at high water is apparently "a terrifying, gigantic river-wide wave that's unavoidable.") No serious problems. As soon as we emerged from Middle Big Drop, I looked ahead. Not far below, the river vanished. Just ended. As if cut off. With a knife.

A respectful distance above the drop-off I pulled ashore, left, tied the raft very securely, and walked down the bank.

Dave Stimson had said, "When you see it, you'll say, 'Holy Shit, am I going through *that*?'" I reached the drop-off, complied.

What I saw, a few feet out from the left bank, was a raging white maelstrom. And I knew my route transected it.

"At higher water you can make a run way over to the right," Dave had said. "You'll see that the river guide says 'scout from the right bank.' But when you're there the river will only be running around four thousand cfs, and you'll have to scout left and run left." He'd gone on to give me more detailed instructions than usual. And now, standing beside the rapid, I read a note he'd written in the guide: "Run is *right* of big mossy rock!" Also a clarification in my handwriting: "Mossy rock is on *left* side of rapid."

I checked. The mossy rock formed the near wall of the maelstrom—which roiled and fumed, white with sustained anger, through a gap or gut between it and two other big boulders. Through a gut perhaps twelve feet wide.

"The trick is to hit it dead center," Dave had said.

If I succeeded, I could now see, there'd be two or three feet to spare on each side. But if I erred either way and hit a boulder while in the grip of that torrent . . .

My eye ran on beyond the gut, across the line of the drop-off, clear to the far bank. A tight, unbroken obstacle course of massive boulders and foaming white water. Unrunnable. Just as Dave had known it would be.

Eye back to the maelstrom. This time, to its approaches. At once, a shock: the maelstrom was not, in itself, the problem. What I had to worry about was getting into it.

So I worried. Worried for more than an hour.

The only way you could enter the maelstrom was down a steeply plunging tongue, so narrow that at first I doubted whether even my little raft could squeeze between the rocks that flanked and formed the tongue. Making it through the gut might be a matter of feet, but at the tongue you measure tolerance in inches. And if you so much as grazed any of those flanking rocks, at the drop-off or in the first few plunging feet, you'd go skitterwise into the gut, wildly out of control. And maybe out of the raft.

I took a deep breath—then realized that the tongue itself was not, after all, the true crux of the problem.

You could not, I saw, float down into it from directly above. A slanting line of small, barely submerged rocks, fringed with white water, guarded the approach like a tank trap. At first that seemed to mean there was no way a raft could reach the tongue. Then I saw that the tongue consumed two bodies of water. One came directly downriver, through the tank-trap rocks. The other angled in below them, from the left. It slanted in smooth and sleek, broken only by one small, white, rumpled flare of foam, no doubt caused by a submerged rock. This flare would persist for a spell, then fade away.

The smoothness was good, up to a point. It would make for easier maneuvering. But its very sleekness posed questions. What line down that smooth, slanting run would take you to the tongue so that when you reached it you were in the right place to pivot left and, throwing your raft upon the waters, plunge down it into the maelstrom? And what about a marker to guide you onto your chosen line and let you hold it?

I spent the next hour chewing at those problems. Making decisions, then unmaking and remaking them.

At first I felt sure about the line that would bring me to the tongue: it ran just to the right—that is, upstream—of the lone white rumple-flare in the smooth approach. For ten or fifteen minutes I hung happily with that decision. Then, belatedly, I enrolled a routine river-runner's aid: I threw a piece of wood into the smooth run, well above the white flare. The stick floated down, exactly as intended, just to the right of the flare. But it dipped over and into the tongue much too far right. A raft approaching on that line would be wrecked on the tongue's far-flank boulders. I launched another stick—on a line that would take it just left of the marker. And this time, when it reached the tongue, it plunged down dead center. Several more trials confirmed this line. I stood considering the import of their message.

If I floated down left of the flare marker, the raft's port tube would hang perilously close to the glassy drop-off. Would there be room for the left oar to help hold us back, dead slow? And also contribute to the small ongoing adjustments I'd have to make? What if . . . ?

All at once I realized I'd been staring intently at rapidly moving water for far too long. My retinas had retained the shifting images, and when I looked at stationary objects they seemed to be moving. To avoid the risk of distorted messages, eyes and brain needed a rest. (I'd been studying the water longer than I may have seemed to suggest. To keep things simple I've reported the launching of only four or five pieces of flotsam. But I had to keep finding new pieces of wood, then throw them out into the river. And not every piece landed where intended. So the trials took time.)

Below the maelstrom, the bank was a staccato jumble of boulders—part of the "block talus cone" that along with its partner on the far bank created the barrier that was Big Drop. Or so the river guide said. I scrambled over the boulders to the foot of the rapid.

Downstream, a bend hid the last two rapids—all that remained of Cataract before the tentacles of Powell Reservoir began to snuff out the living river. Dave Stimson had told me about those last two rapids: "Just big waves, nothing else. And the waves are great for releasing your adrenaline build-up from the Big Drop. Just ride 'em and whoop." But these rapids still lay beyond the bend, out of sight. Besides, although my eyes were now back to normal and I could see clearly enough, anything below Big Drop at that moment hardly seemed real. First things first.

I turned back upriver—back into the roar of the rapid. As the river guide said, "Even the sound of the water is on a different scale: the Big Drop roars a bass to the tenor of the other rapids upstream." I scrambled on. Level with the maelstrom, jammed under a rock, the torn-off lid of an ammo box lay twisted in silent testimony to the river's power.

Beyond the mossy boulder I paused and began trying to imprint the flow of the maelstrom on my mind; then realized that once you were in it there was probably precious little you could do about where you went.

Soon I was back at the entrance tongue, restudying the smooth run that slanted into it—the silk-smooth run with its little white flare of foam that kept fading away. What would happen if that vital marker faded away just when I needed it most? I re-agonized, reached the same conclusion as before: that was just something I had to risk; was part of the package.

Once again I looked out across the whole horrendous rapid. Aside from the maelstrom, it still looked essentially unrunnable.

Checking the guide, I reread a 1960 report that it quoted: "Comparison of photographs taken by E. O. Beaman on the 1871 Powell expedition and the rapid today shows that 10- to 20-foot boulders have been rolled, shifted, and removed from the rapid within the last century." Yes. Time kept eroding this obstacle, the way it did most obstacles, most challenges. If you can wait long enough, things alter, shift, mutate. But mostly you don't have the time. Not the years, let alone the centuries. You're stuck with your day, your hour, your minute; eventually, with your split seconds.

I glanced upstream. For more than a week I'd had the river to myself; but for the first time on the trip—perhaps the first time on any physical journey I'd made—I would have welcomed the sight of someone. Almost anyone.

My eyes swung back to the rapid, to the present, to reality. One last time, I ran through the script I was stuck with.

All easy enough, in theory. Ease down dead slow, paralleling the shoreline, into the start of the smooth run. Just short of the drop-off, angle right, toward the rumple-flare marker. Pray it persisted. Ease forward, still under perfect control, and pass a few inches to its left. Hold clear of the glassy pour-over that would now yawn under the port tube. Reach the tongue. At exactly the proper moment, push with the right oar. Push with the precise force to pivot us directly down the plunging tongue. Plunge straight as an arrow—bisecting to perfection the tongue's flanker rocks with the cascades pouring over them—and hit the maelstrom dead center. Beyond that, probably, back to prayer. Back to invoking Yhprum's Law: "Just sometimes, every damned thing goes right." Once in the maelstrom, though, I'd have to strive to hold us straight—whatever that seemed to mean at any given split second. And through the very maw of the gut it might be wise to lift both oar blades from the water and push both handles as low and far forward as possible so that the oars angled back and up with the blades maybe clear of the mossy boulder and its opposite numbers. Maybe.

Yes, the script was clear enough. I swallowed twice, farted, turned and walked back upriver.

The adrenaline flood peaked at what felt like a record crest. I stepped into the raft, watched the resulting ripples widen out across the smooth river, then sat down in the soft white plastic seat on the black-topped dry box. Check watch: 12:57. I smiled. No problem. Still a lot to do.

First I stowed away in dry boxes everything that might be jolted or washed or ripped loose. Everything. Not just the cameras and food items I'd put away before running other rapids but the binoculars that normally hung around my neck and the water canteen that normally hung in its red canvas holder strapped to the raft frame. I snap-locked both dry boxes and strapped down their lids, then checked the strap securing the dry bags, up in the bow. I slid the toggle on my eyeglass retainer snug against the back of my head, tightened the adjustable strap on my broad-brimmed hat and slipped it under my chin. By the time the housekeeping was done we were long and safely past 1:01.

Then I did my Emmett. During such "trances," time stops. And I don't think I checked my watch when I emerged. But I know I felt extraordinarily relaxed and centered. All but a few leftover crinkles of fear had been smoothed away. I was ready, eager.

I untied the raft, pushed gently out into the current, began to let the script unfold.

We eased down, parallel to the shoreline. We approached the left edge of the drop-off. I was still holding us back without difficulty, and we were moving very slowly. I could see the familiar line of the smooth run now, and I angled us into it. The flaring white marker was there, just where it ought to have been.

Still under perfect control, I let the current ease us forward. The glassy pour-over was already there, beyond the raft's port tube, but we had a bigger margin of error than I'd feared, and enough room for the left oar to play its part in holding us back and making small, vital adjustments to our line of travel. The line still looked good. And the rumple-flare was persisting. We passed a few inches left of it.

Now the tongue was there, just ahead, plunging left, down between its flanker rocks. The angle of plunge looked steeper than before, the flanker rocks more menacing. I suppose the roar must by now have grown louder, but I don't think I noticed it. My eyes monopolized my senses. And my eyes were riveted on the tongue. We inched toward it. I remember feeling elated at the way I still had us under control.

The bow came level with the tongue. Through the oars I could feel the water begin to gather itself. I could still hold us on line, but we were gaining speed. And then the center of the raft, just ahead of me, was moving into position directly above the center of the tongue. I waited another split second, then pushed with the right oar. We pivoted to perfection, down into the tongue. The bow dipped. We began to accelerate. I lifted both oars clear. And then we were plunging as if in free fall and I had a flash-glimpse of the right flanker rocks—bigger and more terrible than ever—and of the Niagaras pouring over them. In the moment of the fall I looked ahead and saw that we were perfectly aligned to bisect the mossy boulder and its opposing cousins. Then we were rocketing into the maelstrom.

All hell let loose. We bounced, bounced again, again, went on bouncing. No sense of air around the raft now, just white foam. Foam that surged and boiled and flung itself in sunlit dervish dances. But this white hell was a heavenly hell, for as we rocketed forward we held line.

The flung foam was all I could see. Or perhaps I caught a glimpse of dark boulders, left and right; I'm not sure. All I knew was that we were holding line, straight as an arrow. I'm not sure I did anything to hold us there. I think it just happened. And then, almost before I'd registered what was happening, before I'd had time to do more than feel the beginnings of exultation, we were through. Through and heading downriver, still arrowlike.

We were clear of Big Drop's last white water before it occurred to me that even during our rocket trip through the maelstrom, when I could see nothing but churning white foam, high and all around me, we had shipped little or no water. I checked body and clothing. Not even damp. We floated on downriver. Floated on air, it seemed, not water.

We eased into the first bend. Now at last the two remaining rapids were real. The reservoir below them, too.

We rounded the bend, entered Cataract's penultimate rapid. As advertised, a straightforward roller coaster. We bounced joyfully through it, hitting every wave head-on. Minutes later we were in the last rapid of all. This time I knew I could let go. As we lifted over the crest of each huge white wave I put my head back and whooped. Whooped and whooped again in celebration of Yhprum's Law. I hoped Dave Stimson could hear me.

The waves diminished, died away. The last white water flattened out. A huge, familiar silence began to build between the canyon walls. We moved slowly into it.

By degrees, the current slackened. Soon, the river was no longer pure river.

Linda Hogan

Plant Journey

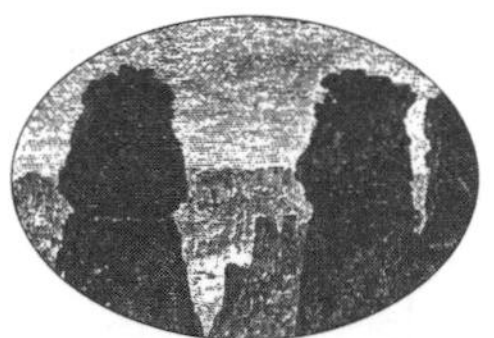

Linda Hogan's "Plant Journey" is one of fifteen contributions by women writers to Writing Down the River, *each essay in the anthology being a unique and personal record of its author's thoughts and impressions of the Grand Canyon.*

This canyon world where water yearns toward the ocean is a place so large I can't take it in. Instead, I am taken in, traveling a near dream as we journey by water, contained by rock walls. In order to see this shorn-away world, I narrow my vision to the small and nearly secret. Never mind the stone's illusion of permanence or the great strength of water. I look to the most fragile of things here, to the plant world of the canyon. The other river travelers seem taken in by stone, time, and water, and do not see the small things that tempt my attention, the minute fern between stones, the tiny black snails in a pond of water. I am drawn in by the growing life and not by the passing. It may be that I am simply a dreamer of the small and alive, or it may be that to see this world at our feet in the midst of the vast world above us requires a gaze shaped by another history than the ones recounted here by our river guides, a history that begins only with the journeys of white men.

This new history of the Colorado River, the one that began so recently, doesn't contain the vision of those who, for thousands of years, have known the land in all its sacred power and detail. This is a land so alive that the

---

From *Writing Down the River: Into the Heart of the Grand Canyon* (Flagstaff: Northland Publishing, 1998).

Havasupai address songs to it. And the Hopi people's place of origin is above the place where waters of the Little Colorado meet with larger waters, a place called Sipapu, opening, center. I know there is a wider way to see the canyon. I look for this wider way by looking down, at the plants. While I see plants as sacred, I am disturbed by the way in which they are unacknowledged by the others, treated with carelessness. It is hard for me to observe this, because I know that even something as small as a plant is not only alive and necessary, but that it can represent the known history and geography of a world.

Of all the plants we travel past, it is the short-lived blossom of the sacred datura that most strongly draws me in with its luminous white flower. Similar to a morning glory, even its trunk-stem glows with life, gold on deep green. I watch for these plants all along the way, and at each rest stop I walk about to find them, thinking of how their seed pods, which gave them the name "thornapple," have traveled along this water as we are traveling, how these plants have washed up and then staked a rooted claim in their place.

Perhaps its transience is what attracts me, because I, too, am only passing briefly through time and rock on the charge of water.

Or perhaps it is the datura's intimate beauty, shining with light and green intelligence. Or that datura has the sweetest of smells when I sit beside it trying to learn its secrets. But mostly probably what takes me in is its history, one that traveled from ancient worlds and times into the present.

For whatever reasons, in the canyon I find that this plant has a language that speaks of what's too large and immense for a mere human mind to grasp. You could say it holds the secrets of the world around it. It tells its story. Part of the story is in its relationships with other life forms. It opens its white evening flower, as if it is made of light, and the night-flying moths arrive, drawn to its sweetness. I see them enter the flower that is delicate as dusk, overpowering in its softness. By day, other pollinators arrive, insects, birds, some intoxicated by the plant's narcotic quality.

This plant is also kin to water. It has traveled many world rivers, not only the Colorado, on a mission unknown to us. Its use has been recorded in India, South America, Russia, and China. The Aztecs painted its likeness on murals. The priests of Apollo used it to treat such illnesses as epilepsy. Datura shines with a power as immense as the passage of water across the world, the movement of it as mysterious as the force that carries water upward through stem and leaf, as powerful as that which carries a river to the sea.

Like all plants, it has its relationship, as well, with light. But most significant is its long, ongoing relationship with humans. Every plant has been an offering to the human world and this relationship is what I wish to understand.

For the first peoples the plant world has always been an offering to humans, of richness, healing, and food. And to those who can read and understand the plants, knowledge resides in the body of the plant itself. For tribal peoples a plant is a living being, considered to be a person, as worthy of existence and survival as a human. To our ancestors, plant knowledge was both medical knowledge and a part of sacred history. In a relationship developed over many thousands of years, plants and people were allies in healing. This has not been the case in the more recent Western model of the world. Most humans in this time haven't been fortunate enough to learn the gifts of plants, have forgotten to regard the plants with their full measure of respect. These days, plants are likely to be overlooked, unseen, and unremembered in their subtle vitality. For this reason, I offer the plants my attention and affection. I know the subtle has power every bit as strong as the water we travel and the years of time shaped into canyon by this downward-rushing Colorado River. In the same way that the river never leaves anything unsaid, the plant expresses itself with every atom of its making.

Datura has been of great value as a medicine and as a spiritual ally for tribes on this continent. I love and admire this plant. I know that the story of this plant, how it was once worshipped and came to be considered a toxic weed, is the same as the story of the canyon itself, one of how the sacred loses its power. It is also the story of water, valuable only in its use to us.

This white-flowered medicine in use since nearly the beginning of all civilizations is now considered a poisonous weed, "rank and noxious" and hard to destroy. It is true that people have died from misusing it, even recently, but for those who know its ways, it is alive in its potence, and sacred. It is clear from the plant's history that it is a beautiful power, a flower of the dream, one used as a passageway to other dreams and places, the supernatural and the sacred. The plant that travels the water is esteemed for its offering of vision, of the spiritual journey to other worlds. In this, it is part of the same story of the luminous canyon that puts travelers in touch with the great beauty of a sacred world.

The world is not here just to be visited by humans. It has its own repose and turbulence, its own journey and destination. The sacred datura itself is one of many travelers. The whole world is a river through which its seed has journeyed. Unlike the Hopis who begin here, no one knows from where datura came. I say it came from here, this dream, this water and light.

But then, this is the land the tribal people sing to, with emotions deeply felt and love unsurpassed.

THE GRAND CANYON

Suggested Reading

Abbey, Edward. *Desert Solitaire.* New York: McGraw Hill, 1968.

Berkman, Richard L., and Viscusi, W.K. *Damming the West.* New York: Grossman Publishers, 1973.

Berton, Francis. *Un Voyage sur le Colorado.* San Francisco: n.p.. 1878.

Clark, Thomas D. *Frontier America: The Story of the Westward Movement.* New York: Charles Scribner's Sons, 1959.

Collier, Michael. *Water, Earth and Sky: The Colorado River Basin.* Salt Lake City: University of Utah Press, 1999.

Crampton, C. Gregory. *Land of Living Rock: The Grand Canyon and High Plateaus.* New York: Alfred Knopf, 1972.

Darrah, William Culp. *Powell of the Colorado.* Princeton: Princeton University Press, 1951.

DeVoto, Bernard A. *Across the Wide Missouri.* Boston: Houghton Mifflin, 1947.

———. *The Course of Empire.* Boston: Houghton Mifflin, 1952.

Edmonds, Margot and Clark, Ella E. *Voices of the Winds: Native American Legends.* New York: Facts on File, Inc., 1989.

Farquhar, Francis P. *The Books of the Colorado River and Grand Canyon: A Selective Bibliography.* Los Angeles: Glen Dawson, 1953.

Fowler, Don D. *John Wesley Powell and the Anthropology of the Canyon Country.* Washington: U.S. Department of Interior, Geological Survey, 1969.

Freeman, Lewis R. *The Colorado River Yesterday, Today, and Tomorrow.* New York: Dodd, Mead, 1923.

Jaeger, Oscar R. *The Grand Canyon Adventure: A Narrative of Rapid-Shooting on the Colorado.* Dubuque, Iowa: O.R. Jaeger, 1932.

Kniffen, Fred B. *The Natural Landscape of the Colorado River*. Berkeley: University of California Publications in Geography, 1932.

Krutch, Joseph Wood. *Grand Canyon: Today and All Its Yesterdays.* New York: W. Sloane Associates, 1958.

Lavender, David Siervert. *Colorado River Country.* New York: Dutton, 1982.

————. *Southwest.* New York: Harper & Row, 1980.

Lee, Watson. *Torrent in the Desert.* Flagstaff: Northland Press, 1962.

Leopold, Aldo. *A Sand County Almanac.* New York: Oxford University Press, 1947.

Lingenfelter, Richard E. *Steamboats on the Colorado River, 1852–1916.* Tucson: University of Arizona Press, 1978.

Merk, Frederick. *History of the Westward Movement.* New York: Alfred Knopf, 1978.

Nash, Roderick. *Grand Canyon of the Living Colorado.* New York: Sierra Club and Ballanatine Books, 1970.

Pike, Zebulon Montgomery. *Exploratory Travels through the Western Territories of North America.* Denver: W. H. Lawrence, 1889.

Powell, John Wesley. *Report on the Lands of the Arid Region of the United States.* ed. Wallace Stegner. Cambridge: The Belknap Press of Harvard University, 1962.

Rusho, W.L. *Powell's Canyon Voyage.* Palmer Lake, Colorado: Filter Press, 1969.

Spamer, Earl E. *Bibliography of the Grand Canyon and the Lower Colorado.* Grand Canyon, Arizona: Grand Canyon Natural History Association, 1990.

Stegner, Wallace. *Beyond the Hundreth Meridian.* Boston: Houghton Mifflin, 1953.

Stone, Julius Frederick. *Canyon Country.* New York: Putnam's Sons, 1932.

Ullman, James Ramsey. *Down the Colorado with Major Powell.* Boston: Houghton Mifflin, 1960.

Yates, Richard and Marshall, Mary. *The Lower Colorado: A Bibliography.* Yuma: Arizona Western College Press, 1974.

Zwinger, Ann Hammond. *Wind in the Rock.* New York: Harper & Row, 1978.